Estate Planning
FOR
DUMMIES®

Estate Planning FOR DUMMIES®

by N. Brian Caverly and Jordan S. Simon

WILEY

Wiley Publishing, Inc.

Estate Planning For Dummies®

Published by
Wiley Publishing, Inc.
909 Third Avenue
New York, NY 10022
www.wiley.com

For general information on our other products and services or to obtain technical support, please contact
our Customer Care Department within the U.S. at 800-762-2974, outside the U.S. at 317-572-3993, or fax
317-572-4002.

Wiley also publishes its books in a variety of electronic formats. Some content that appears in print may
not be available in electronic books.

Library of Congress Cataloging-in-Publication Data:

Library of Congress Control Number: 2002114822

ISBN: 0-7645-5501-4

Manufactured in the United States of America

10 9 8 7 6 5 4 3

1Q/RV/QU/QU/IN

WILEY   is a trademark of Wiley Publishing, Inc.

About the Authors

N. Brian Caverly

N. Brian Caverly, Esq., is a practicing lawyer in Northeastern Pennsylvania with his principal office in Wilkes-Barre. He has practiced law since 1968 and in his practice emphasizes wills and estates, estate planning, and elder law. He is a graduate of Bucknell University in Lewisburg, Pennsylvania, with an AB degree in economics, and from the Dickinson School of Law in Carlisle, Pennsylvania, with a JD degree. He serves on the board of directors of the Angeline Elizabeth Kirby Memorial Health Center in Wilkes-Barre, a charitable organization. Brian is also chairman of the Luzerne County Planning Commission. He presents lectures and writes articles and papers about various legal topics, including those related to estate planning.

Jordan S. Simon

Jordan S. Simon is vice president of asset management at Venture West, Inc., a Tucson, Arizona-based investment firm, where he has worked since 1988. Jordan focuses on real estate investments. He received his bachelor's degree from the University of Arizona and his MBA from the University of Southern California, where he was the recipient of the Quon Award for outstanding university and community service. Jordan is the co-author of *The Computer Professional's Guide to Effective Communications*.

Dedication

To my wife Anne; my children Jessica, Kelly, and Brenna; and my grandchildren Collin, Diarmid, and Fiona (and those to come)

— N. Brian Caverly

To my parents Sandra and Bernard Simon; Credit; and Meghan for their time, love and support.

— Jordan S. Simon

Authors' Acknowledgements

We would like to acknowledge the following individuals for their invaluable assistance with this book:

— Our agent Matt Wagner of Waterside Productions

— Cathy Levi for administrative assistance with the book's manuscript

— Lewis W. Wetzel, Esq., John C. Eichorn, Esq., and David J. Harris, Esq., for their sage counsel and advice

— Our anonymous technical reviewer (an attorney from Indiana who emphasizes estate planning) whose comments and suggestions helped us shape the book's contents

— Alan Simon (Jordan's brother), the author of *Stock Options For Dummies* and *Data Warehousing For Dummies*, who helped us create an engaging and sometimes entertaining book (at least we hope so!) about an often dry and occasionally sobering subject

Publisher's Acknowledgments

We're proud of this book; please send us your comments through our Dummies online registration form located at www.dummies.com/register/.

Some of the people who helped bring this book to market include the following:

Acquisitions, Editorial, and Media Development

Project Editor: Norm Crampton

Acquisitions Editor: Pam Mourouzis

Copy Editor: Chad Sievers

Technical Editor: Richard M. Hall

Editorial Manager: Christine Beck

Editorial Assistant: Melissa Bennett

Cartoons: Rich Tennant, www.the5thwave.com

Production

Project Coordinator: Maridee Ennis

Layout and Graphics: Amanda Carter, Joyce Haughey, Michael Kruzil, Barry Offringa, Jacque Schneider, Scott Tullis, Jeremey Unger

Proofreaders: John Bitter, John Greenough, TECHBOOKS Production Services

Indexer: TECHBOOKS Production Services

Publishing and Editorial for Consumer Dummies

Diane Graves Steele, Vice President and Publisher, Consumer Dummies

Joyce Pepple, Acquisitions Director, Consumer Dummies

Kristin A. Cocks, Product Development Director, Consumer Dummies

Michael Spring, Vice President and Publisher, Travel

Brice Gosnell, Publishing Director, Travel

Suzanne Jannetta, Editorial Director, Travel

Publishing for Technology Dummies

Andy Cummings, Vice President and Publisher, Dummies Technology/General User

Composition Services

Gerry Fahey, Vice President of Production Services

Debbie Stailey, Director of Composition Services

Contents at a Glance

Table of Contents

Introduction

*E*ven *The Sopranos* are worried about estate planning. In a season-opening show of HBO's wildly successful TV series, mob boss Tony Soprano finds himself nagged and pestered by his wife Carmela to work on the family's estate planning. Keep in mind that Tony tells her that they have loads of money sitting in numbered overseas bank accounts, and in the same episode he's stuffing bundles of cash into hiding places around his New Jersey estate. But Carmela isn't satisfied; she's worried about the future and how, if something happens to Tony (quite a possibility, in his line of work!), she and her two children will be cared for.

By the fourth episode, Carmela has Tony sitting down with her cousin, a financial planner, to discuss putting together an estate plan. By the fifth episode, they're covering the pros and cons of irrevocable life insurance trusts, the downside of probate, and even *intervivos trusts,* which Tony calls "in vitro" trusts!

Your lifestyle and line of business (to put it delicately) may be different from the characters on *The Sopranos.* But guess what? You should have the same concerns that Carmela Soprano has, and you need to work on your estate planning...now!

Who Needs This Book

Estate planning applies to everyone, yet a surprising number of people either have only done a very small part of what they need to do (usually just creating a will, which very often is out-of-date) or perhaps have done absolutely no estate planning at all!

That's where *Estate Planning For Dummies* comes in. This book is especially intended for you if you:

- ✔ Have done very little or nothing on your estate planning so far, and feel so overwhelmed that you don't know where to start

- ✔ Have done bits and pieces of your estate planning but all those parts are disjointed, and you're concerned that you have lots of holes in your estate planning

   ✔ Are concerned that you may have serious shortcomings or even outright mistakes in what you've put in your will, how your insurance policies are structured, and other aspects of your estate planning

   ✔ Have done a fair amount of work on your estate planning, but in a haphazard, undisciplined manner; you realize that estate planning is an ongoing, lifelong proposition and you want to become more disciplined in how you approach your will, estate tax planning, and all the rest

In short, *Estate Planning For Dummies* can help you no matter where you are in the estate-planning process.

How to Use This Book

Estate Planning For Dummies is written in easily understood language from cover to cover, with liberal use of examples. Some of the topics we cover are very basic — the estate-planning fundamentals we cover in Chapter 1, for example — while other material, such as the chapters on trusts, is more advanced and complicated.

If you're considering estate planning for the first time, you may want to skim through the book cover to cover just to get an idea of what's here, then settle down and use the book as a reference on specific topics as they come up. If you have had a bit more exposure to estate planning, you may want to selectively read certain chapters, and either skip or skim others. We recommend at least skimming every chapter, even if you currently have (for example) a will, a few trusts, and various types of insurance policies, and understand the basics pretty well.

How This Book is Organized

Estate Planning For Dummies is organized into seven parts. The chapters within each part cover specific topics in detail, as we describe below.

Part 1: Estate Planning Fundamentals

The chapters in Part I cover the fundamentals, and are particularly appropriate for readers who are newcomers to estate planning. (But as we mention earlier, we recommend even those who have started estate planning to skim the chapters and pick up a tidbit or two with which they aren't familiar or haven't yet come across.)

Chapter 1 covers the estate-planning basics that you must understand before moving forward with the many different strategies and mechanisms we discuss in the rest of the book. After all, you need to understand what is in your estate (hint: probably more than you think is in your estate right now!), why you need to worry about estate planning (and what happens if you don't), and — here's some good news — how to build a team of estate-planning professionals to help you through it all.

Chapter 2, as we note in the chapter's title, helps you figure out what your estate is worth. And the result will be, to repeat the hint we have for Chapter 1, "probably more than you think right now!" Your estate consists of different kinds of property, and we help you figure out how to calculate it all and to stay up-to-date on changes in your estate's value.

Part II: Where There's a Will, There's a Way

The Part II chapters get right into the part of estate planning that you may or may not have already tackled: your will. But whether you already have a will or not, read through these chapters to see if you may have made any mistakes and need to rethink your strategy for your will.

Chapter 3 presents a comprehensive discussion of the basics of wills: how they're structured, different ways in your will in which you can leave property to others, safekeeping for your will, and reasons you need to keep your will updated. We also discuss what happens if you die without a valid will, and believe us, it ain't pretty!

Chapter 4 presents a topic that is probably going to be a surprise to many readers. You don't have free reign to do anything you want in your will as you specify all the beneficiary conditions for your property. Your will is governed by your state's *statutes* (laws), and we present an overview of the most common statutes and what they mean to your will. As a preview, if your will violates one or more of those statutes, your will may be partially or totally invalid!

Chapter 5 discusses a topic that most people have heard of but know very little about: probate. We discuss what probate is, how your estate goes through probate, and what part of your estate doesn't go through probate. We also give you some practical tips to help you divide your overall estate between what goes through probate and what doesn't, and what the respective advantages and disadvantages are.

Chapter 6 discusses the general topic of *will substitutes,* which are various ways you can own property and transfer ownership to others without that particular property going through probate. We look at the advantages and disadvantages of the most common types, such as living trusts and joint tenancy with the right of survivorship, and discuss many other types as well.

Part III: Matters of Trust

The three chapters in Part III help you gain a realistic sense of different types of trusts and which ones — if any — make sense for your estate planning. Trusts are the most complicated estate-planning topic that we cover, but we divide our discussion into three chapters so that you can take this topic step by step.

Part IV: Life, Death, and Taxes

Most people are at least somewhat familiar with the federal estate tax, if only from the constant debate over whether or not there should be a "death tax." But did you know that you may actually need to worry about several different types of estate-related taxes in addition to the federal estate tax?

In Chapter 10, we take a broad look at all these estate-related taxes — both federal and at the state level, if your state has either an estate or inheritance tax — and look at the changes that the 2001 tax law made to those taxes at the federal level.

In Chapter 11, we look at the gift tax (no, this tax isn't a tax on Valentine's Day or birthday presents!), including lots of ways to get around the gift tax. Most importantly, we look at the little-known (or at least little-understood) ways in which the gift tax is linked to the federal estate tax system and some tax-planning strategies you can use.

Chapter 12 looks at a tax that you most likely won't have to worry about unless you're very rich — the generation skipping transfer tax (GSTT). We give you the lowdown without the excruciating detail.

Chapter 13 discusses the so-called "death tax," or the federal estate tax. Pay particular interest to how the 2001 tax law has turned the death tax into a moving target not unlike a midway booth at a carnival or the state fair. And, just like at a carnival or the state fair, you need to be very careful with your money and make sure you really understand the game you're playing!

In Chapter 14, we present you with a step-by-step approach you can use to take all the tax information we present in the preceding chapters and put together a tax strategy that takes all these taxes into consideration.

Part V: Estate Planning for Family Businesses

Family businesses present a particular challenge to estate planning. Chances are that you've heard arguments against the federal estate tax that passionately claim that the "death tax" is the ruination of family businesses and farms. True, estate taxes can play havoc with family businesses, but they don't have to.

In Chapter 15, we discuss the nuts and bolts of estate planning for various types of family businesses, including the most pressing estate-related issues such as succession planning.

In Chapter 16, we discuss various ways you can transfer your ownership in a family business to others and the respective advantages and disadvantages, as well as estate-tax concerns — and a few breaks and special considerations — that can help you keep your business in your family even if estate-related taxes come into play.

Part VI: Crafting a Comprehensive Estate Plan

In this part, we discuss three additional topics of concern to everyone's estate planning. In Chapter 17 we look at how various types of insurance not only help you protect your estate, but also can fit into your estate planning by manufacturing cash. (No, we're not talking about counterfeiting; check out our discussion.)

Chapter 18 discusses how your retirement planning and estate planning are closely related. What's that? Right now your retirement planning isn't related at all to your estate planning? Well, proceed to Chapter 18 for some practical, easy-to-accomplish tips.

Chapter 19 is sort of a collection of additional estate-planning topics that apply to nontraditional families (to introduce a theme we occasionally use, a family that doesn't look like one out of a 1950s or early 1960s TV show with never-before-married parents and only their biological children) and non-traditional situations (being declared incompetent, for example). We look at estate-planning implications of divorce, including what happens with stepchildren and adopted children. We also look at estate-planning considerations for unmarried couples (both same-sex and opposite-sex), as well as guardianship concerns for your children and even yourself, if you're unable to care for yourself. We also look at two documents you absolutely need to have in addition to your will: a durable power of attorney and a living will.

(If you wonder why it's so difficult to find information about factoring your beloved pets into your estate planning, we agree and in Chapter 19 we present valuable information about providing for your pets that you need to know.)

Part VII: The Part of Tens

The Part of Tens chapters present you with concise lists, each of which contains ten elements about a key estate-planning topic. Chapter 20 presents ten questions you need to ask yourself before you start your estate planning (or, if you've already begun before reading this book, ten questions to ask yourself before doing anything else!). Chapter 21 lists ten common mistakes people make with their wills that you don't want to make (hint, hint), and Chapter 22 lists ten Internet sites that contain loads of valuable estate-planning material you can use for reference.

Icons Used in This Book

As with all *Dummies* books, the text is annotated with icons to call your attention to various points we make (or try to make!) about estate planning.

When you see the Tip icon, the accompanying material is some action you should consider taking.

The Warning icon is exactly that: a warning of some dire consequence that may occur should you make the wrong move with your estate planning.

When you see the Technical Stuff icon, the accompanying material falls into that category of "thanks, but that's more than I really needed to know." You can certainly get the gist of any chapter's contents by skimming over all the Technical Stuff material, but if you want to get "under the hood" for that chapter's topic, a few moments spent with the Technical Stuff material can help you thoroughly understand that topic — just like the estate-planning professionals!

The Remember icon highlights the key point or two that can help you be a better estate planner.

Part I
Estate Planning
Fundamentals

The 5th Wave   By Rich Tennant

"I just think we need to make provisions in our Will
for disposition of our property. Who'll get Park
Place? Who'll get Boardwalk? Who'll get the thimble
and all the tiny green houses...?"

In this part . . .

This part explains the basics of estate planning: how everyone has an estate, and why estate planning is so important. We describe what you want to accomplish as part of your estate planning, and where you can turn for assistance. We also describe how you can get a handle on your estate's value, which is something you absolutely need to know for estate tax planning, insurance planning, and nearly every other aspect of your estate planning.

Chapter 1

Congratulations: You Have an Estate!

he protection and control that you need.

No, the above phrase isn't the marketing slogan for a new deodorant, instead it expresses the two most important reasons for you to spend time and effort on your estate planning. The two reasons are these:

✔ After you die, the government will try to take as much of your estate as possible, so you want to protect your estate from the government to the greatest extent that you can.

✔ For the portion of your estate that you are able to protect from the government, you want to have as much control as possible over how your estate is divided up. Basically, you want to decide what will happen to your estate rather than have a jumbled set of complicated laws dictate who will get what.

Before you can plan your estate, you need to understand what your estate really is. Many people think that for the average nonbillionaire, estate planning involves only two steps:

✔ Preparing a will

✔ Trying to figure out what inheritance and estate taxes — the so-called "death taxes" — apply (and if so, then how much money will go to the state and federal governments)

But even though wills and the death taxes are certainly important considerations for you, chances are your own estate planning will involve much, much more.

This chapter presents the basics of estate planning that you need to get started on this often-overlooked topic of your personal financial planning. In this chapter (and book), you also discover that estate planning is every bit as important as saving for your child's college education or putting money away for your retirement.

What Is an Estate?

In the most casual sense, your estate is your *stuff* or all your possessions. However, even if your only familiarity with estate planning comes from watching a movie or television show where someone's will is read, you no doubt realize that you aren't very likely to hear words like "I leave all of my stuff to. . . ." Therefore, a bit more detail and formality is in order, which we provide below.

The basics: Definitions and terminology

"All my property."

Think of that phrase when you plan your estate

What's that, you say? You don't own a house or any other real estate, so you think that you don't have any property? Not so fast! In a legal sense, all kinds of items are considered to be your property, not just real estate (more formally known as *real property,* as discussed later in this chapter's "Property types" section), but also your

- ✔ Cash, checking, and savings accounts
- ✔ Certificates of deposit (CDs)
- ✔ Stocks, bonds, and mutual funds
- ✔ Retirement savings in your Individual Retirement Account (IRA), 401(k), and other special accounts
- ✔ Household furniture (including antiques)
- ✔ Clothes
- ✔ Vehicles
- ✔ Life insurance
- ✔ Annuities
- ✔ Business interests

✔ Jewelry, baseball card collection, autographed first edition of *Catcher in the Rye,* and all the rest of your collectibles

As we discuss in the "Property types" section, your estate consists of all the preceding types of items — and even more — divided into several different categories. (For estate-planning purposes, these categories are often treated differently from each other, but we cover that distinction later.)

The types of property listed almost always have a *positive balance,* meaning that they are worth something even if "something" is only a very small amount. Of course, an exception may be your overdrawn checking account, which then is actually property with a negative balance. In the case of an overdrawn checking account, the "property" is the amount that you actually owe a person or company (your bank, in this case). So your estate also includes *negative-value* property such as:

✔ The outstanding balance of the mortgage you owe on your house or a vacation home

✔ The outstanding balances on your credit card accounts

✔ Taxes you owe to the government

✔ Any IOUs to people that you haven't paid off yet

Basically, all debts you have are as much a part of your estate as all the positive balance items.

In addition to understanding what your estate is, you also need to know what your estate is worth. You calculate your estate's value as follows:

1. Add up the value of all the positive balance items in your estate (again, your banking accounts, investments, collectibles, real estate, and so on).

2. Subtract the total value of all the negative balance items (remaining balance of the mortgage on your home, how much you still owe on your credit cards, and so on) from the total of all the positive balance items.

The result is the value of your estate. In most cases the result is a positive number, meaning that what you have is worth more than what you owe!

(If calculating a *net value* by subtracting the total of what you owe from the total of what you have seems familiar, you're right! In the simplest sense, calculating the value of your estate involves essentially the same steps that you follow when you apply for many different types of loans: mortgage, automobile, educational assistance, and so on.)

However, in many cases — including perhaps your own — determining what the parts of your estate are, and what they are worth, can be a bit more complicated than simply creating two columns on a sheet of paper or in your computer's spreadsheet program and doing basic arithmetic. If you are a farmer, for example, you need to figure out the value of your crops or livestock. If you own a small one-person business, you need to calculate what your business is worth. Or perhaps you and six other people are joint owners of a complicated real estate investment partnership; if so, what is your share worth?

In Chapter 2, we discuss more technical and sometimes more complicated ways to determine your estate's value. (***Note:*** For estate planning and estate tax purposes, more is not always better!)

For now, another point to keep in mind is that in addition to what you have right now, your estate may also include other items that you don't have in your possession, but at some point in the future, you will have, such as:

- Any future payments you expect to receive, such as an insurance settlement or the remaining 18 annual payments from that $35 million lottery jackpot that you won a couple of years ago
- Future inheritances
- A loan you made to your sister to help get her business started and when she plans to repay you

If you are familiar with the business and accounting term *accounts receivable* — what people or businesses owe to you — you need to include your own personal accounts receivable along with your banking accounts and home when figuring out what your estate contains and what your estate is worth.

One final term to cover is *estate planning.* By definition, estate planning means to plan your estate. (Duh!) More precisely, you need to follow a disciplined (as contrasted with haphazard!) set of steps that we discuss later in this chapter. Why? Referring back to the opening slogan of this chapter, you want to protect as much of your estate as possible from being taken away and you (not the government or a scheming family member) want to control what happens to your estate after you die.

Your estate plan typically includes the following:

- Your will
- Will substitues
- Trusts
- Tax considerations, with the idea of minimizing the overall amount of taxes you have to pay
- Various types of insurance
- Items related to your own particular circumstances, such as protecting your business or setting aside money to pay for your health care or a nursing home in your later years

All these aspects of estate planning are discussed in this book. If this collection of estate-planning activities seems a bit overwhelming, think of estate

planning as a parallel to how you plan your personal finances and investments. Your investment portfolio may be made up of individual stocks, bonds,
and mutual funds, along with bank CDs or other savings-related investments.
And then, within each type of investment, you have further categories (for
example, different types of mutual funds) that you may want to use.

Your investment objective is to sort through this menu of choices and put
together just the right collection for your needs. You must also do the same
with your estate plan. You need to have the right will and insurance coverage, possibly accompanied by trusts if they make sense for you and your
family (see Chapter 7). Furthermore, you may need additional estate-planning
activities and strategies particular to your own needs.

Property types

You can have several types of property within your estate. Make a distinction
between these types of property because various aspects of your estate planning treat each type differently. For example, in your will (see Chapter 3) you
can use different legal language when referring to various types of property,
so remember to keep these definitions and distinctions straight!

We already mentioned one type of property — *real property* — and noted that
real property refers to various types of real estate, including:

- Your home (a house, condominium, co-op apartment, or some other
  type of primary residence that you own)
- A second home, such as vacation property on a lake or near a ski resort
- A "piece" of a vacation home, such as a timeshare
- Any kind of vacant land, such as a building lot in a suburban development or even agricultural land you might own next to your "main" farm
- Any investment real property that you either own by yourself or with
  anyone else, such as a house you rent out or your share of an apartment
  building

In addition to the actual real property itself, your estate also includes any
improvements that you can't even see. For example, if you and three of your
friends bought 200 acres of land with the intention of turning that land into a
subdivision and you have spent loads of money on infrastructure — water
lines and hookups, sewer lines and hookups, in-ground electricity and cable,
and so on — then those improvements (or, more accurately, your share of
those improvements) are also considered to be part of your estate along with
the original real property itself.

In addition to real property, your estate also contains imaginary property.

No, not really! Just kidding! Your estate has no such thing as "imaginary property," unless some years back you got tripped up by some investment scam such as an oil or gas well that didn't really exist, or stock in some company that turned out to exist only on paper. (And if that's the case, don't even think about leaving that worthless swampland or your share of the Brooklyn Bridge to one of your children in your will, unless you want that "lucky" person to curse your name for all eternity!)

Actually, the other type of property in your estate in addition to real property is called *personal property,* which is further divided into two different categories:

- ✔ Tangible personal property
- ✔ Intangible personal property

Your *tangible personal property* includes possessions that you can touch, such as your car, jewelry, furniture, paintings and artwork, and collectibles (baseball cards, autographed first-edition novels, and so on).

Your house is considered to be real property, not tangible personal property, even though you can touch it. Why? Because your house is permanently attached to (and thus made a part of) the land upon which it is built.

Your *intangible personal property* consists of financially oriented assets such as your bank accounts, stocks, mutual funds, bonds, and your IRA. Of course, you can hold a stock certificate or mutual fund statement in your hand, but the stocks or mutual funds are still considered intangible personal property.

Technically, that stock certificate or mutual fund statement isn't actually what you own; it represents your portion of the ownership of some company (in the case of the stock certificate) or your portion of that mutual fund in the companies' stocks in which it invests. Sound confusing? Don't worry; just keep in mind that financially oriented paper assets are typically intangible personal property, while actual possessions are tangible personal property. If you have any doubt as to what category any particular item of your possessions falls, just ask one of your estate-planning team members that we discuss later in this chapter.

Types of property interest

For each of the three types of property in your estate — real, tangible personal, and intangible personal — you also need to understand what your interest is.

"Of course I'm interested in my property," you may be thinking; "After all, it's my property, isn't it?"

In the world of estate planning, *interest* has a somewhat different definition than how that word is used in everyday language, or even as the word is often used in the financial world (interest that you earn on a certificate of deposit or pay on your mortgage loan). And more importantly, the specific type of interest in any given property determines what you specifically need to be concerned about for your estate planning.

Property interest is an essential part of almost all your estate planning, from the words that you put in your will (Chapters 3 through 6) to how you may set up a trust (Chapter 7), for two very important reasons:

✔ You need to clearly understand what type of interest you have in your property, so you can make accurate decisions about how to handle your property when you plan your estate.

✔ As you decide what to write in your will and perhaps also set up trusts as part of your estate plan, you need to make decisions about what type of interest in each property that you want to set up for your children, your spouse, other family members, or institutions such as charities.

The two main types of property interest are:

✔ Legal interest

✔ Beneficial interest

If you only have a *legal interest* in a property, you have the right to transfer or manage that property but you don't have the right to use the property yourself! For example, Part III of this book discusses the very important (and very complicated) subject of trusts that may be an essential part of your estate planning. By way of a very brief introduction to that topic, when you set up a trust you name a *trustee* who is a person who manages the trust.

Suppose you set up a trust for your oldest son, Robert, as part of your estate plan, and you name your brother-in-law, Charlie, as the trustee. Charlie isn't allowed to use Robert's trust for his (Charlie's) own benefit, such as withdrawing $10,000 for a trip to Paris. That's called "Uncle Charlie goes to jail for stealing!" Assuming Charlie does what he is supposed to do — and, more importantly, doesn't do what he's not supposed to do — Charlie has a legal interest in your son's trust as the trustee.

Unlike his Uncle Charlie, Robert has the other type of property interest in his trust: a *beneficial interest,* meaning that he does benefit from that trust. Basically, you set up that trust to benefit Robert.

Now, to complicate matters a bit more, two "subtypes" of beneficial interest exist:

✔ Present interest

✔ Future interest

If you have a *present interest* (remember that means "present beneficial interest"), you have the right to use the property immediately. So if Robert has a present interest in his trust that is managed by his Uncle Charlie, Robert may receive payments of some specified amount — say $30,000 every three months for this example — from the trust. After Robert receives the money, he can do whatever he wants with it; the money is his to use, no strings attached.

The other type of beneficial interest — *future interest* — comes into play when someone with a beneficial interest (that person is allowed to benefit from that property) can't benefit right now, but instead must wait for some date in the future.

For example, you can set up the trust described to not only benefit your oldest son, but also your other two sons, Chip and Ernest. But you decide to take care of your three sons differently within that same trust. Suppose that after Robert receives his quarterly $30,000 payments for five years, his payments will then stop and Chip and Ernest each begin receiving $30,000 quarterly payments at that point. Essentially, Chip and Ernest have a future interest in the property (the trust) because they can't benefit right now, rather they benefit in the future.

Complicating factors just a bit more (last time, we promise!), someone with a future interest in property can actually have one of two different types of future interest:

- ✔ Vested interest
- ✔ Contingent interest

If you have a *vested interest,* you have the right to use and enjoy what you will get from that property at some point in the future, with no strings attached.

In the world of estate planning, the word *vested* means basically the same as it does in the world of retirement plans, stock options, and other financial assets. After you are vested in your company's retirement plan, you have the right to receive retirement benefits according to the particulars of your company's plan, even if you leave your job. (Unless you worked at Enron, but that's another story. . . .) Similarly, if you have stock options that have vested, you have the right to "exercise" those options and buy your company's stock at your "strike price." Furthermore, if you want, you can immediately sell those shares for a quick profit if your company's stock price has gone way up. (Unless you worked at Enron, but that's basically the same story. . . .)

However, if you have the other type of future beneficial interest — *contingent* — then you have to deal with some "strings attached" other than the simple passage of time. For example, you may set up that trust for your three sons in such a way that for Chip and Ernest to *realize* that future benefit, each must graduate from college and spend two years in the Peace Corps.

(Or you may set up the trust so that Chip only receives his future benefit if he marries and his wife gives birth to a set of triplets, if the above example reminds you of the old television show *My Three Sons*.)

Why You Need to Plan Your Estate

You can, of course, decide to leave what happens to your estate after you die totally up to chance (or, more accurately, the complicated set of state laws that will apply if you haven't done the estate planning that you need to do). But because you're reading this book, chances are that the two fundamental goals of estate planning at the beginning of this chapter — protection and control — are on your mind.

But going beyond the general idea of protecting your possessions and being in control, you have some very specific objectives that you're trying to accomplish with your estate planning, such as:

- ✔ **Providing for your loved ones.** You have people like your spouse or significant other, children, grandchildren, and parents who may rely on you for financial support. What will happen to that financial support if you were to die tomorrow?

  Even if you have a "traditional" family (that is, the kind of family typically shown in a 1950s or early 1960s situation comedy that is in perpetual reruns on *TV Land* or some other cable network), financial and other support for family members after you die can get very complicated if your estate isn't in order. But if your family is one that may be described as (quoting Nicholas Cage in the movie *Raising Arizona*) "Well, it ain't *Ozzie and Harriet*," then you absolutely need to pay attention to all the little details of protecting your family members if you die. Specifically, if your loved ones include former spouses, children living in another household, stepchildren, adopted children, divorced and remarried parents, or an unmarried partner, then you have a lot of decisions to make with regards to your estate about who gets what.

- ✔ **Minimizing what your estate will have to pay in estate taxes.** Yes, we know that we said that estate planning involves much more than the inheritance and estate (death) taxes, but make no mistake about it, death taxes are certainly a consideration. Why pay more than you have to? You can take several steps — such as giving gifts, as we discuss in Chapter 2 while you're still alive — to reduce the value of your estate and therefore reduce the amount of death taxes that will have to be paid.

  Protecting your business. Politicians love to talk about the small business owner or the family farmer when describing how they are "a friend to the little guy," but the fact remains that if you own a small- or medium-scale business, such as a retail store or a farm, that business can be turned topsy-turvy if you die without a solid estate plan in place. (So actually, you want to make sure that if you're a farmer, your farm is protected after you've "bought the farm.")

Sure, it's human nature to just let things happen. You're very busy with your career and your family. And after all, do you really want to dwell on morbid thoughts such as your own death?

But like The Beatles sang in *The Ballad of John and Yoko,* "Oh boy, when you're dead you don't take nothing with you but your soul. Think!" And because you really can't take any of your property with you, you do leave behind people and institutions (charities, foundations, and so on) that you care about along with all your possessions. Why wouldn't you want to take the time to appropriately match up your property with those people and institutions?

Besides, estate planning is as much (if not more) about what you do during your life to manage your estate than what happens after you die. Sure, it makes good theater to have a deathbed scene where the aged family patriarch or matriarch dictates what will happen to the vast family fortune, but the place to begin your estate planning isn't on your deathbed! That last-minute approach usually opens up the probability of one or more disgruntled family members trying to overturn your dying words. More than likely, due to the result of your lack of estate planning, your estate will dwindle away through legal fees and taxes in excess of what should have been paid.

(And not to be morbid, but if you were to die suddenly and unexpectedly, you may not even have the "opportunity" for that dramatic deathbed scene. If you haven't done your estate planning, then chances are nobody in your family will have any idea of what you want to happen to your estate.)

Need more? How about the game that the United States Congress is playing with the federal estate tax? As part of the estate tax laws (see Chapter 13), you have an *exemption* — an amount that you may leave behind that is free of the federal estate tax. (The estate tax doesn't kick in until your estate exceeds the exemption amount.)

As part of Congress's latest overhaul of the tax code, the federal estate tax exemption will rise each year, to $3.5 million in 2009. And then, in 2010, the federal estate tax goes away entirely but only for one year! In 2011, the estate tax not only "comes back from the dead" (appropriately enough, huh?), but the exemption also becomes $1 million, or $2.5 million less than it was only two years earlier!

We spend much more time on Congress's little game in Chapter 13 and what that means to your estate planning. The main point for now is that for federal estate tax purposes, your estate planning is actually a moving target between now and 2011. If you were to die between now (the time you're reading these words) and 2011, the amount of federal estate tax could be all over the map if your estate is very valuable. Indeed, if you die in 2010, then under the current law you won't owe any federal estate tax; however, if you die in 2011, you could owe a lot. Now most people won't try to work "Dying in 2010" into their estate plans for the sole purpose of saving money on federal estate taxes, but the point is that you really need to stay on top of your estate-planning activities to try and minimize the amount of those taxes.

Another reason to plan your estate deals with a mistake that many married couples make with their respective estates. Irrespective of the federal estate tax and varying exemption amounts, you can leave an unlimited amount of your estate to your spouse free of federal estate taxes.

However, sometimes you are better off not leaving your entire estate to your spouse, especially if your spouse also has a sizable estate (not only property jointly owned with you, but personal property that only your spouse owns). Why? Because then your spouse (assuming you die first) now has an even larger estate, which is then subject to a potentially larger tax liability than if you had done something else with your estate. Basically, your children or whomever else you and your spouse are leaving your respective estates to will likely be stuck with paying more in federal estate taxes just because you decided to take the easy step with your estate and leave it all to your spouse.

Many states also impose inheritance and estate taxes which your estate pays in addition to federal estate taxes (see Chapter 10).

The answer? You need to proactively conduct your estate planning, take all the matters in this section into consideration, and create a personalized estate plan.

Why Your Estate-Planning Goals Are Different from Your Neighbors'

You are a unique individual.

No, the above statement isn't part of the latest feel-good pop psychology designed to boost your self-esteem (not to mention make tons of money for the guru with seminars and videotapes), but rather it's a point we want to emphasize to stress why you need to take time to create an individualized estate plan for your own situation.

Many people finally and grudgingly acknowledge that they need to worry about their estate plans but then take a haphazard, lackadaisical approach to estate planning: a generic fill-in-the-blank will purchased in a stationery store, a cursory review of active insurance policies, and checking to see whose names are listed as beneficiaries on the retirement plan at work. But that's all; everything else will fall into place, right?

And besides, is it really worth putting any more time and effort beyond those basic tasks? After all, you're the one who will be dead. Why make all that effort for a series of events that will take place after you've died?

However, consider all the factors that make up many different aspects of your life, including:

- ✔ Your marital status: married, divorced, separated, single, widowed (or "widowered"), or maybe unmarried but living with someone

- ✔ Your age

- ✔ Your health (Not to be excessively morbid, but if you know that you have a potentially fatal condition or illness, or are in generally poor health, time is of the essence for your estate planning.)

- ✔ Your *financial profile*, such as the property (real and personal) you have and what that property is worth

- ✔ Any potentially complicated business or financial situations you have, such as investment partnerships

- ✔ Any money you expect to receive — particularly large sums — such as an inheritance, lawsuit settlement, or severance pay from a job you are leaving

- ✔ What insurance policies you have, the types (we discuss different types of insurance in Chapter 17), and the value of each

- ✔ If any of your assets are particularly risky, such as stock or stock options in a start-up company that on paper is worth millions of dollars, but you can't do anything with those assets for some reason (such as your stock options haven't fully vested)

- ✔ If you have any children and if so, how many, what are their ages, their respective financial states, and their respective marital statuses

- ✔ If you have any grandchildren and if so, if you want to explicitly take care of them as part of your estate planning or, alternatively, leave it to your children to take care of their own children as part of their own estate planning

- ✔ If your parents are still alive and if so, whether they are still married to each other, if either may have remarried, their financial status (together or, if divorced, separately) and if you need to take care of them

- ✔ Your siblings (brothers and sisters) and if you want or need to take care of them as part of your estate planning

- ✔ Any other family members (cousins, aunts, uncles, and so on) or even friends that you want to include in your estate planning

- ✔ Charities and foundations that you support

Just consider the items in the above list — not to mention dozens of others that you can probably think of — and the answers for you and your life. Sure, somewhere in the United States, you can probably find someone else with more or less the same profile as yours, but the point is that no estate plan is a one-size-fits-all plan that you can effortlessly adapt to your situation.

Additionally, even a canned plan that seems to be suitable for your situation may actually be a poor choice after you really dig into the details. Think of the man's suit or woman's evening dress that looks great in a magazine advertisement or even on a store mannequin — one that seems to be bodily proportional to your own — but when you try that suit or dress on, something just doesn't look or feel right.

So we strongly recommend that you make your credo for estate planning be "no shortcuts allowed!" The time and effort, and even expense that you put into developing a solid, comprehensive estate plan will be well rewarded. True, you won't necessarily be alive to fully see the benefits of your efforts, but those people that you care about enough to include in your estate plan likely will be grateful!

Why Estate-Planning Lingo Is Not Really a Foreign Language

Part of the reason many people shy away from doing the proper amount of estate planning is because of the many different disciplines involved, including law, accounting, personal finance and investments, and insurance. And with each of those disciplines comes an entire set of complicated terminology — some more complicated than others, such as the many legal terms that come into play.

Abatement statue. Antilapse statute. Exordium clause. Intervivos trusts. Uniform probate code. The technical terms go on and on and on.

But instead of throwing your hands up in disgust and saying to yourself, "I don't want to learn any more foreign languages; I had enough trouble in high school German," we suggest the following plan of attack to get through the complicated terminology.

Even though we use and explain many different technical estate-planning terms throughout this book, we also provide plain language alternative definitions. For example, in Chapter 3 we discuss the *exordium clause* of your will, but we suggest that you think of that clause as the introductory clause because the clause is your will's introduction.

So you're more than welcome to try and remember all the Latin-root legal terms that we use when discussing wills, trusts, and the other topics, but if you're more comfortable with plain-language definitions, use the easier definitions instead. Leave the legal-speak and technical terms to your estate-planning team members that we discuss later in this chapter.

The Critical Path Method to Planning Your Estate

Estate planning is a process that can be further divided into multiple steps or activities (or, for you computer and business types, *subprocesses*). In business, building computer applications, or even life itself (weddings, for example), most processes tend to take days, weeks, months, or even years from start to finish; rarely does any process happen overnight.

You need to treat your estate-planning activities as a process. The process includes a disciplined method created from a set of steps that lead you from a state of *estate-planning nothingness* (that is, you have no estate plan at all) to the point where you have a well-thought-out estate plan in place. We recommend using the *critical path method* to planning your estate.

If you have taken a college business class in operations research, quantitative methods, or a similar topic, you may already be familiar with the critical path method, which is defined as "the most effective way through a series of steps to reach your objectives." In other words, even when you have a seemingly infinite number of possible paths in front of you, you can find one particular path that is the most effective and efficient of all those alternatives.

In estate planning, you are often faced with many side roads when working on your will or setting up a trust. Before you know, the side road has turned into a detour and your estate plan is in a state equivalent to your car being stuck up to its lug nuts in mud. (For the automotively challenged, the previous sentence means you aren't going anywhere anytime soon.)

If the terms *operations research* and *quantitative methods* cause you to draw a blank stare or if those terms cause shudders and tremors as you flash back to long-forgotten hated college courses that you barely passed, then simply think of the critical path method as a map. If you're standing on a corner in Winslow, Arizona, and you want to go to Phoenix, Arizona, you can get in your car and, after checking a map, drive approximately 190 miles of interstate highway. Or maybe you don't know the area very well and you're one of those I-never-check-a-map-kind of people, so you get in your car and just start driving. First, you head to Los Angeles, then drive up to San Francisco, then maybe go over to Chicago, back to Denver, and then drive toward Phoenix. ("By the time I get to Phoenix, she'll be on Social Security.")

Anyway, the critical path method is fairly straightforward, and includes the following steps:

1. **Define your goals.** Before you begin your estate planning, decide what you're trying to achieve. Are you trying to make sure that your spouse has enough income for some period of time (say, five years, or maybe longer) if you were to die suddenly? Are you trying to make sure that

your children have enough money for college after you're gone? Is your estate worth upwards of $10 million, and are you trying to protect as much as possible from the eventual federal estate tax bite?

As we mention earlier in this chapter, your estate-planning goals are almost certainly different than anyone else's that you know, so make sure that you take the time to define exactly what those goals are.

Write down your goals; don't just think about them. Often by actually writing your goals rather than just visualizing them, you get a better handle on how your goals relate to one another, and you make sure that you haven't forgotten anything.

2. **Determine which estate-planning professionals you want to work with.** Financial planners, insurance agents, attorneys, and accountants (all of whom we discuss in the next section) can provide valuable guidance and service to you. You need to determine which professionals best help you meet your goals. For example, have an attorney work with you on your will to be sure you meet all your own state's requirements for the will to be legally binding. You may also decide to work with other professionals depending on the complexity of your estate and the particular goals you defined in the previous step.

3. **Gather information.** Whether you work with professionals or not (more on this particular decision point in the next section), you need to have as much available information as possible so that you know where you are currently in your estate-planning process. You need to ask yourself the following questions:

    1. Do you have a will right now and if so, when did you prepare that will?

    2. What in your life has changed since you created that will?

    3. What insurance policies do you currently have?

    4. Have any insurance policies expired?

    5. Perhaps most importantly, what property is in your estate and what is the value of that property?

4. **Develop your action plan.** Basically, get ready to do the many different activities we discuss in this book: Work on your will. (Create your will if you don't have one, or perhaps update your will if the will is out of date.) Decide if trusts make sense for you and if so, choose which ones. Figure out what you need to do to protect your business, and so on.

5. **Actually conduct your action plan.** People often trip up on this step during their estate planning (or anything else they like to procrastinate on). Take the plans that you developed in Step 4 and actually do them! If you die without a will, complications may arise even if someone in your family finds a sheet of paper on your desk that reads "Step 4: Prepare my will."

6. **Monitor your action plan.** You may like going through all the previous estate-planning steps, finishing them, and then just forgetting about

them all. But in estate planning, you never really finish. You periodically need to resynchronize your estate plan with any major changes in your life. For example, have you gotten divorced and remarried? You had better get cracking on those updates! Even less dramatic changes in your life can trigger changes, so your best bet is to double-check every-thing in your estate plan once each year so you can make sure that all changes to your life, great and small, are reflected in your estate plan-ning in a timely fashion. You can even tie your "checkup" to an annual occurrence, like your birthday, or the beginning or end of daylight saving time (unless you live in one of those places like Arizona or parts of Indiana that don't "spring ahead and fall back" each year), or to some other occasion that you won't easily forget.

By following these steps and staying on the critical path, you greatly reduce the chances of taking all kinds of unnecessary and potentially serious detours with your estate planning, and can typically get through the tasks with a minimum amount of stress.

Take these initiative to meet with each member of your estate-planning team annually. Or ask someone on the team to remind you annually to review your estate plans — the way your dentist reminds you come in for a checkup.

Getting Help with Your Estate Planning

You can do all your estate planning by yourself, but you don't have to and even more importantly, we don't recommend that approach. But can you turn to someone with a job title along the lines of Professional Estate Planner for help?

Not exactly. As we mention several times in this chapter, estate planning actually consists of several different specialties or disciplines, and if you want, you can work with one or more people in each of those specialties as part of your estate planning.

The number of people with whom you work largely depends on two main factors:

✔ How comfortable you are with the overall concepts and mechanics of estate planning

✔ How complicated your estate is

The material covered in this book can go a long way toward helping you with the first of those two factors. But even if you thoroughly understand little nuances of the clauses to include in your will (see Chapter 3) or the basic types of trusts (see Chapter 7), you may still want to tap into a network of professionals if your estate is particularly complicated. Sure, you'll spend a bit more money on fees, but in the long run, you are more likely to avoid a horrendously costly mistake (financially, emotionally, or both), particularly if your estate is rather complicated.

How to make sure your team of advisers is "FAIL" safe

So with whom do you work? Here's an acronym to help you remember whom you need to think about for your estate-planning team: FAIL, which stands for:

- ✔ Financial planner
- ✔ Accountant
- ✔ Insurance agent
- ✔ Lawyer (or attorney, the more familiar word we'll usually use in most places in the book)

The order of the professionals in the above list doesn't indicate any type of priority (that is, your financial planner is more important than your accountant) or any type of sequence (such as you must work with your accountant before you work with your insurance agent). The order shown is solely for the purposes of the FAIL acronym to help you remember these different professions and how they may help you.

You don't necessarily need a full slate of estate-planning professionals on your team. You may, for example, work with your attorney and accountant. But if you've decided that insurance is only a minimal part of your overall estate plan, then you may not need to work with an insurance agent. Or if you are well versed in investments and financial planning, then you can handle that aspect of your estate plan by yourself, and work with team members from the other specialization areas.

Straight talk

You need to talk candidly and honestly about personal and sometimes sensitive — or even painful — matters with your estate-planning team. The last thing you want is for your insurance agent to recommend a certain type of insurance policy that the issuing insurance company could invalidate because you hid some important fact that was later found out.

And your attorney needs to thoroughly understand all aspects of your relationships with your family to help you create a will that accurately reflects your wishes. For example, if you really want to cut someone out of your will and leave that person nothing at all, make sure that your attorney knows that so your will can be constructed appropriately.

The best professionals sometimes set things into motion that can have unintentional and less-than-desirable consequences if another member of your estate-planning team isn't aware of what was done. For example, you need to be certain that you understand all the tax implications — federal income, state income, gift, estate, and so on — of a trust that your financial planner recommends and that your attorney sets up. Therefore, your accountant needs to work side by side with your attorney and your financial planner before the trust is created to be certain that no unpleasant tax surprises pop up.

Working with Certified Financial Planners (CFPs) and other financial planning professionals

Because a significant portion of your estate is likely to involve your investments and savings, consider working with some type of financial planning professional. You can work with a financial planning professional solely on an advisory basis. If you want, you can make your own decisions about your investments and savings, after consulting with a professional. Your financial planning professional also can play a much more active role, such as making major decisions for your financial life (with your consent, of course).

All financial planning professionals aren't created equal, nor do they necessarily have the same background and qualifications. In the following paragraphs, we provide a brief overview, and you can also find a very candid, no-holds-barred discussion of financial planners in *Personal Finance For Dummies*, 3rd Edition, by Eric Tyson (published by Wiley Publishing, Inc.).

Before you decide to work with any financial planning professional, you need to understand just who these people are, what type of formal training and credentials they have, and how using them relates to your estate planning.

Certified Financial Planners (*CFPs*) provide financial planning services and general financial advice on a wide range of topics from investments to taxes and from estate planning to retirement planning. CFPs are required to pass college-level courses in a broad range of financial subjects, and then a two-day, ten-hour examination. CFPs must also either have a bachelor's degree and at least three years of professional experience working with financial planning clients, or without a degree have at least five years of experience doing financial planning.

You can check with the Financial Planning Association at www.fpanet.org and search for planners by state, city, or zip code or call 404-845-0011 (toll-free 800-322-4237). You can find financial planners who have the CFP credentials. You can then verify a planner's CFP status with the CFP Board of Standards at www.cfp-board.org and click on "CFP Certificants."

Other financial planning professionals

If your financial life is particularly complicated, you may need to work with several types of financial planning professionals in addition to a basic financial planner (who may or may not be a CFP).

Another type of financial planning professional is the *Investment Adviser* (*IA*) or the *Registered Investment Adviser* (*RIA*). IAs and RIAs specifically advise their clients about securities (stocks, bonds, and so on) Any IA who manages at least $25 million in assets must register with the Securities and Exchange Commission (SEC), and you can check this information out at .

Chartered Financial Analysts (*CFAs*) are typically portfolio managers or analysts for banks, mutual funds, or other institutional clients (in Wall Street lingo), but some CFAs also advise wealthy individuals and families who have particularly complicated investment situations. CFAs take a series of examinations covering portfolio management, accounting, equity analysis, and other subjects, and must have at least three years of professional experience in investments. CFAs are also required to sign an ethics pledge every year.

A *Certified Investment Management Consultant* (*CIMC*) works with the wealthiest of the wealthy — high-net-worth private clients. A variety of examinations and continuing education, plus at least three years of professional experience, is required.

A *Certified Fund Specialist* (CFS) works with clients on mutual funds. (Some CFSs also provide general financial planning services.) Examinations and continuing education are required to retain CFS status.

You can regularly check *Money Magazine, Smart Money,* and other personal finance publications for the latest information, and even problems and scandals in the profession.

Make sure you clearly understand how your financial planning professional — CFP or otherwise — gets paid! Some financial planning professionals get paid on a "fee-only" basis, meaning that they don't receive any commissions for selling you financial products. They are only compensated for advice (basically, they're consultants).

Fee-based financial planning professionals not only earn fees from the advice they give you, but also from commissions for selling you financial products, while commission-based financial planning professionals only make money from the products they sell you.

You can certainly find both ethical and unethical people (not to mention competent and incompetent) in any of these three categories. However, always pay particular attention to recommendations from fee-based or commission-based financial planning professionals. Perhaps those investment choices are the perfect match for you, but you need to make that decision, not your financial planning professional who stands to benefit financially from selling you some type of product!

Knowing what to expect from your accountant for your estate planning

Your accountant can do a lot more for you than fill out your tax returns for the previous year. Businesses use accountants for planning purposes, trying to steer what happens in the future for tax purposes by doing certain steps today. Plan on working with an accountant on your estate planning for those very same reasons, even if you do your own income taxes and haven't really worked with an accountant before.

Make sure the accountant on your estate-planning team presents you with scenarios of what can likely happen, based on recommendations from other members of your estate-planning team. If your CFP recommends certain investments or insurance products, then what are the tax implications when you die? What are the tax implications if you die tomorrow versus dying ten years from now?

Your accountant can also have a more active role in your estate planning, suggesting certain tactics with an eye toward reducing your overall estate tax burden, giving gifts in particular.

Never do any financial gift giving (as contrasted with birthday gift giving or holiday gift giving) without consulting with an accountant for all the tax implications; see Chapter 11 for details of financial gifts and the gift tax.

Seek out an accountant who is a Certified Public Accountant (CPA), meaning that the accountant has passed the American Institute of Certified Public Accountants (AICPA) examination.

You may also consider combining two of the roles on your estate-planning team — the financial planning and accounting specialists — by working with someone who is a Certified Public Accountant/Personal Financial Specialist, (CPA/PFS) in other words, a CPA who also provides overall financial planning and has passed the PFS exam. Check out www.cpapfs.org.

Your insurance agent and your estate

Depending on your particular estate-planning needs, various forms of insurance (life, disability, liability, and other types we discuss in Chapter 17) may play a key role. Most people who have dependents (particularly a spouse and children) wind up working insurance into their estate plan to meet the "protection" objective of estate planning.

Therefore, consider your insurance agent a part of your estate-planning team. For example, when you discuss life insurance and make decisions between different types of life insurance policies (see Chapter 17), make sure that your insurance agent is aware of any estate-planning strategies, such as trusts so you can make sure that your policy beneficiaries are listed correctly.

Some insurance companies are *agentless* meaning that unlike traditional insurance companies where you have an assigned insurance agent, your contact with the company is through any one of hundreds or even thousands of customer service representatives, almost always over the phone or the Internet. In these situations, ask one of the customer service representatives whether you can speak with or even work with anyone at the company on estate-planning matters. Chances are the representative will say yes, so even though you don't technically have an insurance agent, you may still have access to short-term estate-planning assistance when you need it.

Working with your attorney

Even though your attorney is last on the list of the members of your estate-planning team (courtesy of the "L for Lawyer" that we used in our FAIL acronym), he or she could quite possibly be the most important member for one simple reason: Your attorney keeps you from inadvertently making very serious mistakes!

All kinds of problems can trip you up and cause serious headaches in the future, if not headaches for you because you've already died, for someone else. For example:

- ✔ How should your will read to make sure that your significant other (to whom you are not married) receives what you want out of your estate?

- ✔ How should the deed to your home be written to make sure that your unmarried significant other isn't forced to move if you die first?

- ✔ If you have an elderly parent who needs to go into a nursing home, what are the implications to your parent's estate and your own?

Basically, think of your attorney as your "scenario-planning specialist." Your attorney takes all kinds of information about you and your estate into consideration. He or she then presents you with options, based on various scenarios, such as you dying suddenly next week (morbid, but definitely an eye-opener for many people when first doing their estate planning) versus you dying at the ripe old age of 134 (courtesy of advanced biotechnology), having outlived everyone else in your family.

Beyond the scenario planning, make your attorney your primary adviser for your will, trusts, legal implications for your business, and pretty much any other legal matter that directly or indirectly relates to your estate planning. (See Chapter 20.)

Chapter 2

Bean Counting — Figuring Out What You're Worth

. . . .

In This Chapter

▶ Taking stock of your assets: What do you really have?

▶ Calculating the value of your real and personal property

▶ Including your debts in your estate's value

▶ Reducing and controlling your estate's value through gift giving

▶ Figuring out adjustments in your estate's value after your life changes

. . . .

*Q*uick: How much are you worth?

You may think that you have a pretty good idea of what your estate is worth — within 5 to 10 percent, give or take — but you may be very surprised when you actually sit down and start taking stock of your assets.

If you've ever filled out a loan application for a new car or a home mortgage, chances are that when you began listing your assets, you thought of several items beyond your savings accounts and mutual funds that turned out to be quite valuable. What about that wardrobe of $2,000 custom suits from London? And how about all those antiques from trips to Europe? Even families with more modest tastes usually have the family silverware, jewelry, household furniture, and several other items that add up to a decent amount of money.

Therefore, to be accurate in your estate planning, you need to know how much all your estate is really worth. And if you're like most people, you need to dig beneath the surface and beyond the obvious — factoring in your debts and the future, too. In this chapter, we tell you how.

Calculating the Value of Your Real Property

Your *real property* (your home and other real estate-related investments) may very well be the most valuable part of your estate. You need to carefully determine the value of all real property, especially if your estate plans call for dividing the value of that real property among more than one beneficiary. You want to be fair, and you want to have a good idea of what each beneficiary will receive, particularly if some beneficiaries will get other (non-real property) parts of your estate and you're trying to divide your overall estate as equally as possible.

Your home on the range

If you recently purchased your home (say within the last year or two), you have a pretty good idea of your home's worth, even if you live in an area where real estate prices are rapidly going up.

However, if you purchased your home a long time ago, you may have no idea of your property's value. For example, maybe you never purchased your home at all — perhaps you're living in the family's ancestral home that's been in your family since the early 1900s.

Either way, you need to get an official idea of your home's value, and you can do so in one of two ways:

✔ You can hire a real estate appraiser who does nothing but determine property value. A paid appraiser is likely to give you the most thorough and accurate idea of your home's value because you pay for that service.

✔ If you don't want to pay an appraiser, you can do what real estate professionals call "checking comparables." You can find the sale price of a comparable property in or near your neighborhood with the same floor plan, the same exterior design, roughly the same lot size, and other characteristics nearly identical to your home.

In most suburban settings, prices and values for nearly identical properties can vary widely depending on what neighborhood the house is in, even if those neighborhoods are right next to each other! So make sure that if you decide to determine your home's value based on comparable properties yourself, you understand the differences in property values between popular, highly coveted neighborhoods and others not quite so prestigious.

If you live in a home that's unique in any way — a farmhouse set on hundreds of acres or a two-centuries-old brownstone in a downtown neighborhood, for example — then you should definitely hire an appraiser. Otherwise, you can be way off in determining what your home is worth.

That timeshare in Timbuktu and other hideaways

If you own a second home of any kind, from a beachfront bungalow to a condominium at the foot of a prestigious ski resort (or even a part of a second home, such as a timeshare), you can figure out what that property is worth in much the same way as you do your primary home.

Your investments as a landlord

If you have any investment real property, such as a rental duplex or a share of an apartment building or office complex, then you probably have some background in how to value residential or commercial real estate. (At least you should, because you had to decide whether the investment you were considering making was a good deal or not.)

If you do your own finances for your real estate investments, you're familiar with terms like *net operating income* and *capitalization rate,* which are used to calculate how much your investment is worth. But if you don't do your own finances for your real estate investments, don't worry. Whoever manages your investment for you does know these terms, so just ask your investment manager how much your investment is worth. If, however, you invested $50,000 ten years ago in rental property because your brother-in-law told you it was a good idea and you have no idea about operating expenses and cap rates, then take the easy way out: Contact a commercial real estate appraiser and get your investment property appraised.

If you hire an appraiser for commercial investment property, make sure that the appraiser is experienced in valuing the type of property you have. (Don't hire a residential home appraiser to tell you what your 20 percent of a commercial farming operation is worth.)

Your real estate partnerships

You may have an investment in real property that isn't a direct investment, but rather is an investment in a Limited Liability Company (LLC) or Limited Liability Partnership (LLP). (LLCs and LLPs are just methods of ownership that have gained favor over the past years primarily because of their tax advantages.)

The value of some LLCs and LLPs can vary greatly from year to year. Additionally, you usually have restrictions on how you can sell or otherwise transfer control of your ownership portion of an LLC or LLP. Those restrictions often result in a *valuation discount,* meaning that your portion of an LLC or LLP is actually worth less than you would calculate using your share of the income minus your share of the expenses. Consequently, you need to keep current — usually through regular statements you receive from the LLC or LLP — and adjust the value of your estate accordingly.

For example, if you have an investment in a shopping center through an LLP, the shopping center's value can be dramatically affected if an anchor (main) tenant files for bankruptcy and shuts down the location at your shopping center. The property's revenue decreases, which in turn decreases the net operating income, ultimately decreasing the shopping center's value when you divide the net operating income by the cap rate.

You typically use LLCs and LLPs to own shares of more valuable investment real properties (such as large office complexes or an apartment complex with hundreds of apartments) rather than shares of properties you invest in directly (such as smaller office buildings or a duplex residential site). Therefore, the value of LLCs and LLPs is likely to fluctuate more than any direct real estate investments you have. Monitor them closely, not only for estate-planning purposes but also for personal investment purposes.

Calculating the Value of Everything Else: Your Personal Property

Get out the notepad or the spreadsheet program, and get ready for some long lists of your tangible and intangible personal property. You need to be as thorough as possible so that you can accurately figure out what your estate is worth.

Tangible personal property — items you can touch

You will likely see an interesting paradox with regards to your *tangible personal property* (cars, jewelry, and other household items). You probably have far more individual items of tangible personal property that you need to catalog and value than the other types of property in your estate (real property and intangible personal property). However, for most people, tangible personal property has the smallest overall value.

Some of your personal property may be almost worthless (or even totally worthless!) in a financial sense, but you still need to catalog those items and decide what you want to happen to them after you die. For example, whom do you want to get the lucky Liberty nickel that your grandfather carried over on the boat when he came to the United States in 1898, the one that was handed down to your father and then to you? Maybe the nickel isn't worth much more than a nickel even though it's more than 100 years old, but it still carries great family sentimental value. So which of your four children will you leave that nickel to, and what other sentimental goodies will you leave to the others?

You could, of course, let your children, grandchildren, and other family members "put in a claim" on some or all your "trinkets" while you're still alive — sort of a grab-bag approach to giving away part of your estate. But even if you decide to take that approach, you need to have everyone's "wish lists" and make sure that your will reflects all those who-gets-what decisions.

But even leaving aside small-value personal property, the rest of your tangible personal property can add up. Just take a look around your living room at the furniture and antiques, or in your den at that autographed 1927 New York Yankees' baseball and your collection of first-edition Hemingway novels.

So get cracking. You need to figure out what your property is worth, after you first figure out what you have. Overwhelmed at the thought? Here are a few tips to help:

✔ Combine your estate planning-related valuation of your tangible personal property with the same activities for insurance purposes. Most homeowner or renter's insurance policies require you to provide a list of your jewelry, collectibles, and antiques to be included beyond your basic coverage (often more than a certain dollar amount, or for certain types of items). If you need to spend the time cataloging those items and determining what they're worth for your insurance company, use those efforts for your estate planning as well!

✔ Cataloging hundreds of items can be very tedious, and even if you aren't prone to procrastinating, you can often find some way to stretch out the process as long as possible. But if you have a video camera, you can take a guided tour through your home (as well as your second home, if you have one) and narrate the tour into the camera's microphone: "Here is that first edition *Batman* that my idiot husband insisted be framed and hung over the sofa in the living room instead of the painting that I wanted to put there; it's worth..."

✔ Appraisal fees can really add up, especially for hundreds of items. You can get a pretty good idea of what your tangible personal property is worth by using eBay or another online auction service for research.

Look for the identical item (or one close enough and in more or less the same condition) that you have and check the final winning bid of recently closed (completed) auctions, or current bids of active auctions about to close.

Intangible personal property — bank accounts, stocks, and bonds

Your *intangible personal property* — your paper financial assets, such as your bank accounts, stocks, mutual funds, annuities, and so on — may make up a substantial portion of your estate, particularly if you've invested your money wisely (and, as we all have learned in recent years, diversified your assets!).

Fortunately, figuring out what most types of your intangible personal property are worth is fairly straightforward. (More about what's not so straightforward in a moment.) You can

- ✔ Check your bank statements for the value of your checking accounts, savings accounts, certificates of deposit (CDs), Individual Retirement Accounts (IRA), and so on.

- ✔ Consult an interest payment schedule to get the current value of savings bonds.

- ✔ Look up the current prices of your stocks in the newspaper or check any of the many online financial Web sites that give you stock prices, and multiply that price by the number of shares you own.

- ✔ Read the paper each morning and find the *net asset value* (NAV, a mutual fund term meaning the actual value of each share) of the mutual funds you own, and multiply the NAV by the number of shares you own.

- ✔ Ask your broker for the value of your government or corporate bonds, or more complicated investments like call-and-put options and commodities futures.

If you use a computer program to track your portfolio's value, you probably already have the information described at your fingertips; just consult the program you use to figure out the value of those investments.

You may have some intangible personal property that is a bit more complicated when it comes to figuring out its value. For example, you may have *stock options* from your employer. (Stock options give you the right to purchase shares of your company's stock at some point in the future at a guaranteed price per share, no matter how much higher — you hope, anyway — your company's stock price goes.)

If you're one of the "Head Honchos" at work and have a sizable stock option package, consult with an experienced investment professional to help figure out what your options are worth.

Valuing your stock options may be complicated, particularly if your company hasn't gone public yet. If your company hasn't gone public, you can't look up your company's stock price in the newspaper or online because your company isn't yet publicly traded. And even if your company has gone public, the real value of your stock options isn't quite as simple as if you actually owned those shares of your company's stock covered by those options, where you simply multiply the number of shares by the price per share. To calculate the precise value of stock options, investment professionals use complicated factors and terms, such as *intrinsic value* and the Black-Scholes Model. Sound confusing? If you want to find out more about valuing stock options, you can check out *Stock Options For Dummies* by Alan R. Simon (Wiley Publishing, Inc.).

Dead Reckoning: Subtracting Your Debts from Your Assets

In Chapter 1, we mention that in addition to your *positive balance* assets — real property, tangible personal property, and intangible personal property — your estate's value must also include *negative balances* (amounts that you owe).

After you figure out the value of your assets, you simply add up all the debts you owe and subtract that total from your assets to give you the net worth of your estate. These debts include the outstanding balances on

- Any real estate-related loans, including the first mortgage on your home, any second mortgage you may have, the unpaid balance on a home equity loan, the mortgage(s) on a second home, and so on
- Your student loans
- Your credit cards
- Any automobile loans or loans on other vehicles, boats, airplanes, and so on
- Any personal loans, whether from a bank or a person
- Department store loans or other retailer charge accounts

✔ Any margin loans with your stockbroker

✔ Future debts you're sure you'll incur, such as paying for your children's college education

If you have any kind of credit-related life insurance — mortgage insurance, credit card insurance, and so forth — that will pay off the balance of a particular debt, then that life insurance effectively cancels out the debt for purposes of calculating your estate. So don't forget to consider any credit-related life insurance when you're adding up all your property and debts. However, credit-related life insurance isn't a particularly good idea if you can get life insurance elsewhere. For more information, see *Life Insurance For Dummies* by Jack Hungelmann (published by Wiley Publishing, Inc.).

Giving Gifts Throughout Your Life to Reduce Your Estate's Value

You've probably seen the expression that was popular on bumper stickers and posters in the mid-1990s: "He who dies with the most toys wins."

Well, not when it comes to estate planning and, specifically, death taxes! As we discuss in Part IV, the more your estate is worth when you die, the bigger the tax bite. So part of your estate-planning strategy may be to give away some of those toys while you're still alive, effectively transferring those assets from your estate to someone else's estate.

You need to remain aware of many complications with gift giving, such as annual limits on the value of gifts, lifetime asset transfer limits, strategies where you and your spouse coordinate your respective gift giving, and tax implications. In Chapter 11, we discuss how gifts and gift taxes apply to your estate planning.

For now, though, realize that as you tally up all the property in your estate and the property's value, you need to work with your estate-planning team to figure out whether gift giving makes sense for you, and if so, how to get started on a sensible, tax-managed gift plan.

You also need to consider gift giving even if financial and tax reasons don't come into play. For example, you may want to give certain items of sentimental value to a family member or friend, or perhaps a charity or foundation rather than waiting until your estate is settled (and you're no longer alive). Even in these sentimentally based situations, consult with your accountant to determine any tax implications.

Calculating Adjustments in Your Estate's Value Due to Life Changes

Like pretty much everything else related to estate planning, you need to be very vigilant about keeping up-to-date with the change in your estate's value over time.

Changes in your life can dramatically alter your estate's value and, in turn, cause you to rethink your overall estate planning and how you want your estate divided after you die.

For example, if you get divorced (particularly if you live in a community property state, see Chapter 5), your estate's value will likely change dramatically as a result of the divorce settlement. Or, on a more uplifting note, if you win the lottery or have the value of your stock portfolio go way up, your estate's value also increases and you may want to rethink your estate plan.

If you ignore dramatic changes in your estate's value, you run the risk of having an out-of-date estate plan that doesn't come close to reflecting what your original intentions had been.

For example, suppose that you have two children, and in your estate you have $200,000 in various certificates of deposit and treasury bills, plus $200,000 worth of stock in an Internet company called NeverShould HaveGonePublic.com that you purchased in early 1999. When you finally got around to preparing your will later that year, fearing that the Y2K computer bugs would cause widespread chaos and who knows what else, you decided to leave the $200,000 in CDs and T-bills to your daughter and the NeverShouldHaveGonePublic.com stock to your son.

By early 2002, NeverShouldHaveGonePublic.com had joined the dot.com graveyard and the stock was totally worthless. If you die before you update your will, your daughter will get the current value of the CDs and T-bills (now a little bit more than $200,000 because of interest earned since 1999), but your son will get a whole bunch of worthless stock. Therefore, if your intention had been to divide your estate equally between your two children, you first need to realize that your estate's value has changed, and then you need to update your will to reflect those changes and a new strategy of who gets what.

(As we discuss in Chapter 3, if your intention had been to leave each of your children equal shares of your estate, you could have — and should have — divided those assets equally between your daughter and your son. If you had done so, you would not have to update your will simply because of the dramatic change in your estate's value.)

Part II
Where There's a Will, There's a Way

"As you know, your uncle died intestate, and in this State we have our own way of distributing assets to the heirs. Now, do you all know what a piñata is?"

In this part . . .

Everyone needs to have a will! The chapters in this part not only describe what your will should contain, but also look at your state's laws that govern what you can — and can't — do in your will and how the probate process affects your will and your estate. We look at ways to get around the probate process by using will substitutes, which are various types of legal arrangements in which you can own property. We also examine the advantages and disadvantages of various will substitutes, such as living trusts and joint tenancy with the right of survivorship.

Chapter 3

Understanding the Basics of Wills

....

....

*Y*our will is the No.1 legal weapon you have at your disposal to make sure that your estate is divided and distributed according to your wishes after you die. Basically, think of your will as your voice from beyond the grave to prevent the government from grabbing too large a share of your estate, to make it absolutely clear who will receive your assets, and to prevent unintended and unpleasant side effects to your well-thought-out estate plan.

But sometimes, the best-laid plans of mice and men (well, make that women and men — we've never seen a mouse that has a will) are thwarted by selecting a type of will that is inappropriate or inadequate for the particulars of a given estate, or by leaving out key wording that is necessary to make a will valid. And sometimes your will can be 100 percent perfect for you and your estate at one point in your life, but you neglect to keep your will up-to-date with changes in your life. By not keeping your will updated, your estate and the people that you want to take care of after you die can have serious troubles.

Getting technical with terminology

One of the primary purposes of creating a will is to take care of your *beneficiaries*. However, if you fail to properly prepare your will, your *heirs* may wind up with less than expected, or maybe with nothing at all. Legal double-talk? Not exactly. People (such as your family members and friends) and institutions such as charities that you take care of in your will are called *beneficiaries*. However, if you don't have a will — or

don't have a valid will, as we discuss later in this chapter — the individuals who benefit from your estate are determined by state law and are usually called *heirs* (or *heirs at law*).

In layman's language, the terms *beneficiary* and *heir* are often used interchangeably. However, the two words technically have a significant distinction.

You must also take care to keep your will very "matter of fact." You may have seen movies or television shows where someone uses a will as a from-the-grave statement of love, hate, indifference, generosity, stinginess, or some other emotion. If you use your will in that fashion (something like "To my eldest son who has always disappointed me his entire life, who never sent me any cards, who married someone whom I despise, I leave absolutely nothing,") you open the door to all kinds of problems. You can make a mistake in your wording choice that can cause your will to be invalid. Even if your will is letter-perfect, you can open emotional wounds and cause psychological scars that could take years (and lots of expensive therapy!) to overcome. So in your will you should stick to — like the detectives on *Dragnet* used to say — "just the facts!"

In this chapter, we focus on the basics of wills necessary to assure that your will is the most appropriate for your wishes and needs, and to be sure that your wishes will be carried out.

Planning for Your Will

We advise that you work with your attorney to create and to take care of the technical and legal details of your will. Even the simplest, most straightforward wills are filled with legal terminology. Your attorney has likely prepared hundreds or thousands of wills. Why not leave the details to someone for whom the legal-speak and technicalities are second nature?

But before your attorney starts putting anything on paper for your will, you need to consult with him or her to determine what your major objectives are for your will. You need to specifically discuss the following items:

✔ What your *tax exposure situation* is based on your estate's value. (We discuss how to figure out what your estate is worth in Chapter 2.) Your estate may have to pay federal estate tax and any state estate or inheritance tax if your estate is worth more than the allowance at which taxes are owed. (We discuss the federal estate tax in Chapter 13 and state estate and inheritance taxes in Chapter 10.) Your will needs to reflect your overall estate planning, including your tax planning, so both you and your attorney need to clearly understand all tax implications to your estate.

✔ Who you want to explicitly take care of — as we discuss later in this chapter. You can write your will in many different ways to reflect those to whom you want to give what portions of your estate. However, you need to have a general idea of which family members you want to take care of, such as:

  • Your spouse and your children

  • All your children (including adopted children and step-children), but only your children

  • Only some of your children

  • All your children and all your grandchildren

  • All your children and your brothers and sisters

  • Your parents and your brothers and sisters

  • Only two of your four children and all except one of your sisters

✔ You also need to decide if you want some part of your estate (or even all your estate) to go to one or more charities, foundations, or other institutions. Later in this chapter, we discuss different ways in which you can divide up your estate among those you want to include in your will.

The first time you sit down with your attorney, make sure you talk about all three items — the value of your estate and your tax situation, the individuals (family members and others) and institutions you want to leave your estate to, and nursing home concerns — so that your attorney clearly understands your motivation and can help you prepare a will that accurately reflects your situation and preferences.

Getting to Know the Different Types of Wills

Before you even think about what wording you should put in your will, you first need to decide which of several types of wills is right for you. The good news is that you can usually stop your search for the perfect type of will with the first type we discuss, the simple will. However, you should be familiar with the other types in case your attorney advises that some unique aspect of your estate makes one of these other types more appropriate.

Simple wills

Almost always, a *simple will* is the will of choice for you. A simple will is a single legal document that applies only to you (unlike a *joint will* for you and your spouse which we discuss briefly in the next section).

A simple will describes

✔ Who you are, with enough information to clearly identify that document as your will.

✔ The names of your beneficiaries, both people — whether those people are family members or not — and institutions, such as charities, and enough information about the beneficiaries, such as their addresses and birth dates so whoever is reading your will can figure to whom you are referring.

✔ The person's name that you're appointing to be the *executor* of your will. The executor is the person who is legally responsible for making sure that your directions are carried out. You also need to appoint a backup executor — or maybe even a backup to the backup — if, for any reason, your designated executor is unable to perform the official duties (sounds like the Miss America Pageant!).

✔ Always check with whomever you specify as an executor or backup executor in your will before putting that person's name in your will. You want to avoid unnecessary complications that may arise if that person is unwilling or unable to serve as your will's executor. (We discuss the factors you need to consider when choosing an executor — also called a *personal representative* — along with the responsibilities that go along with that role in Chapter 5.)

✔ Your directions as to who will care for your children or for anyone else you are legally responsible.

✔ How you want your assets distributed, and to whom, after you are gone.

Your simple will should be *typewritten* — a term that comes from the days of old-fashioned typewriters but which also applies to a printed and produced document by a computer and printer. Other forms of your will, such as written in your own handwriting or spoken (we discuss both forms briefly in the next section), are usually filled with problems and shouldn't be used.

Other types of wills

You do have other options for your will other than the simple, typewritten will we discuss in the previous section. Other choices, along with the drawbacks of each, include:

✔ A *joint will,* which is a single legal document that applies to two people (you and your spouse, for example). Some married couples mistakenly think that they're required to have a joint will, or that a joint will is better for them than two simple wills. Indeed, a single joint will may be less expensive to have prepared than two simple wills. However, joint wills are usually a bad idea. The primary problem is that most courts treat a joint will as a form of *contractual will,* which is a will or contract that is irrevocable and can't be changed after one party dies. Therefore, if your spouse dies first and you want to revise the contents of your joint will for estate planning or tax purposes, you probably can't. Don't even think about a joint will unless your attorney suggests that some particularly unique aspect of your situation makes a joint will advisable, and then ask your attorney to explain, explain, and explain some more!

✔ A *mutual will,* which you can use to coordinate your estate planning with someone else, such as your brother. For example, suppose that you and your brother want to leave a substantial amount of money to be split among two charities — Charity No.1 and Charity No.2 — that both of you have supported for many years. You can create mutual wills in which:

   • No matter which one of you dies first, 75 percent of either your estate or that of your sibling goes to Charity No.1, with 20 percent going to Charity No.2, and 5 percent going to some other beneficiary.

   • When the other one of you dies, 50 percent of that person's estate will go to Charity No.2, with 30 percent going to Charity No. 1, and 20 percent designated for some other beneficiary.

   Basically, because you don't have a crystal ball to tell you and your sibling which one of you will die first (and even if you did, would you really want to know?), you both have set things up so no matter what happens, Charity No.1 receives a larger amount of money first than Charity No.2 does. If you think a mutual will is particularly suitable for some unique aspect of your estate, ask your attorney and then proceed with caution.

✔ A *holographic will,* which is a handwritten will. A holographic will is handwritten and signed by you. A handwritten will doesn't require an attorney to be involved when you prepare this form of will. However, only some states recognize a holographic will as valid, which means that you may think you have a valid will, but in fact you don't.

✔ A *nuncupative will,* a technical term used to describe a spoken will and has nothing to do with Sister Maria or any of the other nuns from *The Sound of Music.* (Everybody sing along: "How do you solve a problem like Maria's estate planning?") Even though creating a nuncupative will is extremely easy — all you have to do is talk and have someone present to listen — you have many complications and limitations. Some states only allow persons who are on their death bed (literally!) — about to die any minute — to use a nuncupative will for a last-minute expression of what they want done with part of their estate. Some states only allow certain types of property or property only up to a certain dollar amount to be transferred with a nuncupative will.

Don't use any of the preceding nonstandard types and forms of wills except in extraordinary circumstances.

Choosing Your Will's Contents

Your will is composed of a number of *clauses* that when put together into a single legal document, accurately and precisely represent your wishes for your estate. The clauses in your will fall into three categories:

✔ **Opening clauses.** These clauses provide basic information about you and also lay the groundwork for the other clauses in your will that follow.

✔ **Giving clauses.** These clauses follow the opening clauses and comprise the main body of your will, and in which your who-gets-what-part-of-my-estate strategy is specified.

✔ **Ending clauses.** These clauses help to make your will valid by making sure that all statutory requirements have been met.

However, just like you put together a bicycle, bake blueberry muffins, or do anything else in which you need to combine parts or ingredients together, you need to make sure of two things:

1. That you select the right parts or ingredients — or in the case of your will — the right clauses

2. That you put those parts, ingredients, or clauses together in the right order, with the right number of each to make sure that the finished product is what you intend it to be

If you leave out or mess up just one essential clause, you can completely change your intentions or even make your will invalid. And because clauses can get very technical with all kinds of legal terminology, have a professional, such as your attorney, prepare your will for you. (See the sidebar that discusses "How about a preprinted, ready-to-fill-in will?")

Opening clauses

Think of the opening clauses of your will as a preamble in which you provide some basic information to set up the giving clauses that follow. Your will's opening clauses include the following:

- ✔ An introductory clause that

  - Clearly identifies you as the maker of the will

  - Explicitly states that you created this document of your own free will (this part is where you write "being of sound mind," like in the movies)

  - Explicitly states any wills you had previously created are no longer valid

- ✔ A family statement clause, in which your family members referenced later in your will are introduced

- ✔ A tax clause (see Chapter 10) — the structure of your will needs to align with your overall tax strategy for your estate. You can include a tax clause to specifically state how you want taxes to be paid — often out of the *residuary* (everything else) part of your estate, as we discuss later in this chapter. But if you want to specify some other tax strategy in your will, you use the tax clause to state how you want taxes to be paid, by whom, and from what part of your estate.

Your attorney likely has a favorite way of preparing opening clauses, based on hundreds or thousands of wills he or she has prepared. Still, before your attorney starts writing anything for your will, make sure that you discuss your overall strategy.

Giving clauses

The heart of your will may contain the giving clauses in which you specify as precisely as possible how your estate is to be divided among your beneficiaries. In general, you can take one of three different approaches to how you want your estate divided and how the contents of your will's giving clauses will be written.

 ✔ You can be extremely general.

 ✔ You can be extremely explicit and detailed.

 ✔ You can be very explicit about part of your estate and very general about the rest of your estate.

The simplest approach you can take for your will is to basically lump all or almost all your property together, identify the beneficiaries who will share that property, and simply leave all that property to the entire group of beneficiaries to be divided up equally. For example, if you have an estate worth $500,000 that is comprised primarily of bank accounts and stock; if your spouse has died before you; if you live in a rented apartment and no longer own a home; and you want to divide your estate up equally among your four children, all of whom are still alive, then you can take the be-extremely-general approach and just leave that $500,000 worth of property to all your children, each of whom will get an equal share of your estate.

But suppose that you have an estate worth $3 million, a significant portion of which is made up of collectible cars and several vacation homes? And suppose that you not only have two living children from your third (and current) wife, but also seven living children from previous marriages, not to mention several stepchildren? And what if you not only want all these children and stepchildren to share in your estate, but also your two sisters, but not your two brothers?

In this example, you must be as explicit as possible in your will about who will receive specific property from your estate. Which child will receive the 1955 Thunderbird? Who will get the 1967 Corvette, and who gets the 1965 Pontiac GTO? Should your sister who works at IBM get your IBM stock and your other sister who still works at General Motors get your GM stock, or should you give your IBM stock to your sister who works at GM and your GM stock to your IBM-employed sister to help each sister diversify their respective portfolios?

The third strategy for your giving clauses — somewhere in between very explicit and very general — can be useful if you want to divide most of your estate equally among your children, but you still want to explicitly leave other smaller amounts of your estate to your grandchildren, parents, brothers and sisters, a favorite niece or nephew, or a charity.

So regardless of which of the three strategies you want to follow, how do you use your will's giving clauses to make it all happen? You have three types of clauses you can use:

 ✔ Real property clauses

 ✔ Personal property clauses for intangible and tangible property

 ✔ Residuary clause

How about a preprinted, ready-to-fill-in will?

Many do-it-yourself preprinted will forms are available, and some people use them to save money (as compared to meeting with an attorney and having a will created from scratch). Chances are, though, that your individual needs most likely require you to customize your will to some extent, meaning that in most cases, preprinted will forms won't be quite right for you, even though many of these will forms are advertised as suitable for complicated situations.

Therefore, you most likely have to do at least some customization if you use a preprinted will form. As soon as you begin customizing, you open up the possibility of all kinds of problems. Why? First, you need to be sure that you're satisfying legal requirements specific to you own state; otherwise, your will may not be valid. If you're going to put the time and effort into preparing your will, you certainly want the finished result to be legally binding.

Second, you are better off to start working on your will with a clean slate rather than preprinted boilerplate language; doing so actually forces you to decide what to include in your will.

However, if you think that your specific situation is so uncomplicated that a preprinted will form may do the trick — and you really are trying to spend as little money as possible on your will and your estate planning — then we recommend that you at least get an attorney to look over your filled-in will form after you're completed it and to advise you if the finished document may have any problems. If you have limited financial resources, you can usually obtain low-cost or even no-cost basic legal assistance within your community; just check around.

Real property clauses

Your real property — for most people, their home, (see Chapter 2 for other types of real property) — is often the most significant asset in terms of dollar value that you leave to your loved ones, quite possibly, far more valuable than all your personal property put together.

If you want to explicitly leave real property to one or more beneficiaries, you use a *real property clause,* which is a straightforward statement that reveals who is to receive your real property, identifies the property to which you're referring, and names who is to get that property.

Personal property clauses

If you're following the be-very-explicit strategy for your will, then your will must contain personal property clauses specifying what will happen to both your intangible and tangible personal property. In the case of your intangible personal property, such as your stocks and bonds, you can specify who your IBM stock goes to, who your GM stock goes to, and who gets your Enron bonds (just kidding about that last one!)

TECHNICAL STUFF

For fans of *L.A. Law* and *The Practice*

We've taken great care to use plain English in discussing your will and the clauses that make up its contents. But if you're one of those people who can't wait for the next John Grisham lawyer novel, and if you counter your son's dinnertime complaints with either "I object!" or "You're out of order!" then the legal-speak of wills may be of interest to you. Here are some of the legal terms you may come across:

✔ *Exordium clause* — the introductory clause in your will where you state "I, John Doe, of the City of Tucson, County of Pima and State of Arizona, being of sound mind and under no undue influence..." and all the rest of the beginning of your will.

✔ *Dispositive clauses* — the technical term for your will's giving clauses in which you specify who is to receive various parts of your estate.

✔ *Devise and devisee, bequeath, bequest, and legatee* — technically, you devise

(give) your real property to your devisee and your personal property is a bequest (also called legacy) given to your legatee. And for bequests, you use the word *bequeath* instead of *devise* to mean "give." However, these types of property and the associated language have blurred over the years. According to the Internet site dictionary.law.com, "The distinction between gifts of real property and personal property is actually blurred, so terms like beneficiary or legatee cover those receiving any gift by a will." Likewise, the same Internet site describes *devise* as "an old-fashioned word for giving real property by a will, as distinguished from words for giving personal property."

✔ *Testamonium clauses* — the technical term for your will's signature clauses.

Even though you plan to utilize the partly-general-and-partly-explicit will strategy, you can still use a personal property clause to identify some stock or other intangible personal property that you want to go to someone different. For example, if you're leaving the majority of your $750,000 estate to be divided among your children, but you want to leave each of your five grandchildren $10,000, you can use this strategy.

For your tangible personal property, you can divide up your personal items among your beneficiaries. Very often, you want to specify what will happen to sentimental, small-in monetary-value-but-large-in-heart-value (whew!) items, such as your grandmother's antique quilt or your great-great-great-great-grandfather's diary that he carried through the Civil War.

The residuary clause

Technically, your will's *residuary clause* covers the leftovers in your estate that you didn't explicitly mention in real property clauses or personal property clauses. The residuary clause gives you and your will a safety net in case you forget to specifically identify some part of your estate in your will. Remember that your estate can change over time, and if you haven't updated your will lately, you may have some particular item (often tangible personal property, such as a valuable painting you may have recently acquired) unaccounted for.

However, you can use your will's residuary clause for far more than just the leftovers — actually, your entire estate or the majority of your estate — if your will strategy is to be as general as possible. You simply don't use any other giving clauses to explicitly mention real or personal property as we describe above, which forces your estate into being covered by the residuary clause.

Or if you want to take that in-between approach to your will — partly explicit and partly general — you use specific giving clauses for whatever real property and personal property you explicitly want to give to someone. You use a residuary clause to cover everything else.

No matter what your will strategy is, don't forget to include a residuary clause! Even though you may want your will to be as explicit as possible, you will almost always have property in your estate that falls into the leftovers category. Make sure to designate one or more beneficiaries to receive those leftovers.

Appointment and fiduciary powers clauses

The section of your will that includes your giving clauses also contains some additional clauses that actually don't have anything to do with how your estate will be divided. You use the *appointment clause* to name the person you have chosen to manage your estate. At the time you prepare your will, you need to decide who you feel is the best person to handle your estate and act as your *personal representative* after you die. (We discuss your personal representative and the role in managing your estate further in Chapter 5.)

The *fiduciary powers clause* is a companion clause to the appointment clause that gives you the ability to provide your personal representative with powers beyond what may be available in your state regulations. For example, use the fiduciary powers clause to specify that your personal representative will provide your children with some amount of income on an interim basis until your estate is settled. Another way you can use the fiduciary powers clause is to allow your personal representative to continue operating your solely owned business that still provides income to your estate.

Ending clauses

After you complete the most difficult part of your will — the giving clauses portion, which should reflect your overall will strategy — you then need to finish up your work with your ending clauses that include the *signature clause*. The signature clause is where you date and sign your will.

Your will's witnesses also sign the will along with appropriate language that indicates that they witnessed you signing your will and that you executed the will voluntarily and did so of your own free will. (In other words, you weren't coerced or perhaps unconscious with a devious family member putting a pen in your hand to make you "sign" your will.)

Most states recognize that a will can be *self-proved*, which is a method of avoiding the requirement of producing witnesses at the time of probate to prove the validity of the signature of the decedent (the person who died). In the usual case (with a "non-self-proved will"), the person making the will simply signs the will in the presence of witnesses, who also then sign their names as witnesses. In a self-proved will, however, the signature of the person making the will is acknowledged in addition to being witnessed, and the witnesses also execute affidavits. The necessity of providing witnesses at the time of probate is therefore avoided.

Safeguarding Your Will

Here's a quick quiz, and the answer may surprise you: On what single point about wills are estate-planning professionals more likely to passionately disagree?

The answer: whether or not you should keep your will in a safe deposit box.

Some contend that you must keep your original, signed will in your safe deposit box, and that you must also make several copies of your will (or have your attorney make several copies) and give a copy to your personal representative. You must also give copies to certain family members or friends (different people than your personal representative) like your children or your brother or sister, for example.

Others argue that your will shouldn't be kept in a safe deposit box but rather in a safe at your attorney's office or a fireproof safe at home. The reason for not using the safe deposit box for your will, they contend, is that because after you die, your safe deposit box may be sealed until probate (depending on what state you live in) or at least be subject to highly restricted access.

For example, your safe deposit box may only be accessible by a person whom you designated on the signature card when you opened the box, and only during a visit supervised by a bank official and possibly audited by your attorney or the taxing authorities. And in some states, the only items that can be removed from the safe deposit box are your will and burial plot deed.

Our suggestion: Ask your attorney what he or she recommends and follow those directions. If you live in a state where safe deposit boxes aren't sealed, your attorney may advise you to keep your signed will in your safe deposit box. But if you live in a state that does seal safe deposit boxes, you may be advised to keep your signed will with your attorney or at home.

You should only keep your will at home if you have a fireproof safe. That stack of to-be-filed receipts, to-be-replied-to-letters, and candy bar wrappers on your desk in your den or a corner of the family room is no place for your will!

Also, regardless of where you safeguard your original will, you must also keep an unsigned copy of your will for yourself so you don't need to touch the original signed copy in your safe deposit box. If you want to double-check to whom you left a particular item or some other detail on your will, or scribble a possible change that you want to ask your attorney about, you won't risk invalidating your will by damaging or defacing it.

You should also give unsigned reference copies of your will to key family members and others, so your family can start planning for what will happen to your estate.

(Of course, if you have a flair for the dramatic and don't want anyone to know what's in your will until after you're dead, you can always do the bad-movie-plot version and give no one a copy at all, but we strongly advise against that approach!)

Changing, Amending, and Revoking Your Will

Now that you have completed your will, you may assume that you're done with your will. Even though you have completed the tough process of formally expressing what you want to be done with your estate, you still must keep it up-to-date. Often, working on your will can be an emotional process for you as you decide who will get your best dishes when three different children and grandchildren have explicitly expressed their interest with comments like "Boy, I sure do love those plates" at your family dinners.

Nevertheless, you have finally made your tough decisions, you want to put the whole process behind you, and you're tempted to simply put your will in a safe place so that someday in the future your "wishes for your dishes" will be carried out.

Don't make the mistake of putting your will away and forgetting about it. You must make sure that at all times, the details of your will reflect changes in your life that occurred after you initially executed your will.

Why you may need to change your will when something happens

Your will is a dynamic, living document. Ironically, although a will's intent is to provide for what happens to your estate after you have died, the reality is that your will needs to change as your life changes. Think about the climactic last scene of some old black-and-white movie, where the stoic attorney reads the deceased's will aloud as the family members gather around to see what rich oil magnate Grandfather has left them. In that last scene, almost everyone is surprised to find out that Grandpa had made changes to his will as family members drifted in and out of favor, and at the time of his passing those who were out of favor receive nothing except a token amount of cash and a stern from-beyond-the-grave lecture (while those family members who Grandpa favored the last time he updated his will are all ear-to-ear smiles).

This classic movie scene can serve to remind you that those shocked family members were probably blindsided because of some change made to the will that they weren't aware of at all. You need to keep this scenario in mind because your life does change — marriages, children, divorces, increases in your estate value, and so forth — and your will may need to change with these life changes.

The reasons you need to change your will vary. The following are typical reasons to change a will:

- **After a marriage.** You now need to include your new spouse in your estate plan.

- **After a divorce.** You most likely want to absolutely, positively, and certainly make changes to the list of what you had previously been planning on leaving to your now ex-spouse.

- **After your spouse's death.** Most likely, you had left a significant portion — or perhaps all — your estate to your spouse in your will, and now that your spouse has died, you need to update your will to adjust to whom you now want to leave your assets.

✔ **After the death of one of your heirs or dependents.** Suppose that your will has specified that a particular person is to receive a specific asset. If that person dies before you do, then you need to update your will to reflect who you now want to receive that asset.

✔ **After you experience a significant change in your estate's value.** For example, your stock holdings may go way up (or way down!). You should now reevaluate who gets what and how much.

✔ **After any other change in your life that causes you to reevaluate to whom you want to leave something.** (For example, you become passionate about a specific cause and decide that you want to leave a large portion of your estate to some charity that champions that cause.)

If the change to your will is triggered by an emotional event, such as being extremely angry with a family member and wanting to write them out of the will, allow yourself some time to clear your head before you act. Make changes or amendments to your will after life changes and not after an emotional reaction that may dissipate over time.

Ways to change your will

You can change your will in one of two ways:

✔ You can create an entirely new will that supersedes your current will.

✔ You can change or delete specific parts of your current will, or add new parts, while leaving the rest of your current will unchanged. You do so through a new, separate document (we explain in a moment) and not by directly altering your original will itself!

Each of the two methods listed has advantages and disadvantages. In most cases, simply creating an entirely new will with the changes, additions, and deletions is what you want to make. Creating an entirely new will is relatively straightforward, especially in these days of computer files and printers. (Your attorney doesn't need to have an entirely new will typed from scratch like in the old pre-personal computer days.)

However, you can add, change, or delete specific parts of your current will without creating an entirely new will through a form called a *codicil.* A codicil is a separate document that adds to your original will.

Codicils are often expressed in the context of specifically referenced portions of your will. Because a codicil needs to clearly reference a specific portion of your will that it's amending, ask your attorney to prepare any codicils rather than trying to do them yourself, no matter how simple it may seem to just write or type a couple of lines of text. If you mess up, your codicil most likely won't be valid.

When should you use a codicil?

- ✔ When your original will is very long and you want to make only a few, minor changes.
- ✔ When your competency at the time of executing the codicil may be challenged. If someone does successfully argue that you were losing your grip in later years, the codicil may be overturned without affecting the will itself.

Protecting Your Loved Ones from Your Unloved Ones

Perhaps your family bears an uncanny resemblance to an episode of *The Waltons* (still showing in reruns on cable!), or maybe a family scene from a Norman Rockwell painting. Everyone gets along most of the time, every holiday dinner creates new lifelong memories (sigh!).

Or, on the other hand, maybe your family is more like an episode of a soap opera, a particularly nasty soap opera. Lots of bickering and arguing, one family member not speaking to another for years; you know the story. Quite possibly, then, your family consists of loved ones and "unloved ones." Suppose then, that you decide that your unloved ones will receive little or nothing from your estate. If you have made that decision and are willing to live with it (so to speak, because they may not find out your decision until you've died) then you need to be concerned with more than just figuring out how to leave those individuals out of your will. You also need to be concerned with protecting other family members — your loved ones — so that they justly get what you want them to receive without interference from the others whom you decide to leave nothing.

You may think that the most logical way to not leave anything to unloved ones is to simply leave them out of your will (basically, not to mention them at all), but that may be the worst thing you can do! Why? Because doing so leaves the door wide open for the unloved ones to contest your will by saying they were excluded by accident. ("You know, he was always so distracted, he obviously forgot to mention us. After all, we're blood relatives, why wouldn't we be in his will?")

Therefore, you need to explicitly state your intentions for your unloved one in your will, no matter how painful it may be to form those words and commit them to paper. Your attorney can help you with the language to include, as well as help you to keep those words as factual and unemotional as possible.

A simple way to handle the wording problem is to mention the unloved ones in your will, but to leave them only a small or token sum. That way, they can't claim that you overlooked or forgot them and you don't have to explain in your will why they are otherwise excluded.

Still, after you die, those unloved ones may still try to overturn your wishes to receive what they feel they rightly deserve from your estate.

Figuring Out Your Will Status

When you die, you have one of three *will statuses* depending on whether or not you have a complete valid will. Your will status may be

- ✔ *Testacy:* all your assets are covered by a valid will, and you're in pretty good shape
- ✔ *Intestacy:* you die, you don't have a valid will
- ✔ *Partial intestacy:* the "no man's land" (or maybe purgatory?) when only some of your assets are covered by a valid will

Testacy: When you've nailed everything down

If you have a valid will, you are said to die *testate.* Basically, you have spelled out your intentions completely and legally in your last will and testament and you have attained one of your two primary objectives of estate planning, as we mention at the beginning of Chapter 1: control. (Your other primary estate-planning objective is protection.)

Not to sound like a television commercial for a funeral home or life insurance policy, but when you die testate, you at least die with some peace of mind knowing that your wishes will be followed through, courtesy of the legal system.

Intestacy: When you die with zero "willpower"

Intestacy: the dark side! Being *intestate* means that you die without a valid will. Depending on your particular circumstances, the implications of your intestacy can be far-reaching. Most important, dying intestate results in your estate being distributed through the *laws of intestate succession* (commonly referred to as the *intestate law*) — a technical way of saying that the legal system decides how your estate is distributed. Essentially, your state writes a will for you — not an actual-on-paper physical will, but (for any computer and technical readers out there) sort of a virtual will, made up of your state's default clauses that apply to the particulars of you, your family, and your estate.

Now, you have no say whatsoever in how your estate is distributed and who receives it. The intestate succession laws vary by state, but are usually similar from one state to another in terms of the primary purpose, basically, to determine who receives your estate. The intestate law establishes a particular priority for distributing your estate. Did you have a spouse? Did you have children? What other relatives are in the picture?

But what about other people — specifically, those people who aren't related to you — that you had wanted to take care of? Most likely, they're out of luck if you die intestate. Suppose, for example, that you had wanted to leave $100,000 worth of IBM stock to the family housekeeper who has been with you for years, and who even worked for your parents. Without you having a valid will specifying that desire — and thus being intestate — your housekeeper will most likely never receive anything from your estate.

(Of course, whoever does wind up with that $100,000 worth of IBM stock according to the intestate succession laws may later transfer that stock to the housekeeper, as you wanted, but don't count on it!)

Also, if you don't have any living family members covered by the state's intestate laws, depending on the state where you live and your particular circumstances, the state's intestate laws could make your state your only beneficiary! Unless you really want to leave your estate to the state where you live, make sure you have a valid will so you don't die intestate!

Partial intestacy: When the vultures start circling

No man's land. Purgatory. Between a rock and a hard place. *Partial intestacy* — when part of your estate isn't covered by your valid will — is an in-between will status, not quite testacy but not quite intestacy, either. Very often, forgetting to include a residuary clause (we discuss earlier in this chapter) in your will is what causes you to be considered partially intestate when you die.

If you have followed all the steps we discuss in this chapter and you've prepared your will, you may be tempted to think that you no longer have to worry about being intestate or partially intestate. Wrong! You may have overlooked some little item in your will that could negate your will completely if a disgruntled family member contests your will's validity.

The result, if that disgruntled person is successful: You may be *rendered* (basically, switched) into intestacy if your will is declared invalid, resulting in your estate being distributed through intestate succession laws — the one thing you wanted to avoid in the first place by having a will! Or you could forget to include the all-important residuary clause. What happens to your collection of 1930s-era baseball player autographs that you neglected to specifically bequeath to someone? Because you are intestate with regard to those autographs, they will pass to your heirs at law under the intestate law.

Be sure to periodically consult with your attorney to make sure that your will is complete, current, and has been properly signed and witnessed, and you will increase the likelihood of your will status being testate (remember, that's good!).

Chapter 4

Tied Hands and Helping Hands: What You Can and Can't Do with Your Will

In This Chapter

▶ Understanding the laws that affect or interpret your will

▶ Grasping the laws that your will can change and what you must do about them

▶ Comprehending the laws that your will can't change

*W*e've slightly altered an old saying: "Where there's a will, there's all kinds of laws you need to worry about." (Well, it could be an old saying in legal circles, anyway.)

Even though your will provides you with a fantastic tool to direct what happens to your estate after you die, you don't exactly have a free hand in what you can make your will do for you. A number of state statutes affect or interpret your will, and consequently the way you transfer assets to others. If you know what these laws provide, you can include appropriate language in your will to amplify or diminish the effect of those statutes.

In this chapter, we discuss those statutes. Keep in mind that because state law — not federal law — governs your will, some of the statutes we discuss in this chapter may not apply to you simply because of where you live. But because you're working with your attorney to create your will (see Chapter 3), don't worry; your attorney is well aware of the particular provisions that affect your will.

Making Your Peace with Statutes That Affect Your Will

Before you start grumbling about those laws or statutes, remember that many of them protect your beneficiaries, particularly your spouse and children, so they're not necessarily bad for you and your estate. Think of these statutes as playing cards: You have to play the hand you're dealt, but if you really know your game, you can give yourself an advantage.

For example, what happens if your will specifically states that $100,000 must be left to each of your two children (a total of $200,000), but when you die, your estate is only valued at $150,000? A statute called the *abatement statute* (which we discuss in the next section) specifies what happens then.

After you die, who is responsible for paying any death tax that is due? Again, a statute is waiting in the wings to say exactly what will happen.

As you figure out what you want to write in your will (see Chapter 3 for a discussion about the basics of wills), you need to keep the list of the statutes we discuss in this chapter handy for easy reference.

Some statutes affecting or interpreting wills are complicated, especially when the fine print kicks in. Furthermore, the particulars of these statutes vary from one state to another, so you really need to work with your attorney when you prepare your will, rather than use a general fill-in-the-blank form that quite possibly doesn't address the impact of these statutes on your estate.

Identifying Statutes that Your Will Can Change

You can write your will in a certain way to address the following statutes:

- ✔ **Abatement statutes.** What happens when your estate isn't worth enough to provide what you want to leave your beneficiaries and to meet any debts you have remaining when you die?

- ✔ **Ademption statutes.** What happens if some of your property is missing when you die?

- ✔ **Antilapse statutes.** What happens if certain beneficiaries die before you?

✔ **Divorce statutes.** Well, these statues are fairly self-explanatory.

✔ **Simultaneous death statutes.** What happens if you and someone else die at the same time?

Abatement — there's not enough in the cupboard for everyone

In Chapter 2, we discuss how you determine what your estate is worth, and in Chapter 3, we discuss how you can use that information to specify in your will how much of your estate will go to various beneficiaries.

But what happens if you die and for whatever reason, your estate isn't worth enough to give everybody what you want them to get? Your state's *abatement statutes* come into play.

Abatement is defined as the process of reducing or lessening something, so you can think of abatement statues as those laws that say "Hold everything, folks! Because your estate doesn't have enough value to go around, here's what we're going to do." Abatement statutes typically provide for a distribution priority in the event that the assets in your estate are not sufficient to pay all of your creditors and to make a full distribution to each of the beneficiaries named in your will. The abatement statutes specify, for example, that property in your estate's *residue* (your "leftovers") may abate — that is, be reduced — before other property you specifically mention in your will.

You should check with your attorney to determine how your particular state's abatement statutes work. However, if you're not satisfied with your state's statutory method of abatement, don't panic! Usually you can make specific provisions in your will to specify how (and in what order) your assets should abate if your estate is not large enough to provide for the payment of all debts (including taxes) and to then carry out your directions for leaving specific dollar amounts or specific items to your beneficiaries.

Your best strategy to avoid your estate being affected by your state's abatement statutes is to use percentage amounts rather than actual dollar amounts whenever possible in your will.

Suppose that you calculate the value of your estate at $200,000, and you want to split that amount equally between your two children. One way to do so is to specifically state in your will that each child receives $100,000.

However, what happens if your estate doesn't grow at all, and instead shrinks? Maybe some stock you own has declined significantly in value, or maybe you had a large amount of medical expenses. No matter what happens, if your estate is now worth $150,000 and you haven't updated your will to reflect the reduced value of your estate, you have a problem!

But if you had used percentage amounts rather than dollar amounts in your will, specifying that 50 percent of your estate goes to each child, you have avoided abatement statutes coming into play even though your estate's value has shrunk.

Abatement statutes can also come into play even if you have enough assets in your estate to cover specific dollar amounts you've specified for your beneficiaries, but you have outstanding debts that need to be settled when you die. For example, suppose that you still have $200,000 worth of cash, stock, and other assets when you die, but you also have $50,000 outstanding on a variety of credit cards and other debts. Your estate isn't worth $200,000 at all, but rather $150,000 — your $200,000 in assets minus the $50,000 in debts.

Can't your family just, shall we say, forget about what you owe? After all, you're dead, right? Sorry. In the probate process (see Chapter 5), valid creditors' claims must be paid.

In Chapter 2, we mention that you need to tally up your debts as well as your assets when you're figuring out what your estate is worth. Don't forget, otherwise you may be way off in your calculations of your estate's value compared with what your estate is really worth! Be sure to consider an estimate of probate costs (see Chapter 5) and death taxes (see Chapter 10) as parts of your estate's "debt," because those items will also diminish the amount of your estate that will be available to distribute to your beneficiaries.

But what happens if the way you write your will (typically, with specific dollar amounts used throughout) causes abatement statutes to apply to your estate? Basically, the abatement statutes determine how your will's property transfers to your beneficiaries will be reduced, and by how much. In the worst case, some of your property transfers may actually disappear due to the lack of funds available to pay them. That $25,000 to your cousin Jane? Sorry, the money is gone! But why?

State law, rather than federal law, regulates property transfers in wills. States greatly vary in the laws or statutes that affect these transfers. Some states follow the Uniform Probate Code (UPC) regarding wills. More than half of the states in the U.S. have adopted in part or in whole the UPC. The adoption of the UPC enables some uniformity of statutes among states, including abatement statutes.

In Chapter 1, we mention that one of the primary roles of your attorney on your estate-planning team is to help you with the what-if scenarios and to help you prevent problems from occurring. When you're working with your attorney on your will, ask about the abatement statutes that apply in the state where you live, and what may happen to your property based on those statutes. And while you're asking, specifically question your attorney to help you prepare your will so abatement statutes won't come into play at all!

Ademption — some property is missing

In Chapter 2, we mention that cataloging and valuing your tangible personal property (jewelry, antiques, collectibles, furniture, and so on) can be tedious and frustrating, but you need to take the time to do it as part of your estate planning.

In your will, you can explicitly leave items to someone through a *specific bequest*. For example, you can leave your valuable collection of 1950s and 1960s baseball cards to your baseball-crazy oldest son, and your collection of autographed first-edition novels to your other son who is working on his PhD in English literature.

But what happens if you die and the baseball cards or the novels — or maybe both — are, for whatever reason, no longer part of your estate? You may have had to sell some of your property to pay for medical expenses. Or maybe you already gave your baseball cards to your son as a gift with the appropriate gift tax implications (see Chapter 11), while you were still alive, meaning that you have already transferred that property from your estate to his.

Regardless of the reason, if your will refers to property that isn't part of your estate when you die, that property is considered to be missing, or *adeemed*, and the *ademption statutes* apply.

Ademption statutes concern whether the specific asset in question is in existence when you die. In general, the statutes provide that your "who gets what" direction will fail if you are not the owner of the asset when you die. However, you will also find exceptions to the rule which may apply in your case, including what happens if you dispose of an asset while incompetent (see Chapter19) but receive another asset in exchange. Ask your attorney to walk you through the various scenarios that specifically relate to your estate's property.

Ademption statutes vary from state to state, and determine whether the beneficiary who can't receive the specific bequest from your will is allowed to still receive something from your estate, and if so, what that beneficiary will receive.

So what can you do to keep ademption statutes at bay? You can include *backup property* for some or all beneficiaries in your will. For example, you can specify that if your baseball card collection worth $50,000 is no longer part of your estate, your son is to receive $50,000 in cash instead. Beware, though: Including backup property in your will can be complicated and have unintended side effects, so work carefully with your attorney on what backup property to use and the wording to use in your will.

Antilapse — someone dies before you do

Antilapse sounds like a doddering old relative. Actually antilapse is your situation when somebody named in your will dies before you do. To cover yourself, you should consider naming a *contingent beneficiary* (your backup beneficiary) for any property distribution in your will by including words such as:

"In the event that my named beneficiary for the property listed herein does not survive me, then I hereby direct that that my bequest be given to John Doe."

If you don't make your own provisions for contingent beneficiaries, and if your state has an antilapse statute, that law dictates who receives the property that is in limbo because of your beneficiary who died. If your state doesn't have an antilapse statute, then typically the in-limbo property goes to the beneficiaries you name in your *residuary clause* (that statement names the beneficiaries who gets anything you haven't explicitly mentioned in a giving clause). Sometimes, though, that is exactly what you want! Be sure to work with your attorney to determine if naming a contingent beneficiary makes sense.

Divorce — high noon at Splitsville

Nearly everyone has heard the statistic, again and again: Approximately one-half of all marriages end in divorce. With that large of a target audience, no wonder states have divorce statutes that you need to be aware of for your estate planning.

Your spouse automatically has a claim on part of your estate after you die. If you live in a common law state (we cover this later in the chapter), your spouse is entitled to claim a percentage of your assets. If you live in a community property state (we also cover this later in the chapter), your spouse generally owns one-half of your property.

You may not want to change your will right away after you're divorced. For example, you may not have initiated the divorce and you subconsciously think that changing your will is equivalent to acknowledging that your marriage has ended. Therefore, estate-planning procrastination is a natural reaction for the recently divorced.

The good news: In many states, if your marriage has ended, but you resist changing your will to reflect this fact, your estate is protected from claims by your ex-spouse. The effect is that typically your ex-spouse isn't allowed to claim his or her share of your estate if you die after you are officially divorced, but before you change your will. But be careful!

Even with the protection provided by such statues, you still need to change your will as soon as possible after a divorce to clarify your intentions as to who your beneficiaries are. If your ex-spouse isn't one of them, make sure that's what your will reflects.

Simultaneous death — sorry, but we have to talk about it

Estate planning can sometimes be a depressing topic because it revolves around the subject of death, and the statutes dealing with simultaneous death are particularly depressing. However, you need to understand the implications to your estate from these statutes if you want to be as comprehensive as possible.

The simplest way to understand simultaneous death statutes is to consider the following situation:

- ✔ You and your spouse both die.
- ✔ The order of your deaths can't be established. (For example, you and your spouse both die in the same fatal car accident, and the order of death can't be determined.)
- ✔ Your state law determines the order of death for inheritance purposes.

All states have adopted a form of the *Uniform Simultaneous Death Act* to deal with simultaneous death situations. This act is based on the assumption that when the transfer of property is dependent on the order of death, the estate is distributed as if each person had survived the other person. For example, if a childless married couple dies in an accident, the wife's estate is left to her relatives and the husband's estate is left to his relatives. Why? Because each person is assumed to have survived the other, the act treats the estate distribution as if the other spouse had already passed away, which is actually good news (if you can consider any news in this type of situation as "good news"). The same assets don't pass through probate twice (once for each spouse), quite possibly subjecting the estate to double estate taxation and twice as much complication. (See Chapter 5 for more on probate.)

To be on the safe side, include a *survival clause* in your will to either confirm or change your state's version of the Uniform Simultaneous Death Act, according to what you and your attorney decide makes sense for you.

A survival clause is important in "closely related death" (though not simultaneous death) situations. You effectively "void out" a directive you had made in your will to leave property to someone if that person dies very soon after you do.

For example, suppose that the same childless couple is critically injured in an accident, but one spouse dies five days before the other. Without a survival clause, property from the spouse who dies first transfers to the surviving spouse and goes through probate, possibly being subjected to death taxes. When the other spouse dies only a few days later, that very same property can once again be subjected to estate taxes. In effect, the estate goes through double-taxation that wouldn't occur if that couple had died simultaneously.

To help prevent these complications, specify in your will that your beneficiary must survive for some period of time — 30 or 60 days, for example — after your death before receiving the assets you've specified in your will. If that beneficiary dies very soon after you do, your property will skip over that person and go to someone else, avoiding double probate and possible double estate taxation.

Living (and Dying) with the Laws that Your Will Can't Change

If you prepare a will that conflicts with certain statutes, you risk spending a lot of time and effort only to find out that you've created a will that may not be effective or valid. If for some reason you decide to treat your will and your estate like a bad soap opera plot and leave as little as possible to your spouse and children (and possibly leaving them in serious financial trouble), your state's statutes may come to the rescue and provide some amount of financial protection for your family.

But even if you aren't deliberately and maliciously trying to hurt your family with what you specify in your will, you still need to be aware of what your state's laws say about what may happen with your estate. Otherwise, you stand a very real possibility of preparing what you think is a valid will, but because you've accidentally run aground of one or more of your state's statutes, your will isn't valid at all.

So read through the following descriptions of statutes so you know what you're dealing with.

Community property

If you live in a *community property* state, any property acquired and any income made while you're married is considered to be owned 50 percent by you and 50 percent by your spouse. More importantly for estate-planning purposes, you're required under those states' community property statutes to leave half of your community property to your spouse.

Eight states are community property states: Arizona, California, Idaho, Louisiana, Nevada, New Mexico, Texas, and Washington. Wisconsin has a system similar to community property called marital property and for purposes of our discussion, we lump Wisconsin in with the other eight community property states.

If you live in a community property state, all property acquired while you're married is considered community property except for property that you personally receive by a gift or by inheritance, which is considered to be your sole and separate property. For example, your grandmother's inherited wedding ring or the $10,000 cash gift from your aunt to you isn't part of your community property. Additionally, property you owned before you were married is also exempt from being included in community property.

A complicated community

Community property laws can be very complicated. For example, property you own before you marry in a community property state is still considered to be your own. However, income you earn on your own property after you're married may be considered to be community property. For example, if you inherit a farm from your parents before you get married, and then marry and live in a community property state, income from that farm may be considered to be community property.

Additionally, you need to be aware of what happens to your estate if you married in a community property state but later moved to a noncommunity property state, or if you purchased investment property in a community property state but live elsewhere.

You absolutely need to consult with your attorney to see if community property statutes apply to any part of your estate, and if so, what those statutes mean to your estate.

Keep your non-community property separate from your community property! You can actually override the "separate stuff" aspect of your non-community property by either specifying in writing that you want that property (again, a gift or inheritance) to become part of your community property with your spouse, or intermixing your non-community property and your community property. For example, you put your $10,000 cash gift from your aunt into a joint savings account you and your spouse have. If you turn your non-community property into community property, either accidentally or on purpose, you lose your sole control over that property and the community property statutes take over.

Spousal elective shares

What if you reside in one of the other 41 states that aren't community property states? You live in a *common law* state and your spouse still has a claim to some part of your estate, though not the automatic one-half specified by community property statutes. In almost all common law states, your spouse is provided for through *spousal elective shares,* or the law that permits your spouse to claim some part of your estate.

The one exception is Georgia, which uses the old English concepts called *dower* and *courtesy,* which we discuss in the section, "Homestead allowance — keeping a house for kiddies and spouse," in this chapter. In all other common law states, spousal elective shares have replaced dower and courtesy.

Your spouse has the right under spousal elective shares to claim a portion of your estate, with the amount depending on your own state's spousal elective shares statutes. But what about your will? Spousal elective shares are sort of like flipping a coin and calling "Heads, I win, and tails, I win, too."

Your spouse basically gets a choice between accepting the amount you specified in your will or the amount specified in your state's spousal elective shares. If your will specifies that your spouse is to receive more than your state's spousal elective shares specify, then your spouse can accept that higher amount. But if your will specifies a lower amount than your state's spousal elective shares, your spouse can opt for the higher amount specified by law. In doing so, your spouse can cause all kinds of complications to your will.

Spousal elective share amounts vary among states. Under some statutes, your spouse's share is a percentage amount that ranges from 3 to 50 percent of your estate, based on how long you were married. Other states' statutes specify an amount equal to some flat percentage of your estate regardless of how long you were married.

In some states, spousal elective shares are based on an *augmented estate* amount rather than your actual estate amount. Basically, certain property that isn't technically part of your estate is added back to your estate's value, and the spousal elective percentage amount is based on this higher, augmented value rather than your estate's actual value at the time of your death. What's the deal? States that use augmented estate amounts are trying to protect a surviving spouse from that person's husband or wife deliberately trying to reduce the value of an estate and leaving as little as possible to the surviving spouse.

For example, property transfers that you made within a certain period of time before your death may be added back to your estate, along with certain property in which you have ownership with right of survivorship (see Chapter 6) and sometimes life insurance proceeds, retirement benefits, and annuities. Make sure that when you work with your attorney to understand the spousal elective share laws in your estate that you also ask if augmented amounts apply to your estate.

If you really don't like your spouse, don't use your estate plan to try to punish him or her by trying not to leave anything as part of your estate. Your estate-planning attorney isn't the person with whom you should be working on this problem; try a marriage counselor, or if that doesn't work, ask your estate-planning attorney for a recommendation for a good divorce attorney! Don't complicate or even trash your estate planning by trying to give your spouse a raw deal and make some kind of point. Your entire estate plan may be defeated if your spouse makes that spousal election after your death!

Homestead allowance — keeping a house for kiddies and spouse

Just as Dorothy discovered in *The Wizard of Oz,* there's no place like home. So you definitely want your home to be protected after you die. Fortunately, the *homestead allowance statutes* may take care of your home. Unfortunately, though, only a few states have these statues.

The purpose of homestead allowance statutes is to make sure that your spouse and any minor children (under 18 years of age) have a place to live after you die. Your homestead is typically defined as your house and may also include a certain amount of adjacent land. (The legal term you may run across is *curtilage*.) The land aspect of homestead allowances is very important if you live on a farm or any property with a large amount of acres.

Homestead allowance statutes come from the old English common law concepts of *dower* and *courtesy,* and you may come across those terms. (We discuss in an earlier section that Georgia law uses dower and courtesy rather than spousal elective shares or community property statutes.) The purpose of dower and courtesy was to provide a surviving spouse with an interest for the remainder of his or her life in the real property owned by the spouse who died, and therefore have somewhere to live. Dower is the word used for a wife's interest while courtesy refers to a husband's interest.

Homestead exemption — how the law protects your house from your creditors

Homestead exemption statutes are closely related to homestead allowance statutes, and apply if your estate needs to pay debts you owe to creditors. If not enough cash is available, the estate is forced to sell off property — real, personal, or perhaps both — to get enough money to pay the creditors. If your estate owes a lot of money for debts, selling off a single high-value item, such as your house, is often easier, rather than trying to sell a lot of smaller items.

So the homestead exemption statutes are intended to prevent your surviving spouse and minor children from being kicked out of your home if property does need to be sold to pay creditors.

Even with homestead exemption statutes, your home can still be subject to a forced sale. Think of these statutes simply as a "first line of defense" rather than an absolutely 100 percent guarantee that your spouse and children can remain in your home if your estate owes a lot of money and that money can't be raised by selling other property from the estate. Therefore, you need to consider the other parts of your overall estate planning, such as life insurance, to help out the homestead exemption statutes and protect your family and your home.

Exempt property — how the law protects your personal property from creditors

Your estate is composed of various types of property: real property and personal property, including both tangible personal property and intangible personal property.

The two types of homestead statutes that we discuss earlier — homestead allowance and homestead exemption — help to protect part of your real property (your home). However, the vast majority of your intangible personal property (stocks, bonds, and so on) isn't covered by protective statutes and therefore may be forcibly sold to satisfy claims from your estate's creditors.

The good news: Some of your tangible personal property (your car, collectibles, jewelry, and so forth) may be protected through *exempt property award statutes.*

With the homestead statutes, exempt property award statutes vary among states so you need to consult with your attorney about what types of tangible personal property your state's statutes protect, and how that relates to your estate plan.

Family allowance — drawing from your estate to protect your family

Your spouse and children may rely on you as the family's breadwinner. And even if you aren't the sole breadwinner, the income you provide to your family may provide a substantial portion of basic care, such as food and shelter, for your family. Therefore, your unanticipated death will often create an immediate financial crisis for your family. But you have several assets and your will specifies what goes to your family, so you don't have this problem, right?

Not necessarily! Your estate may be tied up in the probate process (see Chapter 5) for an extended period of time. Typically, your estate can't make any distributions to your beneficiaries until all debts to your creditors have been paid. Therefore, your family's immediate financial needs, such as the mortgage payment and even paying for utilities and food, may be in jeopardy!

Fortunately, *family allowance statutes* enable the probate court to provide money for support of your spouse and minor children during the probate process. In fact, family allowance statutes are one of the only distributions that can be made from your estate without risk before the claims of your creditors are paid.

The amount of your family's allowance under your state's law may depend on a number of factors, including your estate's size and your family's living expenses. Ask your attorney to inform you what the allowance likely is so you can factor that into your overall estate plan. For example, you may want to set up your gift-giving strategy to transfer enough cash while you're alive to your beneficiaries that they can use to help cover living expenses during the probate process.

Oops! Taking care of VIPs who aren't in the will

You must continually update your will as circumstances in your life change, particularly when you get married, give birth, or adopt.

But suppose that you get married or have a child and you don't update your will before you die. Are family members who aren't mentioned in your will totally out of the picture when your estate is distributed? (In legal-speak, a spouse or child not included in your estate is called a *pretermitted* or *omitted* heir or beneficiary.)

Pretermitted or omitted heir statutes help to protect certain family members that you don't mention in your will, but they only apply to your spouse and children. These statutes, which (as you probably expect us to say) vary from one state to another, govern what part of your estate must go to your spouse and children if you procrastinate and don't keep your will up-to-date.

Chapter 5

Probate: Top of the Ninth for Your Estate

Dealing with *probate* may sound like you've just been sprung from jail and have to walk a straight and narrow path for a while. Actually, that's *probation,* a word that also means "to prove," like when you call Officer Krupke and reassure him you've left your criminal past behind.

Probate, on the other hand, happens after you die — specifically what happens to your estate. Like probation, probate works through the legal system and is probably the most misunderstood aspect of estate planning.

Fear not! This chapter covers the probate process, including both positive and negative aspects of probate, as well as alternative forms of probate. We also suggest a sensible process for selecting your *personal representative,* the person you name in your will who takes charge of your affairs after you've left the scene.

Probing Probate: What You Should Know

Probate is a term that is used in several different ways. Probate can refer to the act of presenting a will to a court officer for filing — such as, to "probate" a will. But in a more general sense, probate refers to the method by which your estate is administered and processed through the legal system after you die.

The probate process helps you transfer your estate in an orderly and supervised manner. Your estate must be dispersed in a certain manner as we discuss in this chapter (your debts and taxes paid before your beneficiaries receive their inheritance, for example). Think of the probate process as the "script" that guides the orderly transfer of your estate according to the rules.

Many people think that probate applies to you only if you have a will. Wrong! Your estate will be probated whether or not you have a will.

- ✔ **With a valid will:** If you have a valid will, then your will determines how your estate is transferred during probate and to whom.

- ✔ **Without a valid will**: If you don't have a will, or if you die *partially intestate,* where only part of your estate is covered by a valid will (see Chapter 3), the laws where you live specify who gets what parts of your estate.

So read on for a few important points about probate you need to know.

The probate process

Even though you won't be around when your estate goes through probate (after all, you'll be dead), you need to understand how the probate process works. At the most basic levels, the probate process involves two steps:

- ✔ Pays debts you owe
- ✔ Transfers assets to your beneficiaries

A state court called the *probate court* oversees the probate process. Because probate courts are state courts and not federal courts, the processes they follow may vary from one state to another. Yet despite their differences, these courts all pretty much follow the same basic processes and steps, which typically include:

- ✔ Swearing in your personal representative
- ✔ Notifying heirs, creditors, and the public that you are, indeed, dead
- ✔ Inventorying your property
- ✔ Distributing your estate (including paying bills and any taxes)

Swearing in your personal representative

In your will (see Chapter 3), you name who you want to be your personal representative — that is, the person in charge of your estate after you die. However, the court determines the personal representative for your estate under the following circumstances:

> ✔ You die without a will.
>
> ✔ You have a will but for some reason didn't specify who you want to be your personal representative.
>
> ✔ The person you selected has died or for some reason can't serve — and you didn't "bring in someone from the bullpen" to replace your original choice.

A family member, such as your spouse or an adult child, can request that the court appoint him or her as the personal representative for your estate. Regardless of who is finally selected, the court gives your personal representative official rights to handle your estate's affairs. As evidence that this person has the authority to act on behalf of your estate, the court gives your personal representative a certified document called the *Letters of Administration* or *Letters Testamentary*.

In either case, the personal representative named in your will or determined by the court has to first be formally appointed by the court before officially entering into office (the term that's used). Usually this involves that the personal representative take an oath of office, after which he or she will then receive the official documentation showing his or her status (the *Letters of Administration* or *Letters Testamentary* we mention above).

Your personal representative files a document called a *Petition for Probate of Will and Appointment of Personal Representative* with the probate court. This petition begins the probate process. If you have a will, the probate court issues an order admitting your will to probate. Basically, the court acknowledges your will's validity.

Notifying creditors and the public

Some state laws require your personal representative to publish a death notice in your local paper. The death notice serves as a public notice of your estate's probate and enables people who think they have an interest in your estate (such as creditors) to file a claim against your estate within a specified time period.

The notice is part of the process to make the matters of your estate part of the public record. Some people view the general public's ability to review your private estate matters as one of probate's disadvantages, as we discuss later in the chapter.

Inventorying your property

The personal representative must inventory the different types of property — real and personal — that make up your estate so that your estate value can be determined. This inventory is important for a couple of reasons:

✔ **To make sure you left enough to cover your debts and distributions to beneficiaries:** If your estate doesn't meet the monetary obligations of both your estate creditors and your property transfers to your beneficiaries, it's subject to *abatement statutes* (see Chapter 4), meaning that one or more beneficiaries may receive less than you had wanted or even nothing at all.

✔ **To ensure that all property is accounted for.** Your personal representative is in charge of collecting and inventorying your estate's assets to make sure that all property is available for distributing at the end of the probate process. (Your beneficiaries, of course, will want to know what assets are in your estate.) If property is missing or not in your ownership at the time of your death, *ademption statutes* (refer to Chapter 4) become relevant. These statutes determine if a replacement asset or cash equivalent should replace the missing property intended for your beneficiary.

You should already have a pretty good idea of what your estate is worth (see Chapter 2 for details) so that you can make intelligent choices for your estate plan. Obviously, your personal representative needs to know this information, too. So make sure that your personal representative has easy access to the list that shows what your estate includes and what your assets are worth. Even a slightly out-of-date list can serve as a starting point so that your personal representative doesn't have to create an inventory from scratch.

Distributing the estate

The final step in the probate process is the distribution of your estate property. In other words, everyone (ideally) — both your creditors and your heirs — gets what's coming to them.

Creditors that have a valid claim are likely to be paid in the following order (though the order varies from state to state):

1. Estate administration costs (legal advertising, appraisal fees, and so on)

2. Family allowances (see Chapter 4)

3. Funeral expenses

4. Taxes and debt

5. All remaining claims

Whatever's left after your creditors get their money is distributed to your heirs or to the beneficiaries you named in your will. If you died without a will, the laws in your state determine how your property is distributed.

If probate proceeds according to plan and all notices and communications are properly handled, your personal representative is usually protected against any subsequent, late-arriving claims. Your personal representative will be protected after some specified time period expires.

Some complicating factors to the probate process

Some probate processes can be relatively straightforward, while others can be particularly complicated depending on how complicated an estate is. The sections describe some of the more common complicating factors about probate that you will likely encounter.

What's probated where: Differences between states

All states have probate, and all the types of property that make up your estate — real and personal — may be part of your estate's probate. Tangible and intangible personal property, like your collectibles and your stock portfolio, are probated in the state where you live, but your real property (your primary home and other real estate, as we discuss in Chapter 1) is probated where the property is actually located. So if you live on a farm in Pennsylvania and also have a vacation condo in Florida, you'll have two probates: Pennsylvania probate for your farm and your personal property, and Florida probate for your condo.

If you have more than one probate, the additional probate is called an *ancillary probate*. Ancillary probate can be costly because your personal representative usually needs to hire an attorney in the state where the real property is located to handle the ancillary administration of probate.

Here's some good news, though: In many cases the second state's courts will legally recognize your personal representative's authority, and he or she can act on your estate's behalf in the second state without the necessity of a duplicate probate proceeding.

Some more legal-speak for you

If you do specify someone in your will to be your personal representative and to handle your estate, that person is often called the *executor* if male or *executrix* if female. If, however, you do not have a will, the personal representative can be called an *administrator* if male or *administratrix* if female. However, the term *personal representative* can be used whether you have a will or not and is a generic term referring to the person in charge of your estate.

UPC states versus non-UPC states

Probate varies among states that subscribe to the Uniform Probate Codes (UPC) and those states that don't. The probate process is more formal in non-UPC states. The administration in UPC states tends to be more flexible by offering different options regarding the amount of court supervision in the probate process. These options include complete court supervision, no court supervision, or a combination of supervision that falls somewhere between the first two alternatives. Find out whether your state follows the UPC so you can determine the available options for your estate's probate and your personal representative.

Probate or not: Differences between types of property

Another common misconception is that probate applies to all of your estate. Actually, probate handles the processing of all assets in your *probate estate.* Your probate estate is made up of all the property that's distributed through probate; the remaining property is called *nonprobate property.*

In a general sense, probate assets are those you own alone, while you own nonprobate assets jointly with others and to whom those assets will pass automatically upon your death. Nonprobate assets also include assets that pass to a named beneficiary: a life insurance policy, for example. Since these nonprobate assets pass to someone automatically, there is no need for probate.

Nonprobate property is your estate's way of saying (well, if your estate could talk), "No thank you Mr. Probate. I can handle this part myself!" Nonprobate property includes *will substitutes,* such as joint tenancy with right of survivorship and living trusts (refer to Chapter 6). Other assets, such as life insurance proceeds, qualified retirement plan benefits, and individual retirement accounts (IRAs) with named beneficiaries (see Chapter 18) are also included.

Knowing the Good, the Bad, and the Ugly of Probate

Be aware of both the positive and negative aspects of probate. Know the pros and cons when you're planning your estate. You need to determine which assets will require probate and which assets should be nonprobate assets and pass to others through a will substitute.

Probate: The good side

The positive aspects of the probate process include the following:

- ✔ Fairness
- ✔ Defined procedures
- ✔ Protection
- ✔ Potential tax savings

Life isn't fair, but probate is

The probate court's independent role allows for an objective processing of your estate. The probate court regulates all parties involved in the process to make sure that everyone is treated fairly.

For example, the fees paid to attorneys, appraisers, or any other outside parties must be fair and reasonable before they can be paid from your estate.

Defined procedures

The probate process provides an orderly administration of your estate. The probate process guarantees that the probate court will correctly transfer your estate's property.

Here to protect you

The probate process allows creditors that have valid claims to receive what they are rightfully owed from your estate by proving the validity of their claims. If mechanisms weren't in place requiring creditors to prove the validity of their claims, your estate could be subject to fraudulent claims.

An early payout

Depending on your state law and the particulars of your estate, your personal representative may actually be able to distribute part — or even most — of your estate to your beneficiaries earlier in the probate process than otherwise would be done through a *risk distribution*. Your personal representative should work with your attorney and accountant to see if doing so is permissible and advisable, and to proceed with caution.

Imagine a sleazy finance company calling a grieving surviving spouse two days after a funeral and claiming that a loan payment of $5,000 is now two days overdue, but if the payment is made that day by certified check, no late charges will be applied. By requiring creditors to go through the probate process, your estate is mostly protected from these types of fraudulent claims.

Potential tax savings (cha-ching!)

If your estate is in a lower income tax bracket than the beneficiaries who receive the property transfers, tax savings may occur from lower income tax rates. (We explain more about tax implications in Chapter 10.) Income tax savings are dependent on current tax rates and thus may not always be advantageous.

Don't forget that many probate costs are tax deductible, and therefore may also reduce death taxes.

Probate: The bad and downright ugly side

Although the positive aspects present a good case for probate, several offsetting negative aspects can make probate an unpleasant process. The negative aspects of probate include the following:

- ✔ A complicated process
- ✔ A lack of privacy
- ✔ Costs
- ✔ An often-lengthy process

Talk about complicated!

The probate process can cause almost anyone to throw his or her hands toward the heavens and yell "Noooooo!" Multiple, often complicated steps are required before your property transfers can occur. The process often requires numerous hearings and professional assistance — for example, from appraisers to determine value and attorneys simply to get through the process.

Privacy? Forget it

Probate and privacy are polar opposites — the only thing in common is that both words begin with the letter *p*. Privacy typically doesn't exist in the probate process because after your will is probated, your will then becomes a part of the public record. Additionally, your estate's inventory and inheritance tax return (if applicable) also becomes parts of the public record. Anyone then can see what your will and estate contain. ("Wow! I didn't know that John had so much money! Let's try to sell his widow all kinds of shady investments!") However, some states may offer additional means of privacy for the probate process, so check with your own attorney to understand what your estate will go through some day.

Many people consider their own financial situation, including what their estate contains, to be a private matter. On the other hand, you may not be a private person or you may figure that after you're dead, you really don't care about the lack of privacy. In this case, the negative aspect of lack of privacy becomes irrelevant.

Costs can be significant

Everything in life comes with a price. And this old adage applies even in death: Even after you're gone, the probate process is going to cost your family (or beneficiaries).

Your personal representative is entitled to reasonable compensation that typically ranges between 2 and 5 percent of your gross estate.

Your personal representative also has the option of waiving the fee and may wish to do so for income tax reasons. You may consider a family member or trusted friend as your personal representative if you know that person will waive the fee, as long as you feel that person is qualified to serve.

Attorneys are also entitled to a reasonable fee that also may range between 2 and 5 percent of the gross estate, but may vary depending on factors, such as the complexity of the estate, the attorney's time spent settling the estate, the attorney's experience, and other factors. If you add other costs like ancillary probate costs for real property located in another state, the costs of probate add up quickly!

Your beneficiaries need to be patient

Probate may be an orderly and defined process, but probate is anything but fast! The probate process for an uncontested will — meaning no one comes forward to say they have an issue with your will — can easily take between 6 and 24 months. And if your will is contested, the process can be even longer, often years longer.

Typically, your beneficiaries can't receive any property transfers until all the valid creditors' claims and taxes have been paid (see "An early payout" sidebar). While your beneficiaries await the completion of your estate's probate, your estate's value may decline — maybe even significantly (think bear market and declining stock prices) — leaving your beneficiaries with a lot less than they would have received if the probate process was faster.

Streamlining the Probate Process

The legal system hasn't failed to notice the negative aspects of probate. Probate courts and personal representatives everywhere face the costly, timely, lengthy, and complicated process again and again.

In response to the drawbacks of the probate process, several alternatives may be available for smaller estates. Some states have attempted to simplify the process with streamlined versions of probate. Remember, you can't avoid probate with your will, but these alternatives attempt to improve the process. (Hey, every little bit helps!)

In your state, you may come across terms such as *probate affidavit, summary probate,* or *small estate affidavit* that describe your state's alternatives to its formal probate process. Some of these probate alternatives have a cutoff amount that your estate would need to be under (that is, worth less than the specified dollar amount cutoff) for your estate to be eligible to use that particular alternative. Your attorney can advise you what alternatives are available in your state, if your estate qualifies for one or more of those alternatives, and whether or not one of those alternatives makes sense for your estate.

Appointing Your Person In Charge

Choose carefully! Your personal representative plays the central role in your estate's administration.

The appointment of your personal representative (and a contingent personal representative as a backup person) is one of the most important actions in your will. Your estate represents your lifetime of work. You, basically, are your own personal representative while you're alive, but after your death, you need to have someone watch over your estate and make sure that your wishes are carried out. Your personal representative performs this function.

If you don't designate a personal representative, the probate court may appoint someone for you one way or another. So whether you have a will or not, someone is appointed to handle your estate administration.

Identifying your personal representative's role

Before you choose someone as your personal representative, double-check that the person understands his or her responsibilities. For that matter, you need to be aware of your personal representative's responsibilities so that you can select the most appropriate person.

The personal representative follows a *critical path method* — a road map of the most efficient way to proceed — in the administering of your estate. The steps of the critical path are:

- Collecting and inventorying estate property
- Managing estate property
- Processing creditors' claims
- Filing tax returns and paying taxes
- Distributing estate property

Collecting estate assets

Your personal representative first must locate your assets and see what you have in your estate for distribution. Think of this part of your personal representative's responsibilities as the same as the objective of an Easter egg hunt: to find the eggs and put them in a basket, or in this case, find and gather together all your property (sorry, no chocolate-filled treats here).

When collecting and inventorying your assets, your personal representative must notify banks and companies where you have investments of your death, change the address of record on your accounts, and make sure all future communication is through the personal representative. Additionally, your personal representative may need to hire an appraiser to determine your property's fair market value.

Your personal representative also serves as your accounts receivable coordinator. He or she collects all amounts owed to you, such as your final paycheck, rent from an investment property or payments from a note or loan. If your estate is still responsible for what you owe to others after you died, you certainly want to make sure that all amounts owed to your will still come into your estate. You're not letting anyone off the hook for what is owed to you!

Your personal representative also collects payments you're due and entitled to receive from Social Security (but must also return any inadvertent payments from Social Security after your death) and any life insurance proceeds, if the proceeds are payable to your estate. (See Chapter 17 for a discussion of life insurance and your estate.)

Your personal representative must transfer all receivables and any other *liquid* part of your estate (liquid is a financial term that means readily available assets, such as cash on hand or amounts contained in your bank accounts) to an account in which he or she controls. Through this account, your personal representative pays valid creditors' claims, fees, taxes, and cash bequests to your beneficiaries after approved by the probate court.

Your personal representative needs to be careful not to commingle estate assets with his or her own, so he or she must use a separate bank account.

Managing estate property

Because probate doesn't happen overnight and can drag on for months (or even years in the worst-case scenario), your personal representative manages your estate during the entire probate process. He or she keeps an eye on your estate and its contents until the assets are transferred to your heirs or beneficiaries. Managing your estate includes:

- ✔ Supervising property
- ✔ Maintaining property
- ✔ Insuring property
- ✔ Securing property

For example, if your estate has income-producing investment property, such as a rental house or apartment, the personal representative must manage the property or retain a property management company.

The personal representative needs to insure both real property and tangible personal property, such as jewelry and household furnishings, against loss until the property is transferred to your beneficiaries. Some of your estate property likely had sentimental value to you and to the beneficiary you intended to receive the property. In addition to insurance, your personal representative should physically secure your property to prevent any theft or damage.

Processing creditors' claims

One of your personal representative's major tasks is the processing of creditors' claims. Typically creditors have a specified period (varying from state to state) to file their claims or they lose their ability to receive a part of the estate. Because creditors must typically be paid before any property transfers can occur to beneficiaries, processing creditors' claims is an important function of the personal representative in order to keep an already lengthy process moving along.

The personal representative provides notice to creditors of your death by delivering specific notices to the creditors or by general public notice through the newspaper. The notice includes information such as

- ✔ Case or file number assigned by probate court
- ✔ Probate court's location
- ✔ Personal representative's contact information
- ✔ Due date for filing a claim
- ✔ Documentation needed to process the claim.

The personal representative must determine which creditors' clams are valid — sort of like being one of the celebrity panelists on the old game show *To Tell the Truth*. If a creditor's claim is valid and filed within the required time period, the personal representative pays the claim from estate assets. (In fact, sometimes the personal representative must turn to the court to decide whether or not a claim is valid.)

Paying taxes and filing returns

Your personal representative must pay all taxes associated with your estate. Taxes can include any of the following that apply to your estate (see Chapter 10):

- ✔ Federal estate taxes
- ✔ State inheritance and estate taxes
- ✔ Federal, state, and local income taxes
- ✔ Gift tax
- ✔ Generation-skipping tax

Feeling overwhelmed and a little bit guilty about what you are leaving your personal representative to do? Don't! Typically, one of your estate-planning team members — your accountant — actually prepares and files all the tax returns. But your personal representative is ultimately responsible to make sure all taxes are paid.

Many of the tax returns have filing date deadlines that are triggered by your date of death. Your personal representative needs to keep track of these deadlines, which means he or she must be organized. We discuss the important characteristics to look for when choosing your personal representative in the section "Deciding who's eligible to be your personal representative" in this chapter.

Distributing estate assets

The final step for your personal representative is your estate's actual distribution. If you have a will (and hopefully you do!), your assets are distributed to your beneficiaries. If you don't have a will or your will lacks a *residuary clause* (the clause in your will to deal with whatever property you don't specifically mention in a giving clause, as we discuss in Chapter 3) so that some of your assets don't have a beneficiary named, your personal representative distributes the assets in accordance with your state's intestate succession laws.

Even if you have a will, your estate distribution can be affected by other statutes (see Chapter 4). Your personal representative follows the statutes' requirements when distributing your estate assets, such as spousal elective shares, homestead statutes, and exempt property awards.

Real property is transferred to your beneficiaries by a deed evidencing legal ownership. Personal property is transferred by either an assignment document to the beneficiary or by a certificate of title if appropriate (for example, a vehicle). For cash distribution, the personal representative provides a check on the estate account payable to your named beneficiary. The property transfers complete the role of your personal representative. The heirs or beneficiaries generally provide receipts as evidence of the distributions, thus releasing the estate and personal representative.

Deciding who's eligible to be your personal representative

So now you know what your personal representative does in administering your estate. But who can be your personal representative? Your personal representative can be practically anyone, but usually is one of the following:

- ✔ Family member
- ✔ Friend
- ✔ Business associate
- ✔ Attorney
- ✔ Corporate executor (from a bank, for example)

You have a relationship with all these people. The corporate executor is typically a financial institution that you have a financial relationship with, like the trust department of a bank.

Now, whom do you choose? You know their responsibilities as your personal representative. The person — or institution — you select must possess certain characteristics that are needed to perform their duty such as:

- ✔ Trustworthiness
- ✔ Honesty
- ✔ Dependability
- ✔ Good organization
- ✔ Common-sense judgment
- ✔ Fairness
- ✔ Geographical proximity to the probate court and your property

Your personal representative needs these characteristics in order to properly administer your estate. For example, your personal representative needs to be fair because one of the hats the personal representative wears is often as a referee to settle disputes that can arise in your estate.

Geographical proximity to your estate property and the probate court is helpful in your estate's administration. (Long-distance relationships are difficult enough when you're alive and even more complicated when you're dead!)

Okay, so you look around and see many choices. (On the other hand, you may think: "If these are my choices, I'm in trouble!") Many people choose their spouse as their personal representative. After all, you have just spent a lifetime (or your spouse has just made it seem like a lifetime) with your spouse and who knows you better? Besides, your spouse most likely is receiving the largest part of your estate.

But the job is time-consuming and tedious. Make sure your spouse and anyone else you are considering understands what is expected. If you have a somewhat complex estate that involves numerous beneficiaries and creditors, inform your personal representative.

Avoiding the pitfalls

You need to be aware of several potential pitfalls when selecting your personal representative, including:

- ✔ Being perceived as favoring one family member over another
- ✔ Keeping your business going (if applicable to your situation)

If you have three adult children, all about the same age and equally well off financially, you run the risk of slighting two of those children if you select the other as your personal representative. Never mind that pretty much anyone who has ever served as a personal representative agrees that the job is basically one of dealing with details and complications — and plenty of aggravation — for months on end. The other children may conceivably think that the child selected as your personal representative is somehow favored, and this can cause all kinds of family strife and hard feelings for years to come.

If you find that you're in a similar situation, you may be tempted to designate two or more of your children as co-personal representatives of your estate. Think carefully! You open your estate up to unnecessary disputes and complications if two or more people share that role and then start to use your estate as a battleground for disputes between themselves. As Abe Lincoln (or, for *Seinfeld* fans, George Costanza) may have put it, "A personal representative divided against itself can't stand!"

A better alternative than co-personal representatives is to ask your attorney or perhaps your lifelong best friend (hopefully a trustworthy one, remember the key characteristics!) to be your personal representative.

If you own your own business, or are one of the handful of owners (along with several partners of a closely held business), you need to pay special attention to whom you designate as your personal representative. Your personal representative may have to keep your business going. But if that person has no experience in your business, or doesn't have the time to devote to your business, a significant portion of your estate's value may go down the drain if your business collapses. Therefore, if you own a small business (see Chapters 15 and 16), you need to either select a personal representative who can represent your interests and keep your business going, or make other business continuity arrangements separate from the usual personal representative responsibilities.

Paying your personal representative

Now that your personal representative has done all this work, what does he or she get? You really can't personally say, "thanks for a job well done" because you're dead! Your personal representative is typically entitled to receive a personal representative fee. The fee varies among states, and the probate court approves the personal representative fee. Your personal representative receives payment at or near the end of the probate process.

Thinking Things Through When Someone Asks You To Be a Personal Rep

What if your brother asks you to become his personal representative? Suddenly the tables are turned and you have to decide whether to take on that role. You now know what responsibilities are expected of you if you say yes.

But what factors do you consider in making your decision? If you accept the role as a personal representative, are you personally liable for anything to do with the estate? Well, the answer is no — most of the time. You aren't personally liable for any claims, lawsuits, or other monetary obligations of the estate itself as a personal representative.

Traditionally a personal representative is held to a standard regarding investment responsibilities and liabilities known as the *Prudent Person Rule*. In many states, the Prudent Person Rule has been recently replaced by the similarly sounding — but functionally different — *Prudent Investor Rule*. The difference between the two relates to the personal representative's investment focus. The newer Prudent Investor Rule imposes significant new duties on the personal representative for how investments are managed, with resulting increases in potential liability if those duties aren't properly performed. Make sure you completely understand the specific rules and obligations that govern how you serve as a personal representative, should you find yourself in that role.

As a personal representative, you're entitled to receive a fee for your services. The fee is typically a percentage of the probate estate. Many times personal representatives waive their fee for a family member or good friend. Be aware that if you do accept the personal representative fee, the payment you receive is taxed as ordinary income. Compare tax rates between ordinary income and estate-related taxes to see if receiving payment or property is the most tax advantageous for you.

If you're also an heir or beneficiary of an estate for which you're serving as a personal representative, the distribution you receive is free of income tax (any applicable estate tax is usually taken before you get your share). If you're both a personal representative and beneficiary of the same estate, you should consider waiving the taxable personal representative fee in exchange for a tax-free larger distribution.

Despite the hassles and occasional aggravation, the vast majority of personal representatives find the job to be at least a little bit personally rewarding. You have a feeling of helping a friend or family member complete his or her final wishes and intentions. But again, as with anything in life, make sure you know what you're getting into before you agree to become someone's personal representative.

Chapter 6

Dodging Probate: Saving Time and Money with a Will Substitute

*I*n other chapters, we point you toward two main objectives of estate planning: protecting your property and controlling it as long as possible after you die. Your will is your No.1 legal weapon, of course.

But you have other ways to reach your goals of maintaining protection and control — various types of contracts, agreements, and legal documents that are called *will substitutes*. We discuss them in this chapter.

Understanding Will Substitutes

For many of us, having a substitute conjures up memories of school days. When you heard that a sub was coming in for the regular teacher, you wanted to know whether the stand-in was harder or easier than your regular teacher. (We all hoped the sub would spend the entire period talking about growing up on a ranch in Colorado or working as an extra in a Hollywood movie. Any old story was better than drilling multiplication tables or conjugating verbs.)

As with substitute teachers, you're wise to be prepared and do your homework about various types of will substitutes and figure out which ones, if any, make sense for your estate planning. Some will substitutes (like some substitute teachers) can give you peace of mind by filling in the gaps and working hand-in-hand with what you've specified in your will. Other will substitutes (like the occasional nasty substitute teacher who for some reason seemed to pick on you) may actually have very little benefit for you, other than wasting some of your money and triggering unpleasant down-the-road consequences.

In your will, you specify your instructions for what you want to happen to your property after you die. You can specifically mention various items and who will get those items, or you can use your will's residuary clause to instruct how anything you haven't specifically mentioned should be distributed and to whom. If you forget to include a residuary clause in your will, or if you die without a valid will, your state's intestate laws come into play and "write a will for you" that determine who gets what.

However, the covered-in-your-will-or-not distinction has a little wrinkle, and that's where will substitutes come in. Will substitutes treat property transfers by designating who receives the property at your death through *operation of law*. The same way that certain *statutes* (see Chapter 4) can interpret and may override what your will says, will substitutes can take precedence over both your will and your state's intestate laws.

Why would you want to use a will substitute rather than your will for certain property? We have a one-word answer for you: probate! Actually, make that three words: outside of probate. Property covered by a will substitute is transferred outside of probate, which may provide you with some significant advantages in the following:

- ✔ **Time.** In Chapter 5, we discuss that the probate process can be lengthy (especially if you have a complicated estate) and the actual transfer of property typically doesn't occur until probate is mostly or totally completed. With will substitutes, however, property is typically transferred immediately upon your death, even if other parts of your estate are just beginning what may be a lengthy probate process.

- ✔ **Money.** Will substitutes may save you and your estate some money, depending on whether or not your state's version of the Estate Recovery Act applies to your estate after you die. We discuss the Estate Recovery Act, used to recover certain government-provided health care expenses you may receive, in Chapter 10. For purposes of discussing will substitutes, remember that your state's version of the Estate Recovery Act may apply only to your probate estate. In Chapter 5, we note that by definition, your probate estate only includes your property that is passing through probate, and certain property — including what is covered by various forms of will substitutes — isn't part of your probate estate. Therefore, if the government is trying to grab part of your estate after you die under provisions of its Estate Recovery Act, you may be able to protect property from the government's grasp by using will substitutes rather than your will.

If the resulting transfer of nonprobate property results in a death tax — whether state, federal, or any other tax — the taxes must still be paid. Will substitutes only help you do an end run around probate; applicable death taxes must still be paid. However, in many cases, will substitutes may reduce your taxes, so work with your accountant and attorney to coordinate your tax strategy with what you plan to do for will substitutes.

Sorting through the List of Will Substitutes

You can hold property in a variety of will substitute types, including:

- ✔ Joint tenancy
- ✔ Living trusts

We discuss each of the preceding types of will substitutes in detail in the following sections. Additionally, try to have at least a passing familiarity with some other will substitutes, including:

- ✔ Tenancy by the entirety
- ✔ Payable on death accounts (PODs)
- ✔ IRAs, life insurance annuities, and other assets paid to named beneficiaries

Will substitutes predetermine who gets your property upon your death by one of two ways:

- ✔ Right of survivorship
- ✔ Beneficiary designation

Joint tenancy, tenancy by the entirety, and payable on death accounts use right of survivorship, while the other will substitute types use beneficiary designations.

Figuring out joint tenancy

Joint tenancy means that you and others have an equal and undivided ownership of some property. Basically, each joint tenant has the same right to use whatever property the joint tenancy agreement applies to. Joint tenants must own an equal percentage of the property. If two people hold interest in property as joint tenants, each owns one-half of the property; if three people hold interest, then they each own one-third; four people, each own one-fourth, and so on.

The distinguishing characteristic of joint tenancy as a will substitute is the *right of survivorship*. In fact, joint tenancy is usually referred to as *joint tenancy with right of survivorship,* sometimes abbreviated JTWROS. The key feature of joint tenancy is that when you die, the other co-owner (or co-owners) receives your share of the property by *right of survivorship.* Whether you have a will or not is immaterial to the property transfer. If you have a will, the property transfers outside of your will. If you don't have a will, the property transfers outside of intestate succession laws. The surviving joint tenant(s) receive(s) the property.

Family members often create joint tenancy to automatically leave property to the surviving joint tenant family member. However, as we discuss later, joint tenancy has some significant disadvantages, so work with your attorney to figure out whether joint tenancy, or perhaps some other form of a will substitute (such as living trust) best suits your needs.

For example, Tom and Meghan own a house and they hold title to the property as joint tenants with right of survivorship. At Tom's death, Meghan automatically receives Tom's share of the house because of the right of survivorship feature as joint tenants.

Now, suppose Tom, Meghan, and Avery — three people now instead of two — own the house as joint tenants with right of survivorship, meaning that each of them owns one-third of the house. Again, Tom dies. In this case, Tom's share of the house is split equally between Meghan and Avery, who now each have a one-half interest in the house as joint tenants with right of survivorship. Later, upon one of their deaths, the surviving joint tenant will own the house.

In most states, during his or her lifetime a joint tenant can sever the joint tenancy without the consent or notification to the other joint tenants. The joint tenant who severs the joint tenancy then owns the property as a tenant in common with the other former joint tenant. But if more than one joint tenant remains, they still own their share of the property as joint tenants between themselves.

What? An example clarifies the preceding confusing scenario. Suppose Tom, Meghan, and Avery still own the house as joint tenants from the previous example. But Tom decides to *deed* (basically, to give) his interest to Sandra, thereby breaking his joint tenancy with the other co-owners. Now, the property is owned as follows: Sandra owns a one-third interest as a tenant in common and Meghan and Avery own two-thirds interest as joint tenants between themselves.

Don't confuse me!

A sort-of-related form of ownership to joint tenancy that isn't a will substitute form is *tenants in common*. With tenants in common, equal ownership of the property isn't required as with joint tenancy. Additionally, no right of survivorship feature exists so ownership interests can be given to anyone. However, many people confuse these two types of ownership because both use derivatives of the word *tenant* (*tenancy* in one form, *tenants* in the other).

Also, don't let the word *tenant* or the phrase *joint tenancy* confuse you. Joint tenancy (or, for that matter, tenants in common) doesn't mean that you and others are renting (and are tenants of) some particular property like an apartment or a townhouse.

Remember, Meghan and Avery still own the property as joint tenants so they have retained the right of survivorship with each other for their portion of the property. If Avery dies, Meghan receives Avery's share of the property by right of survivorship and would then own two-thirds of the property as a tenant in common with Sandra.

Later, if Sandra dies before Meghan, her share of the property goes to her heirs or beneficiaries and not to Meghan as the other co-owner because at that point, Sandra and Meghan own the property together as tenants in common. No right of survivorship feature exists because long ago, Tom (the original one-third owner who had deeded his interest to Sandra) broke his side of the joint tenancy relationship. Likewise, because Meghan no longer has a co-joint-tenant, her interest also passes to her heirs or beneficiaries at her death and not automatically to Sandra.

Advantages of joint tenancy

Why should you consider joint tenancy specifically as a will substitute? As an alternative to probate, joint tenancy provides you with several advantages:

- ✔ **Cost savings.** The formation and eventual termination of joint tenancy is inexpensive. Unlike other forms of will substitutes, such as a living trust that an attorney should at least review and ideally prepare, you may save money by not necessarily needing to use an attorney to create a joint tenancy. (However, we strongly recommend that as with all other aspects of your estate planning, you work with your attorney as you plan your strategy and figure out what techniques best apply to you.)

- ✔ **Clear title transfer.** Because joint tenancy is based on right of survivorship, joint tenancy allows for a clear transfer of title to the surviving joint tenant. No questions exist about the intent of who is to receive the property upon the death of one of the joint tenants. (To be certain that no question about intent exists, some states require that the wording "as tenants with rights of survivorship and not as tenants in common" be added.)

✔ **Creditors claim reductions.** One of the main steps in the probate process is the payment of valid creditors' claims. Before any of your beneficiaries can receive property transfers after you die, your personal representative must first pay any valid creditors' claims. If your estate doesn't have enough cash or cash equivalents to satisfy the creditors' claims, your estate may be forced to sell property to pay the claims. However, because property held as joint tenants isn't part of the probate process, creditors don't have ready access to property held as joint tenants. Thus the amount of creditors' claims may be reduced.

If the court can prove that you transferred title of property to joint tenants to hide from creditors, your creditors may still make a claim against part of your joint tenancy property.

✔ **Convenient and fast.** You can easily create and ultimately dissolve ownership as you craft and later refine your estate plan. Furthermore, by not having to deal with complex legal documents — wills, trusts, and living trusts — you can use joint tenancy without worrying about the legality and hassles of the wording in these documents. Just a few simple words added to the property title and you're done. In estate planning, you can't get any faster than that! Beware, though: Even though you can dissolve the joint tenancy after it's created, you can't turn back the clock to the way things were before you created the joint tenancy without the permission of the other joint tenant or tenants.

✔ **Private.** If you value your privacy, even after you've died, joint tenancy offers you a better alternative than probate, where your will and estate become part of the public record. Note, however, if your state has an inheritance or estate tax you may be required to file a tax return and pay a tax on the decedent's share of the jointly owned property. Because the tax return is usually a matter of public record, your wishes for privacy will be defeated.

Work out the tax scenarios with your accountant as part of your overall estate planning before you put joint tenancy wording on any property titles!

Disadvantages of joint tenancy

So far, so good with joint tenancy. The concept seems straightforward and the advantages sound pretty good. So why hold property any other way? Well, you know the old saying: If it sounds too good to be true, it must be an estate-planning concept! Holding property as joint tenants has significant limitations and disadvantages that you need to be aware of, including:

✔ **Forced disposition.** The surviving joint tenant(s) receive(s) your share of the property. Period! You can't decide to leave a portion of that property to your joint tenant and another portion to someone else; the law forces you to leave your share to your joint tenant. So depending on the property in question and what you want done with that property after you die, joint tenancy may not be the right estate-planning tactic.

✔ **Lack of control in property transfer.** The right of survivorship feature may not control the final transfer of property under joint tenancy. The death of the next-to-last joint tenant leaves the property to the surviving joint tenant as sole property; no right of survivorship exists when you own something by yourself. So unless other arrangements are made (even creating a brand new joint tenancy with other people), the property may ultimately become a part of the sole surviving joint tenant's estate.

✔ **Undesirable property transfers.** After the next-to-last joint tenant has died, the surviving joint tenant can dispose of the property in any way he or she wants, even if the disposal is contrary to the intentions of any other joint tenants who have died earlier. In effect, if you're involved in a joint tenancy, you have to let go of any desires you have for the ultimate disposal of the property beyond the other joint tenants.

For example, suppose Kathy and Greg, who aren't married and have no children, own a house as joint tenants. They discuss their intentions to leave the house upon their deaths to their favorite local charity. But after Kathy dies, Greg owns the house as the surviving joint tenant and can direct the property transfer to anyone he chooses at his death. Suppose Greg changes his mind and decides that instead of the charity, his sister — who didn't get along with Kathy — gets the house at his death. So Greg's sister receives the house and Kathy's intentions for the property are out the window. (If the property was named in a will or held in a trust, they may have set up a chain of property transfers. The will could state that the survivor had use of the house while he or she was alive and upon his or her death, the charity is guaranteed to receive the house. In effect, choosing joint tenancy prevented Kathy from achieving her ultimate objective for the property.)

✔ **Exposure to other joint tenant's creditors.** We mention that joint tenancy may protect property from your creditors' claims after you die, but what about protection from creditors' claims against your joint tenant? For example, if your joint tenant loses a court battle and has a large judgment against him, the property you hold as joint tenants can potentially be subject to the judgment resulting in a forced sale of the property.

✔ **Numerous tax disadvantages.** Perhaps the biggest disadvantage of joint tenancy is in the area of taxes. A tax disadvantage? Didn't we say earlier that a potential income tax savings from joint tenancy by the surviving joint tenant in a lower tax bracket may occur? Well, yes, but taxes are funny: In estate planning what often saves you money in one tax area increases your taxes (sometimes significantly) in another tax area. In this case, the savings in income tax may be more than offset by the increase in estate tax.

For example, if you're the surviving joint tenant from a property that you once held with two others as joint tenants, this property may inadvertently cause a payment of a larger estate tax. In Chapter 10, we discuss how property held as joint tenants between spouses only receives one-half of the *stepped-up tax basis,* which is a way of resetting some of the figures that are used to calculate the amount of taxes you owe. Furthermore, if your estate is large enough to be in a federal estate tax bracket, joint ownership and particularly a joint tenancy (or a tenancy by the entirety between husband and wife, as we discuss later in this chapter) may preclude the ability to save or reduce federal estate taxes. For now, think of joint tenancy as having potential tax disadvantages when compared with wills or other will substitutes such as living trusts.

Setting up a living trust

We examine trusts in-depth in Chapters 7, 8, and 9, but here, we introduce the living trust due to its popularity as a will substitute form. A *living trust* is created while you're alive (thus the use of the word *living*), unlike a *testamentary* trust, which is created at your death through your will. (Technically, a testamentary trust is similar to a will because it provides for property transfers at your death.)

You place certain property called *trust principal* into a living trust. (You may also see the word *corpus* referring to the property used to fund the trust, which often makes people nervous, considering how similar that word sounds to corpse — makes sense because both corpus and corpse come from the same root meaning "body.")

When you create a revocable living trust, you can be in charge of your own living trust. When you die, the revocable living trust becomes *irrevocable* (meaning you can't "undo" the trust — we discuss irrevocable trusts in Chapter 7) — and the trust principal (again, the property that you have placed into the trust) then passes to your beneficiaries without having to go through probate.

By making a trust revocable, you can dissolve the trust at any time up until death or until the trust document makes the trust irrevocable (such as in the event of your incapacity).

Joint tenancy and unmarried couples

Many unmarried couples (either same sex or opposite sex) use joint tenancy with right of survivorship as a way to transfer their respective ownership shares to their partner. As we discuss in Chapter 19, most estate-planning laws are oriented toward "traditional" families (a married couple, 2.53 children, and so on). If you're in an unmarried relationship and you co-own your home with your partner, joint tenancy with right of survivorship may be an ideal way to protect your partner's right to stay in the home after you die (and vice versa), even though the law doesn't recognize your relationship in the same way as — and with the same rights of — a married couple.

Roles for everyone!

The best way to examine a living trust is to look at the parties and roles involved. Living trusts involve the following roles (note that one person can play more than one role, as we explain later in this chapter):

- Trustor (or settlor)
- Trustee
- Successor trustee
- Income beneficiaries (or current beneficiaries)
- Remainderman (a "special class" of beneficiary)
- Designated person managing minor beneficiaries

Don't panic at the legal jargon! In a typical trust, the *trustor* (or *settlor*) creates the trust, and the *trustee* has the legal interest in managing the trust for the *income beneficiaries* who will have beneficial interest or right to use the trust property. After the beneficiaries receive their portion of trust, the *remainderman* is the trust beneficiary who receives the remainder or what is left over.

In Chapter 1, we discuss two main types of property interest: legal, the right to manage property, and beneficial, or the right to benefit from the property. Trustees have the legal interest to transfer and manage property in the trust while beneficiaries have the right to use the property.

The *successor trustee* is the person you name to become trustee when you die (or become incapacitated) if you're currently the named trustee. Think of your successor trustee as the personal representative of your trust. Look for a successor trustee who has the same attributes we recommend for a personal representative in Chapter 5. Typically, people name a spouse, child, or trusted friends as successor trustees.

You need to appoint someone (usually referred to as a guardian or a custodian) to manage the property of *minor beneficiaries* — those beneficiaries who aren't of legal age.

The paperwork — ugh!

The actual living trust document varies just as wills do. (We strongly recommend working with your attorney to make sure you get all the necessary information correctly on paper.) The variations may include:

- ✔ Designating the trustor and the initial trustee
- ✔ Defining trust property
- ✔ Naming a successor trustee
- ✔ Defining ways to revoke or amend the trust
- ✔ Administering trust by trustee during trustor's lifetime
- ✔ Administering trust by the successor trustee after trustor's death or incapacity
- ✔ Defining trustee's power
- ✔ Restricting beneficiary assignments *(spendthrift clause)*

You can find more details about the paperwork associated with trusts in Chapters 7, 8, and 9. The trust sets forth in detail how the trustor must handle the trust after you've died.

Advantages of living trusts

So why the frenzy over living trusts? Living trusts are a convenient way to avoid additional probates if you have real property like a house, vacation home, or income-producing investment property located in more than one state.

Real property must be probated in the state where the property is located (we discuss *ancillary probates,* or additional probates, in Chapter 4). More than likely, your entire probate process will be slowed down because of the need to administer more than one probate and the increases in fees and costs.

Some states consider real property held in a living trust to be intangible personal property enabling your estate to avoid ancillary probate. If you have real property in more than one state, check to see how your state views real property held in a trust.

Privacy (as compared with probate) is another advantage of a living trust. As with other will substitute forms, your trust is a private agreement — a contract between the trustee and trustor. However, some county recorder offices require the filing of trusts as part of the public record.

To retain the privacy of trusts, your attorney can draft a separate document called a *memorandum of trust,* which identifies the most basic information of the trust. Therefore, your trust usually doesn't become public record as your will does in probate.

However, if your state has an inheritance tax, the trust's details may be required to be filed with the state through an inheritance tax return or other document. You may need to include the amount of trust principal and the identification of beneficiaries or remainderman.

The real attraction of living trusts stems from the advantages offered beyond the typical will substitute form advantages. Living trusts offer unique advantages:

✔ Better planning

✔ Better protection from probate

✔ Better prediction of the future

✔ Ability to name alternate beneficiaries

✔ Ability to name guardianships

In preparing a trust, you place property into the trust (called *funding the trust*), and that property is thereafter known as your *trust principal.* By thinking through what property to include in your trust principal, you examine what property you have.

Unlike joint tenancy, where ultimately the last surviving joint tenant holds the property that can become part of the probate estate, living trusts provide you with better assurance of avoiding probate. In our earlier example, if Tom and Meghan own a house as joint tenants and Tom dies, Meghan, as the surviving joint tenant, now owns the house individually, making the house part of her probate property.

But instead of joint tenancy, suppose Tom and Meghan use a living trust to hold title as co-trustors and co-trustees to the house for both of their lifetimes. If Tom dies, Meghan still owns the house in trust and the house is not part of the probate estate. Upon Meghan's death, the house passes from the trust to the designated beneficiaries without being subjected to probate.

And what does predicting the future have to do with living trusts? Plenty, sort of. A living trust provides you with a peek into your estate's future and how it will be handled. If you establish a trust as the trustor and name someone other than yourself as the trustee to manage your trust, you can preview how he or she handles the management of the trust property and determine if adjustments in your estate need to be made. No need for guesswork on how he or she will perform when you're dead, when you can't make any changes (for obvious reasons). You can preview the future now.

If your trust is set up to make distributions while you're alive, you have the opportunity to see how both your trustee and beneficiaries may handle the trust principal distributions affording you the opportunity to make adjustments if needed.

A living trust also allows you to name alternate beneficiaries if something happens to your primary beneficiary. You can't name an alternate with other will substitute forms like joint tenancy or, as we discuss later, payable on death accounts.

And if you're incapacitated and not able to care for your own affairs, you can set up a living trust to provide for you in the case of incapacity. This advantage is part of the reason living trusts are touted for the elderly. In such a case, you can avoid the necessity of a court-appointed guardian or conservator, or at least assist those persons in carrying out their duties.

Another method of avoiding guardianship or conservatorship is by the popular *durable power of attorney* (see Chapter 19), usually in addition to a living will.

Disadvantages of living trusts

Keep this adage in mind when you're planning your estate: No good will substitute goes unpunished! Disadvantages exist no matter what road you choose, even with living trusts. These disadvantages include:

- ✔ Funding
- ✔ On-going maintenance
- ✔ Longer creditor claims period

The up-front funding of the living trust is a deterrent to many people. Remember, to hold title as joint tenancy, all you have to do is change the title to property with the appropriate wording. It's not so simple with living trusts.

Living trusts require you to execute a trust document. But beyond the paperwork, the next step in the process is the trust's actual funding. You as trustor must transfer your property's title to the trust. So what's the problem? Every time you acquire property — from stocks to real estate — you must transfer title of the property into the trust. For active investors, transferring your property's title to the trust can become a hassle. (Then think about other property, such as cars, furniture, collectibles, and so on, which can be even more hassle!)

If you forget to put property in your trust, the property is treated as if it was never part of the trust and is handled through probate if you have a will, or intestate succession laws if you don't have a will. For example, if you're the beneficiary of someone's life insurance or if you receive property that was formerly held as part of a joint tenancy — and you forget to take care of this property for living trust purposes — then that property isn't part of the living trust.

Trusts require monitoring to make sure that everything is proceeding in accordance with the terms of the trust. Don't just sign a trust document and put it away. The only way to achieve the advantage of previewing the future is to monitor the trust on an on-going basis, which takes time and may not be for everyone.

Another living trust disadvantage is the potentially longer period for creditors' claims. Why? In some states, trusts don't protect property from being subject to creditors' claims. Consequently, trustees may delay distributions to beneficiaries and remainderman until they're certain all claims have been paid. Remember, no probate for trust principal exists so consequently no probate process exists for the controlled processing of creditors' claims.

If a trustee doesn't perform certain required duties after the trustor's death, he or she can have substantial personal liability. This reason is why trustees often delay property transfers until they're certain all creditors have been paid.

Focusing on the costs of living trusts

You may have noticed that we didn't mention the costs of living trusts as either an advantage or disadvantage. Why? Because the costs to set up a living trust can vary greatly. As with your will, you can prepare a basic living trust with preprinted legal forms or alternatively, with an attorney.

Accordingly, the costs can range from a few dollars if you go the do-it-yourself route to more than $1,500 for each living trust that an attorney prepares. Because a living trust is considered a contract between the trustor and trustee, we strongly suggest that you don't mess around with a contract that may contain glitches. A living trust requires careful preparation and thinking. So just like with your will, if you decide to try to create a living trust on your own (which, again, we don't recommend), at least have an attorney review it before execution.

Interestingly, the promotion and marketing of living trusts as part of estate planning has been anything but subtle. Some financial advisers hype living trusts especially to older citizens — giving sales pitches on how living trusts are the solution to all the world's ills, and bombard them with offers of expensive how-to seminars, workshops, and books on living trusts. Before exploring any of these options, make sure you understand what is being offered and what it will cost you. Although these preparations are touted as cost saving, you will probably find it less expensive to work one-on-one with an attorney on your living trust rather than buying an expensive, boilerplate sales pitch.

Identifying Some Less Common but Worthy Will Substitutes

Beyond joint tenancy and revocable living trusts, you have some other options for will substitutes available. Although not as common as the first two methods, the ones we discuss still provide you with the opportunity to use will substitutes in your estate planning.

Tenancy by the entirety — the spouse's option

Tenancy by the entirety — also called *interests by the entirety* — is related to joint tenancy. Similar to joint tenancy, the property's co-owners have a right of survivorship feature that enables property to automatically transfer at the death of a co-owner to the surviving co-owner. Different states have different rules for tenancy by the entirety, so make sure your attorney advises you as you consider this type of will substitute.

The distinguishing characteristic of this form of will substitute: Only spouses can use it. Unlike joint tenancy, which can have any number of unrelated parties, a husband and wife are the only persons eligible to hold property as tenancy by the entirety. The surviving spouse becomes the sole property owner.

Tenancy by the entirety follows general guidelines for marital life. Always tell your spouse what you're doing! Accordingly, one spouse can't transfer his or her interest in the property without the consent of or notification to the other spouse. (Remember, a joint tenant can transfer his or her share to another person without the consent or notification of the other joint tenants.)

Some states don't allow property to be held as tenancy by the entirety. Specifically, tenancy by the entirety isn't recognized in most community property states (Arizona, California, Idaho, Louisiana, Nevada, New Mexico, Texas, Washington, and Wisconsin), and even some common law states don't allow it. Where tenancy by the entirety is available, a divorce changes property ownership from tenancy by the entirety to tenants in common. If you decide to explore using this will substitute form, check with an attorney to see if your state recognizes it.

Joint tenancy bank accounts

A joint tenancy bank account is a form of joint tenancy where two or more people take title to property — in this case a bank account — with the surviving joint tenant receiving the proceeds from the account.

With joint tenancy, a joint tenant can sever the joint tenancy without the consent or notification to the other joint tenants. Here, the bank account joint tenant can sever the relationship by withdrawing funds from the joint account.

Gift taxes (see Chapter 11 where we discuss how you're taxed on certain types of gifts you give, and how those gift taxes affect your estate planning) may come into play with joint tenancy bank accounts. Before you use this will substitute form, talk to your accountant and attorney to understand the implications. Don't just ask the person at the bank who helps you fill out the forms!

Savings bonds

Yes, the same savings bonds that along with green stamps, Hula-Hoops, and first-run shows of *Leave it to Beaver* are often thought of as icons of days long ago. But savings bonds actually are a form of will substitute.

Savings bonds can be issued in two ways:

- ✔ Alternative payee
- ✔ Beneficiary payee

A tip about estate-planning legal-speak

You may have noticed a pattern in legal terminology. Words ending in *or* like trustor and
grantor are always the person in control of the
property. Conversely, words ending in *ee* like
trustee or grantee are always the person

receiving something from the *or*. An easy way
to remember this is that *ee* receives something
from *or*. Put it together as *ee-or* and you have
Winnie-the-Pooh's buddy!

When you use the *alternative payee* option on a savings bond, payment of the
bond can go to either co-owner of the bond (you or your alternative) similar
to the joint tenancy provision of right of survivorship. After one of you dies,
the surviving payee is the bond's sole owner.

By using the other option — a *beneficiary payee* — you and another person
have a similar relationship to a beneficiary named in your will. If the savings
bond is yours, the beneficiary you have named receives the bond's proceeds
after your death.

 If you have a stash of savings bonds locked away in your safe deposit box or
some other safekeeping place, double-check to see what the estate-planning
impact is of each individual bond when you're inventorying the contents of
and determining your estate's value (see Chapter 2).

PODs — payable on death accounts

We know they sound rather morbid, but *payable on death accounts* (PODs)
are a simple will substitute form that keeps personal property out of probate.
You fill out a form at your financial institutions and designate your account
beneficiary. After your death, your beneficiary provides the financial institution with a copy of the death certificate and proof of identity, and then collects what is in the account. (Doesn't get much simpler than that.)

 Because your beneficiary receives the account proceeds at your death, periodically review the accounts for two reasons. First, verify that the named
beneficiary is still who you want to receive the proceeds. Remember you can
change your mind at any time while you're alive. Second, some accounts may
also grow faster than others, causing disproportionate proceeds to different
beneficiaries that you may not be aware of without reviewing the account.

Your beneficiary doesn't have beneficial interest in the account and thus
can't withdraw money from the account until your death. You have the

flexibility to change your mind and name a different beneficiary, or you can even decide that you want to use the funds in the account. Easy come, easy go!

Deeds

For real property like your house, a deed is a weapon in your will substitutes arsenal available for your use.

A *deed* is the legal evidence of real estate ownership. Deeds, like wills, have several legal requirements to be valid including being in writing with an accurate legal description of the property.

You can write wording into a deed to create a will substitute for your real property. Work with your attorney to make sure the wording in your deed accurately reflects the type of will substitute you want to set up.

If the deed is used only as a property transfer mechanism at the grantor's death, the deed may not be considered a valid will substitute form and is subject to probate. Check with your attorney about state laws to find out what requirements are needed for a deed to be considered a will substitute form.

IRAs and your other retirement accounts

Even if you're just beginning your estate-planning efforts, you may already have will substitutes as part of your estate and not even know it!

Most of your retirement savings accounts — your IRA, 401(k) or 403(b) plan, your Roth IRA, and other retirement-oriented investments we discuss in Chapter 18 — are forms of will substitutes. See Chapter 18 for details on these accounts, how you designate a beneficiary, and tax implications.

Part III
Matters of Trust

The 5th Wave   By Rich Tennant

"You put in your height, weight, and marital status here. At the end of your workout, it shows your heart rate, blood pressure, and the type of insurance you should be carrying."

In this part . . .

A trust can be the super-weapon of your estate plan, providing you with additional methods for transferring property to members of your family and others, and protecting your estate in many ways. This section introduces you to the various kinds of trusts that are appropriate in estate plans, including both the upsides and potential downsides. We look at the basics of trusts and the times when you may want to use a particular trust in your estate plan.

Chapter 7

Understanding Trusts

. . . .

In This Chapter

▶ Defining trusts

▶ Looking at how trusts can enhance your estate planning

▶ Examining major categories of trusts

. . . .

*H*urry, hurry, step right up! Come see, with your very own eyes, the eighth wonder of the world: the trust! You can use a trust to save on estate taxes, to protect property in your estate, and to avoid probate! You can even use a trust to get dents out of your car and clean the toughest stains in your carpet!

Okay, we went a bit overboard on the last two items above, but various types of trusts may be the secret weapons in your estate planning. Beware, though: Trusts are also the most over-hyped part of estate planning, as well.

In this chapter, we help you make sense of the extremely complicated topic of trusts: what trusts are and why you may want to consider trusts for your estate plan. Before you seriously start considering trusts, you must understand the basics that we discuss in this chapter so you can make informed decisions about what does — and doesn't — make sense for you.

Defining Trusts, Avoiding Hype

Trusts can be difficult to understand when you hear some estate-planning professionals talk about them. But those people may be more interested in selling you expensive investment vehicles than making sure you understand enough about trusts to make wise and informed decisions yourself.

Don't worry. In this chapter, we help you get a handle on trusts — with three definitions:

- ✔ An incredibly oversimplified definition
- ✔ A slightly more complicated definition, but still using plain language
- ✔ An "official" definition that uses just enough legalese, but still won't cause your head to start spinning

Shazam! An oversimplified definition of trusts

In many comic books and related movies and TV shows, an ordinary person goes into a "special place" and comes out a superhero with a new identity and, very often, with super powers. Bruce Wayne goes into the Batcave and comes out as Batman. Clark Kent goes into a phone booth and comes out as Superman. Billy Batson says "Shazam!" and turns into Captain Marvel.

Think of a trust as a special place in which ordinary property from your estate goes in and, as the result of some type of transformation that occurs, takes on a sort of new identity and often is bestowed with super powers: immunity from estate taxes, resistance to probate, and so on.

So in many ways, a trust is your own personal Batcave — a place to go where you want to change the identity of some of your estate's property. And even though Batman doesn't have any super powers, he does pick up that nifty utility belt with all kinds of weapons while he's in the Batcave. So although property is in your trust, it can "pick up its own utility belt" and do things that aren't possible outside of the trust.

Adding a bit of complexity with an ingredient list

Suppose that you want to set up a trust. Just like with a cooking recipe or building something in your garage workshop, you need to make sure you have everything you need before you start. To cook up a trust, you need these seven basic ingredients:

- ✔ The person setting up the trust (that's you)
- ✔ The reason you want to set up the trust, and certain objectives you want to achieve
- ✔ The trust document itself

✔ The property that you decide you're going to place into the trust

✔ The trust's beneficiary (or beneficiaries, if more than one), whether that beneficiary is a person (your oldest daughter, for example) or an institution, such as a charity

✔ Someone to watch over and manage the trust and the property that is now in the trust

✔ A set of rules that tells the person watching over and managing the trust what he or she can and can't do

All the items in the preceding list come together, and when everything is done properly, presto! You now have a trust!

Adding some lawyer talk to the definition

If you're comfortable with a little bit of legalese — just a little bit, we promise — we explain in a somewhat more "official" manner than comic book analogies and simple recipe-style lists. Including some attorney talk to the seven basic elements:

✔ **Person setting up the trust.** The person is commonly known as the *trustor,* though you may sometimes see the terms *settlor* or *grantor.*

✔ **Objective of the trust.** You use different types of trusts to achieve a variety of specific estate-planning objectives. You can use some trusts for a single estate-planning objective, while others help you achieve more than one goal. Some of the most common estate-planning objectives for trusts (we discuss later in this chapter in more detail) are to reduce the amount of estate tax liability, to protect property in your estate, and to avoid probate for certain property. Before you decide whether you need one type of trust or another, you must think about what you're trying to accomplish in the first place!

✔ **Specific kind of trust.** As we discuss later in this chapter and in Chapter 8, trusts come in many different varieties. And just like ice cream, yogurt, or pudding, you find different colors and flavors, some of which you may like and others which just don't do it for you. Regardless, when you're setting up a trust, you need to decide what type of trust you want and make sure that you follow all the rules for that particular type of trust to make sure that it's proper and legal, and carries out your intentions.

✔ **Property.** After you place property into a trust, that property is formally known as *trust property* — that is, just like with our Batcave analogy, the property now has a different identity and in one way or another, isn't quite the same as it was before you placed it into trust.

✔ **Beneficiary.** Just like with other aspects of your estate plan (your will, for example), a trust's *beneficiary* (or, if more than one, *beneficiaries)*

benefits from the trust in some way, usually because the person or institution will eventually receive some or all of the property that was placed into trust.

✔ **Trustee.** The person in charge of the trust is known as the *trustee*. The trustee needs to clearly understand the rules for the type of trust he or she is managing to make sure everything in the trust stays in working order.

✔ **Rules.** Finally, some of the rules that must be followed are inherently part of the type of trust used, while other rules depend on what is specified in the *trust agreement*. You will find still more rules in state and federal law.

Putting all the preceding information together, the trust agreement is a document that spells out the rules that you — the trustor — want followed for the property that you've placed into the trust to benefit the beneficiary (or beneficiaries) of the trust, as managed by the trustee. (Got all that? If not, keep rereading the above until it makes sense, checking back with the list above to help clear up the parts that seem difficult.)

Consider the following simple example. You decide to put $300,000 in a trust for your two twin 10-year-old daughters, and you want your sister to oversee the trust. You specify that neither daughter is allowed to receive anything other than interest on the property in that trust before reaching the age of 25, and then can only receive a maximum of $10,000 each year on her birthday until the age of 35, at which time the remaining money in the trust (which hopefully has been growing along the way because of your sister's wise investment choices) will be split 50-50 between the two of them.

In this example, you are the trustor, your twin daughters the beneficiaries, and your sister the trustee. The conditions about when your daughters can start receiving money, how much, and until when are part of the terms of the trust agreement.

But what kind of trust can you set up? Ah-hah! That is often the $64,000 question (or $300,000 question, or $1 million question or perhaps the $5,000 question . . . all depending on the value of the property you place in the trust). As we mention, you can use different trusts to achieve different objectives, and later in this chapter we begin to discuss the major categories to lead into Chapter 8's discussion of different types of trusts.

Attaching all the bells and whistles to a trust

Beyond the basic definition (or, in our case, multiple definitions) of what a trust is, you need to be aware of several little tidbits about trusts. When

Batman enters the Batcave, he needs to know where his utility belt is, if the Batmobile has enough fuel, and where he's headed as soon as he gets outside. Otherwise, he may be in big trouble.

The same is true for trusts, which is why you need to work with your estate-planning team — particularly your attorney — to make sure that before that trust goes into effect, you have everything in order and haven't set yourself up for the estate planning equivalent of an ambush by the Joker.

The following list may seem a bit nitpicky, but you can use the items in this list when you work with your attorney to avoid any problems. For example

✔ Make sure the trust agreement is in writing. An oral trust may be considered legally valid, just like an oral (nuncupative) will, as we discuss in Chapter 3. Certain trusts, such as those dealing with real estate, must be in writing. However, just like with your will, you should put the trust agreement in writing instead of relying on word of mouth so misunderstandings or other problems don't arise!

✔ A trust must provide duties and obligations for the trustee (again, the person in charge of the trust). Typical duties and obligations include how and when to make payments from the trust, or how to manage or oversee the property in the trust (such as paying property taxes on real estate in the trust, renewing certificates of deposit in the trust, and so on). In legalese, a trust that adequately features such duties and responsibilities is known as an *active trust.*

✔ If the trust doesn't adequately include trustee duties and obligations, a court may consider it to be a *passive trust.* Watch out! The court may deem it as "no trust at all." Furthermore, the law automatically transfers the trust's property to the beneficiary or beneficiaries, and everyone loses out on whatever the objective of the trust was, such as tax savings. So make sure that when you (or, more accurately, your attorney) set up a trust that the trustee's role is well defined so you won't have any down-the-road problems.

✔ The wording of the trust agreement must clearly specify that you're actually setting up a trust and indicate what property you're placing in the trust (or intend to place in the trust at some future date).

✔ The trust agreement must clearly identify the beneficiary or beneficiaries — the person or people by name and other identifying characteristics ("my daughter Ellie Mae Clampett," for example) or an institution ("The Meow Cat Shelter of Tucson, Arizona").

✔ Don't take the process of deciding on and appointing a trustee lightly! Make sure that whomever you select as a trustee has the right background — education or profession, for example — for the job at hand. If you want someone to manage a trust containing lots of money, make sure that the trustee understands and has adequate experience in portfolio management, diversification strategies, and other investment management techniques. But just as important (maybe even more important) than education and professional background is that your trustee has the honesty, character, and integrity to fulfill the responsibilities. Sometimes being in charge of lots of money intended for someone else (the trust's beneficiary or beneficiaries) can be, shall we say, a bit too tempting.

In Chapter 1, we discuss how a trustee may have a *legal interest* in the property in a trust but doesn't have a *beneficial interest*. The trustee is responsible for managing the trust's property, but he or she can't benefit from the trust other than receiving the agreed-to trustee compensation (fees and costs) for taking on this job.

Designate a *successor trustee* — a pinch hitter to step in if the primary trustee can't serve or continue to serve for some reason — when you set up a trust. Otherwise, the court that has jurisdiction may appoint a successor trustee, and that may not be someone whom you want.

Trust Power — Making Your Beneficiaries Smile

You're probably thinking: "Why should I care about trusts?"

In a very general sense, the primary reason you set up a trust is to benefit a person or institution more than if you didn't set up the trust. After all, trusts are often complex, can be time consuming to set up and oversee, and cost you some amount of money (a modest amount for a straightforward trust, or perhaps a lot of money for a very complex setup involving multiple trusts, different jurisdictions' laws, and so on). So you should have a good reason to go to all this trouble!

By benefiting a person or institution better, we mean examples like the following:

- ✔ You have some part of your estate or your overall personal financial situation, such as a life insurance policy, that under applicable law is likely to cost your estate some amount of money in estate taxes. But by setting up a trust, your estate can avoid paying some or all taxes, meaning that more money is left over for your trust's beneficiaries.

- ✔ As we describe in Chapter 5, the probate process can cause problems for your estate, anywhere from minor annoyances and delays to major costs and inconvenience. However, you can use trusts for certain property that you absolutely, positively don't want to be subjected to the problems and delays of probate. Your beneficiary may gain ownership and use of that property more quickly if you had set up a trust than if you used the regular method of having that property as part of your probate estate.

The following sections look at the most significant objectives you likely want to achieve by using trusts.

Avoiding taxes

Some trusts have the "special power" (or maybe that's "super powers") to avoid estate-related taxes that otherwise may apply. One of the most common tax-saving trusts is an *irrevocable life insurance trust.* As we discuss in Chapter 17, after you die, the proceeds from your life insurance policy (the death benefit amount) are added back into your estate, often turning an estate that isn't subject to federal estate taxes into an estate that needs to write a substantial check to the IRS!

However, an irrevocable life insurance trust is one of several ways you can shelter life insurance death benefit proceeds from estate taxes, as we discuss in Chapter 8. After setting up the trust, you still have life insurance, and your beneficiary or beneficiaries still receive the proceeds from your policy upon your death. But now, estate taxes may not be a problem.

Avoiding probate

In Chapter 6, we discuss *living trusts* as a form of will substitute to help you avoid probate.

By keeping certain property out of your *probate estate* (as we discuss in Chapter 5, the part of your estate that is subject to probate), you may be able to avoid many of the hassles, costs, and lack of privacy concerns related to probate.

You have a number of other means at your disposal to avoid probate for other property — joint tenancy with right of survivorship, payable on death (POD) accounts, and others as we discuss in Chapter 6 — so work with your estate-planning team to figure out for each type of property in your estate what the best probate-avoidance tactic may be. For some, the costs of a trust may make sense, particularly if you're not only trying to avoid probate, but also trying to accomplish one of the other goals we discuss in this section (avoiding estate taxes, protecting your estate, and so on). For other property, a simpler, less costly way to avoid probate, such as joint tenancy, may be a better choice for you.

Protecting your estate (and your beneficiary's or beneficiaries' estate)

One of the primary uses of trusts is to protect your estate — not only while the estate is yours, but also when your estate becomes someone else's estate (and so on).

For example, suppose that you want to leave $500,000 to your only son, but you're concerned that if you were to die while your son is still relatively young (say, under 30), he won't be responsible or mature enough to adequately manage a large amount of money. Before you can say, "sail around the world," you're afraid he will have spent the entire half million.

You can use a trust in the manner that we describe in our example earlier in the chapter to parcel out the money to your son as you see fit. The trust can give him a little bit each year for some duration, and then a final lump sum at some age when you think he'll be mature enough to protect the money as if he had actually earned it himself. Or you can add conditions to how the money in the trust is dispersed, such as your son receives a little bit of money until a certain age, and then he gets the rest only if he graduates college or meets some other criteria you determine when you set up the trust.

Trusts are an important part of your estate plan when you want to leave money to your minor children and make sure that

- The money is available to them when they reach certain ages

- The money is set aside (think "officially reserved" meaning that nobody else can touch it) for your children and managed by a trustee, rather than just leaving it to your brother-in-law and saying "Please don't spend this money on a Rolls Royce; make sure you keep it safe for my kids." (Yeah, right!)

Providing funds for educational purposes

Another common use for trusts is to make money available to your children, grandchildren, other relatives, or even nonrelatives (your employees' children, for example) for educational purposes, such as college tuition and living expenses.

You can set up and fund trusts that parcel out money for educational purposes but that also come with the restriction of "no school, then no money!"

In Chapter 8, we look at various trusts particularly suited for educational purposes.

Benefiting charities and institutions

You can help out charities in many ways: gift giving (see Chapter 11) or by leaving money or other property to one or more institutions as part of your will (see Chapter 3).

Alternatively, you can set up some type of *charitable trust,* as we discuss in Chapter 8, that may, for example, annually give money to the charity while you're still alive, give a larger amount upon your death, and then from what is left in the trust after you die continue to make regular payments to the charity. You can even set up a charitable trust to make regular payments to the charity for some amount of time but eventually "give back" whatever is left to you or, if you've died, to someone else in your family. Alternatively, you can set up a charitable trust to work the other way — pay you while you're still alive, and upon your death, the remaining amount in the trust goes to the charity.

Sorting Out Trusts — from Here to Eternity

In Chapter 8, we indoctrinate you into the complex world of trusts that's filled with alphabet-soup acronyms and a number of similar-sounding trust types. Before we do that, though, we look at different categories of trusts.

In general, you have two different ways of categorizing trusts:

- ✔ Those trusts that are in effect while you're still alive versus those that take effect upon your death
- ✔ Trusts you can change your mind on versus those that are absolutely, positively, unchangeable

Trusts for when you're alive versus when you're gone

We apologize in advance. We're sorry about the legalese, but here goes. An *intervivos trust* is a trust that you set up and is in effect while you're still alive. In contrast, if you set up a trust under your will and that trust doesn't take effect until your death, you're using a *testamentary trust.*

Here's a quick example to emphasize the distinction between these two categories. Suppose that you want to help out your favorite charity and, after consulting with your estate-planning team, you decide that a trust is the best way to go. If you set up a particular type of charitable trust (see Chapter 8) that makes annual payments to the charity while you're still alive, then that trust is an intervivos trust. If, however, you set up a trust under the terms of your will to become effective (and start making payments) after your death, you've set up a testamentary trust.

The following sections look at both of these categories of trust in more detail.

Selecting intervivos trusts for your estate plan

If your primary objective of creating a trust is to provide an economic benefit (cash payments, transfer of real property that is currently in your estate, and so on) to specific people or institutions (again, your children, your favorite nephew, your favorite charity, and so forth) or for yourself, then you should strongly consider setting up some type of intervivos trust.

With an intervivos trust, payments and other types of property transfers may begin while you're still alive rather than waiting until your death (in this case, "sooner" is better than "later" when it comes to money). Furthermore, you usually have a better handle on the amount and value of your property with which you fund an intervivos trust than a testamentary trust, as we discuss in the next section.

With an intervivos trust, you know what your estate is worth and how much is available to fund such a trust. Essentially, you have a higher degree of control with an intervivos trust than with a testamentary trust. When you set up an intervivos trust, you can initially fund the trust with certain property from your estate, add more property throughout your lifetime, and even make arrangements for additional property to be added to the trust upon your death. For example, if you initially fund an intervivos trust with stock, you can always add more later to cover any shortfalls if the shares you used for the trust have decreased in value. Or if your portfolio has skyrocketed — including the stock you used to fund the trust — and you're feeling particularly generous, you can increase the trust's value.

Choosing testamentary trusts for your estate plan

If you aren't particularly concerned about providing economic benefit to a trust beneficiary while you're still alive, you can still set up an intervivos trust, or you can hold off on creating the trust until after your death and instead, create a testamentary trust under your will.

So how exactly do you set up a testamentary trust if you're already dead? Actually, you lay the groundwork for a testamentary trust in your will while you're still alive, which means the following:

✔ Along with all the other contents of your will that we discuss in Chapter 3 — specific giving clauses, the residuary clause, and so on — you include appropriate language to set up a testamentary trust that, just like everything else in your will, doesn't actually "come alive" until your death. (Ironic, huh?)

✔ Your will goes through probate and must be in compliance with various will statutes (see Chapter 4). Your testamentary trust also needs to be in compliance because it's technically part of your will. If you make any goofs in the language you use relating to the trust (or trusts) you want to establish, all kinds of complications set in, just as with any other part of your will.

✔ Unlike a testamentary trust, an intervivos trust generally doesn't have to go through probate, but the probate court still has jurisdiction over an intervivos trust if any controversy or problems arise, just as it does for a testamentary trust.

✔ The funding of a testamentary trust can often be up in the air because the actual funding doesn't take place until your death. Just like with other parts of your will, if your circumstances have changed and property you had anticipated using for the trust no longer is in your estate or is worth far less than it once was, you and the trust's beneficiaries may be out of luck because, quite simply, the necessary funds aren't available.

To help prevent unpleasant surprises, such as an underfunded or even unfunded testamentary trust, review all aspects of your trust when you do your annual review of your will. (After all, the provisions for a testamentary trust are contained in your will, so doing so is only logical.) If the property you had planned to use to fund the trust is no longer worth enough to accomplish your goals, then you can either look for additional property in your estate and adjust your will accordingly, change the details of the trust to reflect a reduced value, or in the worst case, cancel your plans for the testamentary trust.

Deciding if an intervivos or testamentary trust is better

Which is better for your estate plan: an intervivos trust or a testamentary trust? The favorite answer of estate-planning professionals: It all depends! As with most other aspects of estate planning, you and your estate-planning team need to carefully look at many different factors to put strategies and instruments in place that are specific to your needs.

Intervivos trusts, together with plain old gift giving (see Chapter 11), are a good way to reduce your estate's value and reduce or negate the effect of federal estate taxes. And, as we mention earlier in this section, you can give early and give often with an intervivos trust, benefiting people or institutions sooner than if they had to wait for your death.

Looking closely at revocable trusts

Estate-planning advisers often point to revocable trusts — particularly living trusts, which we discuss in Chapter 6 — as "the perfect way to totally avoid probate." Put all your property into revocable trusts and you can have control over that property, the pitch goes, and because none of your property is now in your probate estate (that is, it's all held in trust) your estate doesn't have to go through the probate process because your probate estate is "empty!" And, by avoiding probate, you avoid the costs of probate, the lack of privacy, and the other disadvantages to the probate process we discuss in Chapter 5.

Not so fast! True, you can avoid probate costs, but do you really think setting up and maintaining trusts is free? No way! Your costs to set up a revocable trust vary depending on attorney fees and other costs, but be prepared to pay to have your trust managed.

You also need to make sure that everything you own is held in trust form. If you fail to include any part of your estate in your trust(s), then you have a probate estate that is subject to the probate process. So every time you buy a new home, open a new brokerage account, or make

any changes to the your estate's inventory, you need to make sure that you transfer that property into your trust(s). Can you say "what a pain"? Sure, we knew you could!

Remember also that probate isn't always bad, either. The probate court, which has the responsibility of making sure that property in your probate estate is disposed of properly with no behind-the-scenes funny games, supervises your probate estate. Without the probate court's supervision, part or all your estate that is held in trust or other nonprobate form (joint tenancy with right of survivorship, for example) can be in for problems if someone close to you in a position of authority has, shall we say, a lack of ethics. Eventually all the beneficiary problems may get straightened out, but quite possibly because of prolonged, costly legal battles.

Also keep in mind that you may be required to file state or federal estate or inheritance tax returns, even though you have no "probate estate" (or "probate assets"). At the state level, at least, those returns are usually considered to be public records. Therefore, if privacy concerns are important to you, your desire for privacy may be defeated.

On the other hand, suppose that you only want a trust to come alive if you die before a certain age and you want to make provisions for your minor children's care, education, and so on. You can use a testamentary trust as part of your will. If you live long enough so that your children are no longer minors and are out on their own and don't need to have money parceled out, you can revise your will and eliminate the testamentary trust provisions.

Our advice: If you do a good job at outlining your objectives for setting up a trust in the first place, the most appropriate category of trust — intervivos or testamentary — is fairly obvious along with the particular type of trust that we discuss in Chapter 8.

Changing your mind: Revocable and irrevocable trusts

An intervivos trust — again, a trust you set up that goes into effect while you're still alive — can be either:

- ✔ *Revocable,* meaning that you can change your mind
- ✔ *Irrevocable,* meaning sorry, what's done is done

Irrevocable trusts are the easier of the two to understand. After you place property into an irrevocable trust, you can't retrieve the property. For all intents and purposes, that property now belongs to the trust, not to you!

With a revocable trust, however, you can place property into the trust and at some point in the future, undo the transfer by removing the property and terminating the trust.

Very often, if you die or become incompetent, the provisions of a revocable trust call for the trust to become an irrevocable trust. Consider a revocable *burial trust* as an example, which you can terminate at any time, usually before death or incompetency. However, if the burial trust is still in existence when you die (or become incompetent), the trust becomes irrevocable and the money is used for your funeral expenses.

The most significant distinctions between revocable and irrevocable trusts are the estate tax considerations. Property that you place in an irrevocable trust is no longer considered part of your estate, meaning that the property typically isn't included in your estate's value when it comes to determining if you owe death taxes and, if so, how much. However, you still own property that you place into a revocable trust, and therefore that property is still subject to death taxes. (Which is very logical, if you think about it! If you can change your mind about the trust and retrieve the property from the trust at any time while you're still alive, the property is really yours and should be considered part of your estate.)

You most likely have gift tax consequences when you establish an intervivos irrevocable trust, so make sure your accountant is "in the loop," along with your attorney. Also, certain transfers within certain time periods prior to your death can be included in your estate as "gifts in contemplation of death" under both state and federal statutes. So watch out for possible death tax implications!

So if you only get a break on estate taxes with an irrevocable trust, why would anyone want to use a revocable trust without the estate tax break?

Recall that earlier in the chapter, we discuss how estate tax savings is only one of the reasons you may consider including a trust in your estate planning. If your estate's value is no where near the federal estate tax exemption amount magic number, then you really don't need to be concerned about federal estate-tax-saving tactics — for now, anyway. Your motivation for setting up a trust may have more to do with estate protection or helping out a charity, but you also may want a safety valve that allows you to pull money out of a trust if circumstances change in some way.

Make sure to work with your accountant to understand any and all tax implications — gift, federal estate, and state inheritance or estate — for property transfers to both irrevocable and revocable trusts. He or she can help you set up the right provisions and avoid unpleasant tax-related surprises from the government because of some provision of the tax code you didn't know about.

Chapter 8

Trusts You May Want to Trust — or Not

. . . .

In This Chapter

▶ Getting hitched to a marriage trust

▶ Considering whether a charitable trust makes sense

▶ Deciphering protective trusts

▶ Utilizing trusts to administer and distribute assets

▶ Understanding grantor-retained and irrevocable life insurance trusts

. . . .

*W*hen it comes to trusts, you not only need to trust (pun intended!) your estate-planning team, but you also need to have at least some understanding of the various types that are available to you. Chapter 7 shows you how trusts work. This chapter is your handy reference to the kinds of trusts that people use the most in estate planning.

If, for example, you want to start giving gifts to your minor children, you can ask your estate-planning advisers about minor's trusts. Or if you want to give something to your favorite charity, you can read about charitable trusts and find out the differences between a *charitable lead trust* and a *charitable remainder trust*.

We explain the basics in this chapter and prepare you for an informed discussion with your estate-planning advisers.

Saying "I Do" to a Marriage-Oriented Trust

In this section, we assume that you're married and that you die before your spouse does — nothing personal, it's just an example. (If you're not married, feel free to skip to the next section.)

One of the most popular uses for all trusts and certainly for a marriage-oriented trust is to buy time on paying any applicable estate taxes until both spouses in a marriage have died, or to skip over your spouse for purposes of transferring property but still give your spouse the right to income from a trust.

Marital deduction and QTIP trusts

A *marital deduction trust* allows you to put property in trust with your spouse as the beneficiary. Upon your death, your spouse has the right to use the property in the trust. No matter how valuable the property in the trust is even if it exceeds that year's federal estate tax exemption amount (see Chapter 13 for a discussion of the exemption amounts), your spouse won't owe any federal estate taxes.

Later, upon your spouse's death, the leftover amount, if any, transfers to the beneficiaries that your spouse determines.

Suppose, though, that you want to determine who receives the trust property after your spouse dies? (Again, assume that you're already dead when your spouse dies.) Consider instead using a *Qualified Terminable Interest Property trust,* commonly known by its acronym as the *QTIP trust.* (We can't help but wonder how many hours went into thinking up that name just to get that acronym.) A QTIP trust (feel like you need to clean your ears out yet?) operates much the same as a marital deduction trust, with one important exception: You, not your spouse, specify who receives the remaining property in the trust after your spouse dies.

When should you consider using a marital deduction trust instead of a QTIP trust, or vice versa? Consider the following: Suppose that you and your spouse were only married once (to each other), you have a happy, contented marriage, and both of your children act like they stepped right out of a 1950s or early 1960s TV show, such as *Ozzie and Harriet* or *Leave it to Beaver.* You both want the other provided for no matter who dies first and want to set up some type of a trust to delay or diminish federal estate taxes, but then after the second spouse dies, you both want the remainder to go to your children.

In this case, either a QTIP trust or a marital deduction trust probably works equally as well, because you both agree (at least for now) about how you eventually want to distribute the remaining property in your estates. If you set up a marital deduction trust and you die first, your spouse can later designate your two children as equal beneficiaries of the property left in the trust. Or perhaps one of your two children makes millions of dollars in business or in the stock market (don't laugh; it may happen again someday!); your spouse can decide to leave the entire leftover estate to the other child who wasn't quite so fortunate or skilled. Whatever the rationale, a marital deduction trust allows the beneficiary-designation decision to be delayed as long as possible.

Now consider the following, however. You and your current spouse are each on your second marriage, and you each have children from your first marriage. You and your spouse's first-marriage children (to put it delicately) don't quite see eye to eye. The word "freeloaders" comes to mind every time you hear their names, but your spouse thinks of those first-marriage children as "my angels."

Regardless of your cool relationship with your spouse's children, you and your spouse have a happy marriage, and you want to provide for your spouse if you die first. And, because you both are fairly well off financially, a marriage-oriented trust makes sense to delay estate tax impacts.

But do you want your spouse to decide what happens with any leftovers from your estate upon his or her death, as would be the case in a marital deduction trust? Probably not. In this case, you want a QTIP trust, in which you designate what happens to those leftovers. After all, this estate is yours, and for all intents and purposes you are just "loaning" it to your second spouse for the duration of his or her life if you die first. Afterwards, you want the leftovers to go to your children, your favorite charity — *anyone* but your spouse's children from that first marriage, which is what may happen if you leave the decision up to your spouse by using a marital deduction trust.

Bypass trusts

Another way for a married couple to shelter property from estate taxes is to use a type of trust sometimes referred to as a *bypass trust* because of the way the trust works, as we explain in a moment. Suppose, as in the examples in the previous section, that you die before your spouse does but instead of either a QTIP trust or marital deduction trust, you've set up a bypass trust.

Instead of the property being held in trust for your spouse (as in a QTIP or marital deduction trust), the property in a bypass trust "bypasses" your spouse (thus the reason for the often-used term) to someone else, such as your child, for whom the property is held in trust. However, unlike the relatively simple process of giving property to your child as a gift or leaving your child property in your will, your spouse can still benefit from the property under a bypass trust. Although the property is held in trust for the ultimate benefit of your child, your spouse (while living) can have the benefit of the trust assets.

Because your spouse never takes possession of the property in a bypass trust, he or she never is considered to be the property owner and therefore never has to include the property in his or her estate — and possibly be subject to estate taxes on the property. Along the way, the trust agreement that you set up for the bypass trust spells out all the rules that you want followed: how much interest will be paid to your spouse and when, for example.

An incredible number of rules apply to bypass trusts and, specifically, the estate tax consequences. The IRS has all kinds of restrictions. In order to determine the exact amounts you want to use to fund a bypass trust, consider the exemption amounts, your estate's value, the value of your spouse's estate, and other factors. Rather than even attempt to go into all this detail — which we could write an entire book on by itself — we recommend that you work very carefully with your estate-planning team not only in setting up a bypass trust (like all other trusts), but also deciding which type of trust (a bypass trust, QTIP trust, or marital deduction trust) makes the most sense for you and your spouse.

Considering Charitable Trusts

A marriage-oriented trust may have little appeal to you, for a variety of reasons. Perhaps you're not married. Perhaps you're married but you and your spouse don't have any children or other blood relatives with whom you're particularly close. Or suppose that you're married and do have children who are very well off, and really don't need (or maybe don't even want) anything from your estate other than a couple of antiques and some items of sentimental value. What other trust strategies can you employ?

We discuss in Chapter 11 how you can give gifts to qualified charitable organizations and take advantage of the charitable deduction to avoid gift taxes. Another way to leave property to charitable organizations, particularly on a time-release basis, is to use some type of *charitable trust*.

We discuss two main types of charitable trusts in the following sections. The two types are:

- ✔ Charitable lead trust
- ✔ Charitable remainder trust

Charitable lead trust — everything has its limits!

You can use a *charitable lead trust* (a type of irrevocable trust) to make a series of payments (for example, an *annuity* of the same amount each year) to a charitable organization. At some point in the future, the remaining property in the trust:

> ✔ Reverts back to you
>
> ✔ Transfers to someone else that you specify, such as your spouse or your child

Charitable remainder trust

You place property in a _charitable remainder_ trust and your beneficiary receives a specified amount of money regularly for a period of time. After that period of time has elapsed, whatever is left over goes to the charity.

Instead of some finite period of time, you can set up a charitable remainder trust to cover the life of your beneficiary. When the beneficiary dies, the payments end at that point.

Many people set themselves up as the beneficiary who receives the payments from the trust, but you can also specify your spouse, your children, or someone else to receive those payments. If you specify anyone other than your spouse or yourself to receive the payments from the trust, gift taxes most likely apply, unless the payments are under the $11,000 annual exclusion that we discuss in Chapter 11. The payments are considered to be a gift. (Gifts to your spouse don't trigger the gift tax because those payments are treated the same way as if they were gifts with the unlimited marital deduction, as we also discuss in Chapter 11.)

If you're trying to reduce your estate by using a charitable remainder trust and specify your spouse to receive payments, you may be increasing the value of your spouse's estate where estate taxes eventually kick in or, if they already apply, they may be higher than they otherwise would. As with all the other estate-related tax strategies we discuss elsewhere in this book, you need to think several moves ahead and discuss any foreseeable down-the-road complications with your accountant.

Everybody into the pool!

Chances are that your college alma mater or a charity has pitched a _pooled interest trust_ (even if not identified as such by that name). They tell you that you can make a donation and receive interest back on that donation for some period of time, such as until you reach a certain age.

What happens is your contribution is _pooled_ (lumped together) with other contributions from other people. You don't have to take on any expenses for setting up some type of charitable trust, but at the same time your options for the trust are limited and are established by the charitable institution themselves.

Now you know the estate-planning basis for that pitch from dear old State U.!

Protecting Your Estate With Protective Trusts

You can use a *protective trust* to protect your beneficiary's property. The following sections discuss the different types of protective trusts:

- ✔ Spendthrift trusts
- ✔ Supplemental needs and special needs trusts
- ✔ Education trusts
- ✔ Minor's trusts

Spendthrift trusts — "you get it when I say so!"

Several times in this book we use an example of setting up a trust to parcel out money to the trust's beneficiary, rather than giving that person a whole lot of money all at once. Essentially, the reason a spendthrift trust is considered to be a protective trust is that it protects the beneficiary from himself (or, to be fair and gender-neutral, herself).

The rules that apply to a spendthrift trust are rather straightforward. The beneficiary (for sake of this example, your somewhat spoiled son) can't touch any of the property in the trust; he only owns the payments that have been made.

Additionally, your son's creditors can't seize the property in the trust. The creditors can, of course, go after the money in dribs and drabs as it comes out in payments to your son, but they can't grab the entire property itself.

Despite the spendthrift provisions that keep creditors at bay, the courts allow certain types of claims (alimony and child support, for example), which you need to consider when setting up the trust.

Supplemental needs and special needs trusts — keep the "recovery agents" away

God forbid if you become disabled or incapacitated and need extensive personal care in your lifetime. But if you do need long-term treatment, you already know that the cost can be ferociously high. One serious and extended hospital or nursing home stay can wipe out your life savings.

Getting technical about spendthrift trusts

In addition to a spendthrift trust, you can specify spendthrift provisions on other types of trusts, such as a *discretionary trust*. With a discretionary trust, the trustee — the person in charge of the trust — has vast and far-reaching powers (to get a bit overdramatic) to control the trust's payments to the beneficiary or beneficiaries. Included in those "vast and far-reaching powers" is the discretion to make no payments at all!

For people with an estate — remember, that's most of us — how do you protect your assets from seizure by state government if you're receiving assistance for your long-term care?

In Chapter 17, we discuss different types of insurance (long-term disability and long-term care). In Chapter 19, we also discuss issues of guardianship and the durable power of attorney, and how both apply to incompetent or incapacitated people.

But we also discuss in Chapter 10 how the *Estate Recovery Act* may cause the government to go after part or all of a person's estate after death if that person received certain types of government assistance. In addition to insurance, you also need to consider if a *supplemental needs trust* or *special needs trust* makes sense for your estate planning.

A supplemental needs trust is designed to support a disabled, elderly, or handicapped person in such a manner as to not jeopardize or reduce that person's eligibility and qualification to receive private or public benefits, such as Medicaid. Furthermore, a supplemental needs trust also protects the assets in the trust from creditors' claims. The supplemental needs trust adds funds to cover the beneficiary in addition to the public or private funds.

If your disabled beneficiary receives state medical assistance and is under the age of 65, a *special needs trust* repays the state. You place property in the trust and a trustee manages it, for the benefit of the beneficiary, just like the typical trust. However, instead of providing income to the beneficiary, the trustee makes payments as required to reimburse the state for care it provides. At some point in the future, often after the beneficiary dies, any remaining balance is paid to other beneficiaries (often other family members).

Essentially, the trustee repays the state as the beneficiary uses the services, instead of reimbursing the state after death under the Estate Recovery Act. Either way, you need to have both long-term disability and long-term care insurance as part of your overall estate planning to help protect you and your estate if you become seriously injured, incompetent, or incapacitated.

Educational trusts — "you're going to use it only for school!"

As you guess from the name, an *educational trust* provides payments to the beneficiary for education-related needs: tuition, books and supplies, and so on. Educational trusts usually contain provisions that halt payments if, for example, the beneficiary drops out (or flunks out) of school.

You can use an educational trust for a single beneficiary — your oldest daughter, for example. Alternatively, you can set up a single educational trust for all your children, your children and grandchildren, your nieces and nephews, or any other combination of beneficiaries that makes sense.

When you talk with your advisers, make sure that you cover these items:

- ✔ What happens to any leftover funds in the trust?
- ✔ What happens if nobody from the beneficiary list decides to go to college?
- ✔ What happens if everyone on the beneficiary list receives full scholarships and nobody needs the money?
- ✔ When does the educational trust terminate?

You have several alternatives for each of the preceding questions and many others, so ask your estate-planning team members for advice based on their experience with other educational trusts. Also ask about any worst-case situations so you can avoid those same problems!

Minor's trusts — "I'm thinking about your future!"

You use a *minor's trust* to establish funds for someone who worked in the coalmines.

No, we're not serious! We just wanted to see if you were still hanging in as we continue through this long list of different types of trusts. (Besides, a trust for someone who worked in the mines would be called a "miner's" — spelled differently! — trust.)

A minor's trust is a way for you to make gifts to minors (for example, your three children, ages 5, 7, and 10) and still take advantage of the annual exclusion from gift taxes ($11,000 per person, as we discuss in Chapter 11).

When the minor reaches majority, the property in the minor's trust becomes his or hers, because he or she is no longer a minor. (Happy birthday!)

GRAT, GRUT, GRIT: Chewing over the Grantor-Retained Trusts

You can create a trust that pays you a fixed amount of money at regular intervals. That's a GRAT — a grantor-retained annuity trust.

You can create a trust that pays you a specified percentage. That's a GRUT — a grantor-retained unit trust.

Or you can create a trust that allows you to transfer ownership of certain assets but retain the income or use of that property during the trust. That's a GRIT — a grantor-retained income trust.

Earlier in this chapter we discuss the charitable remainder trust, in which you create a trust containing property that eventually goes to a charitable organization. But along the way, income from that trust or use of property in that trust (a house or building, for example) either comes back to you or some other beneficiary whom you specify in the trust agreement.

GRATs, GRUTs, and GRITs give you a way to create a "noncharitable" variation on the theme. By *noncharitable,* we mean that instead of the property in the trust eventually going to a charitable organization, the property goes to (for example) your child or your favorite cousin.

Grantor-retained trusts are irrevocable (see Chapter 7), so think and plan carefully before putting one in place.

The primary difference among the varieties of grantor-retained trusts is how the income you receive is determined. In general financial lingo, an *annuity* typically refers to a fixed amount of money, and a GRAT pays you an annuity from the trust.

In contrast, a GRUT pays you some specified percentage of the trust rather than a fixed amount. So with a GRUT instead of a GRAT (stay with us!), your payments likely vary from one year to another, depending on the property's value in the trust, which is affected by any earnings (or losses).

The third type — the GRIT — is useful if you want to place your family home in trust and still keep living there. Part of the income applicable to the trust is your right to live in that house.

To be extremely precise, placing your house in trust and continuing to live in it is actually a *qualified personal residence trust,* which is a specific form of a GRIT that's still permitted under current tax law. Other older GRIT varieties no longer are permitted, but estate planners often use GRIT and qualified personal residence trust interchangeably, even though the latter is technically only one form of a GRIT. Why? Estate-planning advisers do so most likely to keep with the common acronyms (GRAT, GRUT, GRIT) and to prevent too much alphabet soup and complicated terms from slipping into the estate-planning vocabulary (and confusing their clients).

With all three types of grantor-retained trusts, after the trust goes away, the property in the trust transfers to the beneficiary. Again, instead of a charity (as with a charitable trust), that beneficiary often is a relative.

The tax laws for all the varieties of grantor-retained trusts are extremely complicated! For example, you and your beneficiaries may need to worry about gift taxes and estate taxes. At the same time, you may realize some tax savings depending on factors, such as the value of the property you place in trust and changes in that property's value. Not only do you need to work with your attorney when deciding if a grantor-retained trust is for you (and if so, what type), but also make sure you work with your accountant to clearly understand all the tax consequences — for you and also for your beneficiary.

Sidestepping Estate Taxes with an Irrevocable Life Insurance Trust

Beware of the life insurance tax trap! In Chapter 17, we discuss how various forms of life insurance are likely to be an important part of your estate planning, from protecting your estate to creating cash that goes to one or more of your beneficiaries. However, the tax laws dictate that the death benefit from your life insurance policy gets added into the rest of your estate when calculating your estate's value and the amount of estate tax you owe. As a result, you must look ahead to various tips and tricks to help get around this tax trap!

One common way to get around estate taxes on your life insurance is to create an *irrevocable life insurance trust*. You transfer the ownership of your life insurance policy to the trust, effectively taking advantage of a loophole to get around estate taxes.

If you think an irrevocable life insurance trust makes sense in your situation, you need to be aware of the following:

✔ As the name implies, your life insurance trust must be irrevocable, otherwise goodbye, estate tax break! As we discuss in Chapter 7, with a revocable trust, you can change your mind about the trust, or the property in the trust (or whatever is left over) transfers back to you. In order to qualify for the estate tax break, the trust has to be irrevocable. After the trust owns the life insurance policy, you can never get it back nor make any changes!

✔ You can't be the trustee of an irrevocable life insurance trust that contains your own life insurance policy, even though you don't own the policy (the trust does).

✔ You need to act now! The IRS also says that if you set up an irrevocable life insurance trust but die within three years of the transfer of the life insurance policy, then the IRS acts as if the trust never existed and you still owned and controlled the policy. And then, you lose the estate tax break.

Another estate tax saving strategy for your life insurance policy, instead of an irrevocable life insurance trust, is to transfer ownership of the policy to someone else, as we discuss in Chapter 17. The secret recipe is for the IRS to agree that you didn't own and control the policy, which means you get an estate tax break! But note that the same three-year period for the gift inclusion will apply.

What a Crummey deal!

If you don't own and control your life insurance policy because it's owned by an irrevocable life insurance trust, how can you pay your premiums to keep the policy in effect? You can, of course, have someone else pay the premiums for you — your spouse or the beneficiary of the policy, for example. Or you can set up a *Crummey trust* to take care of the payments.

Crummey trusts are very complicated and best explained by your estate-planning attorney doing a John Madden drawing of a football play, showing how money transfers back and forth, how the gift tax annual exclusion applies, and all kinds of pretty complicated rules and restrictions. But if you and your estate-planning team decide that an irrevocable life insurance trust makes sense for you and your beneficiaries, ask whether a Crummey trust makes sense, too.

Chapter 9

Working a Trust Into Your Estate Plan

*H*ow can you make sense out of the vast number of trusts available for your estate planning? Many of them have similar names but are subtly different from each other. (Quick: What's the main difference between a charitable lead trust and a charitable remainder trust? And, more importantly, which makes sense for your estate plan? See Chapter 8 for the answer.)

Not only do you need to decide among similar-sounding and -functioning trusts, you also need to decide if you even need any trusts at all for your estate plan. In many cases, you have two main courses of action that you may take: one that involves trusts and one that doesn't involve trusts.

So we ask the question again: How can you make sense out of all this trust business?

Help is on the way! In this chapter, we present some disciplined steps to help you make sense out of trusts, figure out which ones — if any — are right for you, and if so, how to get your trusts underway.

Linking Your Estate-Related Tax Planning with Your Trust Planning

Don't even think about creating a trust — any type of trust — unless you've already started your estate-related tax planning. Your estate-planning team may already be on the tax topic. But if not, take a quick look at Chapter 14 where we discuss the approach you need to take for estate-related tax planning.

The initial steps of your estate-related tax planning are exactly the same ones you need to complete before even thinking about trusts. Specifically, you need to:

- Assess your current financial and estate picture, starting with inventorying your estate and determining its value today.

- Look into the future and, as best you can, try to predict what your estate will look like and what it'll be worth at various points in the future.

You conduct these two preceding acts primarily for your estate-related tax planning, so we discuss the details of each in Chapter 14. However, one of the primary reasons to consider trusts is so that you can avoid, diminish, or at least delay estate-related taxes — if your estate is valuable enough that various types apply. If your estate isn't valuable enough to be impacted by federal estate taxes and if you live in a state that doesn't have a state estate tax or an inheritance tax, you may not need to give much consideration to tax-oriented trusts.

So make sure that you begin your trust planning in concert with your death tax planning. If you've already done your death tax planning, then take the next step. But if you haven't begun death tax planning yet, then go no farther with your trust planning until you shift gears and start looking at your estate from a tax liability point of view.

Looking at Your Goals and Objectives for Setting up Trusts

In Chapter 7, we mention five primary goals and objectives that may cause you to consider trusts for your estate:

✔ Reducing or avoiding estate-related taxes

✔ Steering clear of probate

✔ Protecting your estate and your beneficiary's estate

✔ Providing money for education

✔ Benefiting charitable organizations

Some types of trusts directly relate to one of the listed objectives (charitable trusts to provide for charitable organizations is fairly obvious), and also have characteristics that secondarily meet other goals on the list.

But you first need to look at your goals and objectives before worrying about which trusts satisfy which objectives. Based on linking your death tax planning with your trust planning, you now have a pretty good idea how vulnerable your estate is to various types of estate-related taxes. If your estate is very vulnerable, then you certainly want to look at various techniques to reduce or avoid estate taxes, such as a charitable trust. In contrast, if you're not the charitable type, then you probably shouldn't waste any time looking at various types of charitable trusts. True, some of them may have tax-savings properties, but if your favorite characters from the movies and literature are Scrooge and The Grinch (of Dr. Seuss fame), you may find better and more tax savings trusts without all the "bother" of that charitable nonsense! (Bah, humbug!)

We also recommend that you take a second — and even third or fourth — look at some of your long-standing objectives to understand just how important they really are to you. For example, in order to avoid probate, we discuss in Chapters 5 and 6 that probate can be a nuisance and you have a variety of will substitutes (joint tenancy with right of survivorship, for example) to keep certain property out of your probate estate. But how important is avoiding probate? For example, do you want to go to the trouble and expense of placing every single piece of your property in some type of nonprobate form, including one or more trusts? Or are you satisfied keeping some or even most of your estate in nonprobate form (again, including trusts)?

Finally, protecting your estate property — particularly keeping the property safe when your beneficiaries, such as your children receive it — may be extremely important to you. But suppose that you don't have any children or other beneficiaries to whom you plan to leave substantial amounts of money? Most likely then, you don't have to worry about trusts whose primary objective is protecting your estate when it passes to your beneficiaries.

So make sure that you have a clear idea of which trust-oriented estate planning objectives are important to you, and which ones aren't.

Deciding What Property to Place in Trust

In theory, you can put every single piece of your property in a trust. But in practice, concentrate your efforts on putting your property where you can get the most bang for your buck. After all, trusts cost money to set up and administer, and you need to worry about finding the right trustee. You also have to make other decisions, such as whether the trust takes effect while you're still alive (an *intervivos trust,* as we discuss in Chapter 7) or upon your death (*a testamentary trust,* we also discuss in Chapter 7). You also need to decide if you want a trust to be revocable or irrevocable (whether or not you can "change your mind" about a trust — see Chapter 7 also), and because some trusts are only one or the other, you often need to search around to find the right type of trust.

But do you really want to go through all this work for every single asset in your estate? We didn't think so! Instead, you may want to consider a trust for only some portion or portions of your estate assets. In deciding whether or not to consider some type of trust, focus your efforts in four main areas:

✔ Your life insurance policy or policies

✔ Real property, including your primary residence, vacation homes, and any real estate investments that you intend to hold for many years

✔ Intangible personal property, such as bank accounts and stocks, that you plan to transfer to someone else while you're alive or after you die — basically, money that you don't intend to use for yourself

✔ Property in your estate of any type — real property or intangible personal property, as we previously list, but also tangible personal property (your antiques, for example) that you intend to transfer to a charitable organization

Most of the trusts that we discuss in Chapter 8 are most effective and provide the most benefit when the property used to fund the trust falls into one of the preceding four categories. So don't worry that every single item on your 25-page estate inventory needs to be placed into trust. Focus on the areas that give you the most benefit.

Linking Your Estate-Planning and Trust Goals with Specific Property

A significant part of your estate planning is to answer the beneficiary question: Who gets what? You may transfer some of your property while you're still alive, and other property upon your death. You made a lot of decisions when you completed your will (see Chapter 3) as well as when you set up certain will substitutes (see Chapter 6).

Now you want to take a second look at all your beneficiary decisions and match them with your specific trust-related objectives. For example, why exactly are you setting aside $75,000 for your nephew while you're still alive? If you're doing so to help pay for his college education, that's a great gesture; but what happens if your nephew decides not to go to college or begins college and later drops out? Do you still want him to have the money?

The reason you need to link your goals and the who-gets-what picture for your estate planning is so that when you compare your trust and nontrust options, you can make the right choices for how to transfer property — or, in some cases, how to not transfer property.

Stepping Back and Comparing Both Trust and Nontrust Options

Don't be in such a big hurry to start setting up all kinds of trusts! In many cases, nontrust options may be better suited for what you're trying to accomplish. (Many times nontrust options cost less and have less hassle.)

Continuing with the same example, suppose that you plan to set aside $75,000 for your nephew. Suppose also that whether or not he goes to college, you want him to have that money at the age of 21. You can set up a simple *minor's trust* that eventually contains $75,000 from your annual below-the-gift-tax-radar contributions (see Chapter 8)that pays income to your nephew while he is a minor and with the provision that your nephew can start drawing principal from that trust when he's 18 if he goes to college, but otherwise, when he turns 21, the money is his.

Alternatively, you can set up an *education trust* that eventually contains $75,000 by the time your nephew goes to college — if he goes to college. If not, the trust agreement specifies "no college, no money" and the trust principal may be "diverted" for some other relative or perhaps donated to the school.

But you can also simply set aside money in your own bank account and if your nephew goes to college, you can pay his tuition free of gift taxes because of the education exclusion (see Chapter 11). No trusts involved!

The point is that after you decide what property to transfer to whom — along with when those transfers take place and under what circumstances — only then should you start looking at which type of trust may work for you. Furthermore, you also need to look at whether techniques that don't involve trusts may be equally suited or even better suited to what you're trying to accomplish.

Here's another example. Suppose that you want your favorite charity to have $500,000. You can simply give the charity the $500,000 at any point and use the charitable deduction to avoid gift taxes. Or, if you want to wait until your death for the $500,000 to go to the charity, simply leave the $500,000 in your will.

You can also set up some type of charitable trust, such as a charitable lead trust or charitable remainder trust (both of which we discuss in Chapter 8). Or you can set up yet any other type of trust with "strings attached" that make annual payments as long as the charity continues to meet certain requirements. Again, you have many options — trust-related and nontrust — available to you.

And are you worried about estate-related taxes taking a chunk out of your life insurance death benefit? Consider an irrevocable life insurance trust, as we discuss in Chapter 8. Remember, you can also just give the policy to someone else and not bother setting up a trust, at least for your life insurance!

For each beneficiary decision that you're examining to see if a trust makes sense, you need to look at all the tax consequences — not only gift and estate-related, but also income and capital gains — to make sure you don't fall into any tax traps. Work with your accountant who understands all the tax laws.

Weighing Trust Tradeoffs

Even when you're fairly certain that a trust makes sense for a particular aspect of your estate planning, take at least one more look at the various options you have to make sure that you choose the right one.

For example, in Chapter 8, we discuss both marital deduction trusts and *Qualified Terminable Interest Property trusts* (QTIP trusts), along with bypass trusts. All three are marriage-oriented trusts with the primary purpose of helping you with an estate tax problem (that problem being too much federal estate tax, of course!). However, all three operate differently from one another, so you need to think carefully about which one makes sense.

Depending on your particular family and circumstances, one type may be perfectly suited while another type may be an estate-planning nightmare! (See our examples in Chapter 8, particularly those involving a second marriage.)

Beware of the pitchmen!

As you consider whether or not trusts make sense for your estate, watch out for scenarios that seem to describe your particular situation as the "perfect reason" for using this trust or that trust.

We absolutely encourage you to do your estate planning homework, and we guarantee that you'll come across some type of pitch along the lines of "Bob is a 50-year old married man with two children and a total estate of $1.2 million. Bob's house is worth $600,000, blah, blah, blah. (A few more blah, blah, blahs. . . .) Bob needs to set up a Thingamajigerdo Trust for his house and a Doowhackie Trust for his stock account, and. . . ."

In some cases, these scenarios are little more than sales pitches from estate-planning professionals trying to sell you something — trusts, mostly. But even if the scenarios are genuine and aren't part of a sales pitch, you still need to be careful! "Bob" in the scenario may sound pretty similar to you, but does the scenario mention if Bob's parents are still living and if so, what their respective health situations are? Does Bob have an incapacitated brother he's taking care of, as you do? "Scenario Bob" may be encouraged to set up education trusts for his daughter, but suppose that your daughter of the same age was accepted to the Air Force Academy and will start next fall, all tuition and expenses covered by the appointment?

As we mention throughout the book, estate planning is very much an individualized exercise. Not only is your estate plan likely to be different from your neighbors, but also it likely is different from "scenario people" who on the surface seem to be just like you. By all means use examples from scenarios as ideas to bring to your estate-planning team, but treat those ideas as just that — ideas — rather than an edict ordering you to set up this type of trust or buy that kind of insurance policy.

As another example, look at the different types of charitable remainder trusts and grantor-retained trusts that we discuss in Chapter 8. Do you want to receive a fixed amount of money each year from the property you've placed in trust, or a percentage of the trust's principal (and consequently a varying amount of money) each year? Do you want to set up your own charitable remainder trust, or lump your contribution in with other peoples' contributions in a pooled interest trust?

Decisions, decisions, decisions . . . hey, we didn't say these decisions were easy! If you've reached the point where you're trying to decide if you want your grantor-retained trust to be a GRAT, GRUT, or GRIT, then congratulations! You've reached this point by following a very disciplined, well-thought-out course of action rather than looking at a list of different trust types and thinking "I'll have one of these and two of those."

Finalizing Your Choices —
Dotting I's and Crossing T's

At this point, you're ready to finalize your trust choices (as well as your non-trust choices, if you've decided against using a trust.

Now is the time to sit down with your estate-planning team and finalize your list of trusts and fill in those last details that you still need to decide. Do you want the trust to go into effect while you're still alive or upon your death? Do you want the trust to be revocable or are you comfortable with it being irrevocable?

As we point out in Chapter 8, some trusts are only revocable and others are only irrevocable. Other trusts only make sense if they're intervivos (in effect while you're still alive), while other trusts may be better as testamentary trusts (taking effect upon your death).

You need to fill in the blanks for each trust and decide what property to place into trust, who the trustee is, who the beneficiary or beneficiaries of each trust are, what all the provisions of the trust agreement are, and so on.

 Think of this step as a dress rehearsal for the trust portion of your estate plan. Now you can make last-minute adjustments because your estate-planning team (think of your team members as you would a play's director) takes a front-to-back, top-to-bottom look at the entire trust plan in concert with your estate-related tax plan and your total estate plan.

This step also includes the paperwork! As your attorney sets up each trust, you need to fill in lots of blanks on many sheets of paper, and double-check lots of fine print.

 If you're setting up a number of trusts as part of your estate plan, don't do them all at once! For example, do your irrevocable life insurance trust first (because the clock is running; see Chapter 8 for the three-year consideration), and then perhaps shift gears to the charitable trust for a charity that really needs funding badly! Then maybe set up an educational trust for your children or grandchildren, and then shift gears again to whatever type of marriage-oriented trust you want to set up for tax purposes.

Take your time with each trust agreement, and indeed with your trust plan as a whole. You don't want to make any serious mistakes, especially with an irrevocable trust that can't be changed!

Part IV
Life, Death, and Taxes

The 5th Wave   By Rich Tennant

SNOW CONES

FLAVORS

"We really should put the business into some sort of trust. I'd hate to see how the state would probate all this inventory."

In this part . . .

Beware! The government wants your money (big surprise!), and it has lots of ways to try to make you pay up — even after you die! In this part, we talk about all the taxes you need to worry about, one by one, and then present you with a straightforward approach to estate-related tax planning that you can follow now and keep up-to-date for years.

Chapter 10

Preparing for the Tug of War with the Taxman

In This Chapter

▶ Understanding the "Big Three" federal estate-related taxes

▶ Figuring out if you have to pay state inheritance or estate taxes, too

▶ Defending hearth and home against the Estate Recovery Act

*T*he Beatles' 1968 hit song *Taxman* makes a dead-on-the-mark commentary about death, your estate, and taxes. George Harrison's lyrics astutely point out that the government firmly believes in the old saying, "You can't take it with you." So, the taxman figures out ways to grab whatever he can — even the pennies holding your eyelids shut!

In this chapter, we give you an early warning about various types of estate-related taxes that you need to factor into your estate planning. We introduce you to the *federal tax triangle* of estate tax, gift tax, and generation skipping transfer tax. And because it may not be only the federal government that wants a big cut of your estate — depending on where you live — you may have to worry about state inheritance or estate taxes. We present an overview of those considerations as well. Finally, we introduce you to an important *sort of tax* — the Estate Recovery Act — and some considerations for you if you ever need to tap into government-provided health care at some point in your life.

Navigating through the Bermuda Triangle of Federal Taxes

The Bermuda Triangle, as you recall, is that stretch of ocean where ships and airplanes have disappeared without a trace. The federal tax system has its own Bermuda Triangle — a trio of taxes that work together to make as much of your estate as possible disappear without a trace. They are

- The gift tax
- The generation skipping transfer tax (GSTT)
- The estate (death) tax

But just like with the Bermuda Triangle, you can counteract this mysterious force by planning ahead and, basically, understanding what you're facing.

If you don't have a very valuable estate, the various federal taxes may not apply to you. (See the exemption amount "magic numbers" in Table 13-1 of Chapter 13 to figure out if, for federal estate purposes, your estate is "valuable.") But you or those beneficiaries who survive you still have a substantial amount of tax-related paperwork to file, so you're not totally in the clear even if you don't actually have to pay any of the taxes.

But you may very well find yourself dealing with at least some of the estate-related taxes, and you need to know what you're up against. In Chapters 11 through 13, we discuss the federal gift tax, the generation skipping transfer tax (GSTT), and the federal estate (death) tax. To introduce you to these taxes, we provide a very brief discussion in the following sections, and suggest that you spend time with the more detailed discussion of each in Chapters 11, 12, and 13 as you find yourself needing to know more about each.

The folks who wrote the laws and rules for the federal estate, gift, and GSTT created some confusing relationships among the three taxes. You absolutely, positively want to use the experts on your estate-planning team — particularly your accountant and your attorney — to help you make sense of the odd relationships among these taxes.

The gift tax

The federal gift tax is imposed on taxable gifts that you give to others. The premise behind the gift tax is fairly straightforward. If you try to avoid estate taxes by giving away a significant portion of your estate while you're still alive, the government applies a tax on those gifts — sort of a "pay me now because you're not going to be paying me later!" approach.

The sort-of-good news is that you have a variety of exemptions and allowances to work with in your gift giving to help you minimize the actual tax bite or even escape the tax bite completely in some cases. Also, even if you make taxable gifts, you may not ever have to actually pay gift taxes (that is, to actually write a check for the amount you owe) because you can credit the amount of gift tax you owe against any down-the-road estate tax after you die.

You can find the particulars of the gift tax in Chapter 11.

The generation skipping transfer tax, or GSTT

The GSTT closes a loophole that the upper class has used to reduce estate taxes. Briefly, the story is:

Members of very wealthy families who have a strong desire to keep as much wealth within their family as possible can use a variety of tactics to help shelter family wealth from a tax bite. For many years, wealthy people directly transferred some of their property to members of lower generations — for example, to grandchildren rather than children.

The idea was that if, for example, a wealthy grandfather gave or left lots of money to his own children who were wealthy in their own right, then they'd never need to spend that money — and most of what the grandfather gave as gifts or left in his will was taxed. Then, when the grandfather's children died, that same money that they didn't need to spend or otherwise get rid of once again was taxed when it was passed to their own children. So the grandfather thought ahead and just gave or left the money directly to the grandchildren or set up certain types of trusts, and essentially the money was taxed (for estate purposes, not for income purposes) only once instead of twice because he (the grandfather) had skipped over an entire generation within his family.

Think of the GSTT as "closing the generation skipping loophole" (at least, GSTT proponents position and explain the tax that way) by adding an additional tax — and at pretty hefty rates — to property transfers that can be classified as generation skipping to make up for the amount of tax that you're trying not to pay.

The good news, though, is that you have a sizable exemption amount to work with, and you can work with your attorney and accountant to minimize the GSTT bite. In Chapter 12, we explain the basics of the GSTT, but we caution you in Chapter 12 and we caution you now: The GSTT is very complex and once you get beyond the basics, you definitely need to work with qualified, experienced professionals on your estate-planning team if you have a sizable estate and could conceivably be subject to the GSTT. In other words, as they sometimes say on TV, "Don't try this at home!"

The estate (death) tax

Good news! The federal estate tax is scheduled to go away in 2010! So who needs to worry about it anyway, as long as you think you'll live past December 31, 2009?

The answer: You — and everyone else — absolutely, positively still need to worry about the federal estate tax, no matter how big (or small) your estate is. Even looking past the obvious — sorry, but none of us has any guarantee that we'll live to see 2010 — all kinds of little quirks in the 2001 tax law changed the rules and consequences of the federal estate tax that you can't afford to ignore.

Most importantly, as we discuss in the next section, the death of the estate tax may only be for a single year! Unless Congress explicitly acts to extend the federal estate tax repeal (meaning that 2010 has no estate tax), the estate tax comes back in 2011! And to make matters worse, the amount of your estate that is exempt from estate taxes — in 2009, that amount is $3.5 million after rising steadily throughout the decade — goes back down to the 2002-2003 amount of $1 million!

So you need to worry about the federal estate tax if for no other reason than you're dealing with a moving target through at least 2011. And you have no guarantee that new tax laws won't be passed sometime in the middle part of the decade (say, 2005 or 2006) that totally overhaul the estate tax system and change the rules yet again! For example, the pre-2001 tax laws had tables going out to 2006 for gradual, annual increases in exemption amounts.

When lawmakers passed the 2001 law, new figures superseded the old figures for 2002-2006. Suppose in 2005 or 2006 lawmakers pass another law, but this time when the rules change, the estate tax rates increase instead of decrease and exemption amounts go down instead of up — the result being higher estate taxes for everyone. You never know!

But before we all worry about what may happen in the future, focus on the federal estate tax rules now. Chapter 13 goes into detail about the estate tax and what you need to know.

Deciphering State Inheritance and Estate Taxes

Depending on where you live, your state inheritance and estate tax situation will be one of these four scenarios:

1. No estate-related taxes at all — lucky you!

2. A state estate tax, which operates much the same way as the federal estate tax does. A tax is imposed on your estate's value and is paid out of your estate (typically by your personal representative).

3. A state inheritance tax, which actually taxes your beneficiaries on what they receive, rather than the estate itself. Don't forget that the primary responsibility for filing the inheritance tax return and paying the tax usually falls on the personal representative.

4. A *pick-up* or *soak-up* tax, which is a *sort of tax:* Your estate doesn't actually owe any additional money to pay that tax, even though a state estate tax return likely needs to be filed. The state gets a cut of what would otherwise be paid to the IRS (but your personal representative still probably has to file a lot of state tax paperwork anyway!)

Keep in mind several points about state death taxes. First, some states are repealing or phasing out their inheritance or estate taxes, but don't be surprised to see other states that currently don't have estate-related taxes instituting either an inheritance or estate tax! Whereas most state governments had budget surpluses throughout the 1990s, the early 2000s have been quite a different story with deficits coming back as a result of economic slowdown. As a result, states are looking to all kinds of new or increased sources of revenue to help cover shortfalls — so why not estate-related taxes?

Keep alert wherever you live and if you see either a state estate or state inheritance tax coming, make sure that you work with your accountant and attorney to adjust your estate planning as necessary.

Additionally, pay attention to the details of any existing inheritance or estate taxes that may apply where you live, such as your state's tax-rate structure. For example, your state may impose different inheritance tax rates on different people, depending on their relationship to you (for example, parents and children in one group or class, other relatives in a second class, unrelated people in a third class, and so on).

Also, don't forget about any exemptions your state has, such as excluding life insurance, pensions, or fixed dollar amounts for different classes of recipients. You definitely need to work with your accountant, but if you want to get a quick idea of the various state laws and amounts, you can check out *Plan Your Estate,* 6th Edition, by Denis Clifford and Cora Jordan, (published by Nolo). (In Chapter 22, we mention www.nolo.com, Nolo's online presence, as a Web site you can check out for up-to-date information about various estate-planning topics.)

Another topic about state death taxes you need to be aware of is the soon-to-disappear credit on your federal estate tax return (IRS Form 706) for any state estate taxes that you have to pay. Whereas most of the 2001 tax law helps with lower tax rates and higher exemption amounts, one part of the 2001 tax law can cost you (or, more accurately, your estate) more money if you live in a state that has a state estate or inheritance tax.

Through 2004, the state estate tax credit will be reduced each year by 25 percent (25 percent in 2002, 50 percent in 2003,and 75 percent in 2004), and then finally be repealed in 2005 when it will be replaced with a deduction rather than a credit. (Without getting overly complicated, tax deductions save you less money than tax credits.)

So if you do have a state estate or inheritance tax where you live, plan ahead with your accountant to determine the impact (if any) of the reduction and eventual repeal of the state estate tax credit.

Even if you don't live in a state with a state estate tax, part of your estate may still be subject to a state death tax! How? If you own property (specifically, real estate) in another state, estate or inheritance tax may apply for your out-of-state property if the state where the property is located does have death taxes. Make sure your accountant knows if you have any out-of-state property so you can factor that into your estate plan.

Protecting Your Property (Including Home Sweet Home!) from the Estate Recovery Act

The Estate Recovery Act technically isn't a tax, but because it involves the government trying to take money out of your estate after you die, we include it in this discussion of various estate-related taxes.

In 1993, the U.S. Congress passed an act that requires each state to demand repayment for Medicaid benefits that had previously been provided to certain citizens for certain services. Specifically:

- ✔ *Certain citizens* — people over the age of 55 who have received Medicaid payments within a specified period of time

- ✔ *Certain services* — payments for nursing homes and nursing care facilities, home and community-based services, related services at hospitals, and prescription drugs

The idea behind the Estate Recovery Act is simple (but devious): If you need to accept help from Medicaid for health care services, you have no problem while you're still alive. But after you die, the government wants its money back!

In fact, the Estate Recovery Act can have a far more devastating impact on your estate than any estate tax does! We explain why in this section.

A helping of philosophy with a side order of ideology

Make no mistake about it: Various kinds of estate-related taxes involve much more than laws and rules, calculations and numbers. The battle lines are drawn between opponents and proponents of estate taxes, gift taxes, and generation skipping transfer taxes, and the two sides may as well be the opposing armies at Gettysburg in 1863!

Opponents of estate-related taxes make arguments like these:

✔ The property in your estate has been "taxed on the way in." For example, the income you earned from your job or business was subject to income taxes and should not also be "taxed on the way out" because doing so represents double-taxation of the same property.

✔ Much of the increased value of property in your estate, such as interest you earn on your bank accounts and certificates of deposit, also has been taxed along the way. So, why tax what you have left over yet one more time?

✔ Owners of family businesses and farms are especially hard hit by estate taxes and often have to sell part or all of their business to raise cash to pay estate taxes.

✔ What's so wrong about keeping hard-earned wealth within your family rather than "turning it over" to the government?

On the other side of the battle, estate tax proponents argue that

✔ In many estates, particularly those of wealthier individuals, much of the value has *not* already been taxed: specifically, gains on stocks, real estate, and other property.

✔ Family businesses and farms actually have the use of special credits and deductions to help defray the tax impact.

✔ Keeping large amounts of wealth concentrated in your family is "socially bad." After you die, your heirs and beneficiaries should be willing to give up some of that family wealth for "the greater social good" because, after all, they didn't earn that money, you did — and now you're gone!

Unlike the Civil War, where less than two years after Gettysburg the two opposing forces had reconciled, don't expect the opposing sides of the estate-taxes-good-or-bad battle ever to come to agreement. You're likely to see a seesaw battle of philosophy and ideology for years to come. For example, the overall reductions in tax rates, increases in exemption amounts, and repeals found in the 2001 tax law can certainly be viewed as the handiwork of opponents of estate-related taxes. But on the other hand, if the repeals don't stick around past that magical year of 2010, don't be surprised if the proponents of estate-related taxes (if they are in power) wind up increasing the tax bite.

The battle continues.

The Estate Recovery Act can be the most detrimental tax (or sort of tax), because the people most likely to require Medicaid assistance are people who probably have the least property or assets. Chances are that most of what they do have is in their respective houses or residences. So guess what the government will go after for reimbursement once a "targeted" person dies? You guessed it: the family home!

However, your state may have some type of homestead exemption or personal residence waiver to protect your house if you ever need Medicaid and fall within your state's guidelines to seek reimbursement after you die. For example, your house may be safe as long as your spouse is still alive, and only then will the state try to pursue a forced sale if no other assets are available for reimbursement. You also can look into other estate-planning and gift-giving strategies to protect your house, such as joint tenancy (see Chapter 6 for more information about the *right of survivorship* aspect) if you want to protect your house because, say, one of your children lives there.

The particulars of each state's version of the Estate Recovery Act — and the names they go by — vary, but chances are that your state's version may not apply to property that passes to others outside of probate (that is, your *nonprobate estate*). Your nonprobate estate may include property in which you and someone else (or more than one other person) have joint tenancy with right of survivorship (see Chapter 6). So as part of your overall estate planning, you need to factor any Estate Recovery Act considerations into your strategy.

Make sure you spend time with your attorney going through all the details of your state's version of the Estate Recovery Act. For example, find out when the state will seek repayment. For example, the state may wait until your surviving spouse (if any) has died, your children have grown, or some other factors. Your state may also have other exemptions (such as a below-the-poverty-line exemption), or you may be allowed to apply for a waiver.

Make sure you tell your personal representative that he or she may be personally liable for Estate Recovery Act-related claims! Specifically, if your personal representative transfers property to others (such as family members) without first satisfying a claim for recovery from your state, the state can come after the personal representative for payment. And if you're someone else's personal representative, make sure you know whether the person's estate that you are a personal representative for is subject to a claim by the state. Not following the rules (or not paying attention) can be very costly!

Your attorney can explain all the rules governing personal representative responsibility to you, both for your own estate as well as any personal representative responsibilities you have for someone else's estate. For example, you need to know how long the personal representative has to notify whatever department in the state government that administers the state's recovery plan, and how to actually do the notification (for example, by certified letter). Our advice: Be careful and pay attention!

Chapter 11

The Gift Tax: Isn't Giving a Gift Enough?

*T*hink about this idea.

If your estate is worth enough to be subject to federal estate taxes after you die, why not transfer some — or maybe even all — of the property in your estate to others while you're still alive to avoid federal estate taxes? Basically, why don't you just give everything away?

Unfortunately, the federal government has already thought about this strategy and has stayed one step ahead with the gift tax. In fact, those sneaky tax guys went a step farther. The government linked many aspects of the gift tax with the federal estate tax to further limit your ability to avoid paying taxes when you transfer your property to others — while you're still alive, as well as after you die.

Still, despite the potential bite of gift taxes, gift giving can be an important part of your overall estate planning. In this chapter, we present you with enough basic information about the gift tax so you can understand the tax implications of gifts you give. And we also help you understand the implications of gift giving and the associated taxes for your estate. Because of the linkage between gift and estate taxes, you absolutely need to think several moves ahead, just as if you're playing chess, to understand the long-range impact.

Giving a Gift: The Basics

At the simplest level, the gift tax is very straightforward, and works like this:

1. You give a gift to someone.

2. You determine if the gift you gave is taxable.

3. If the gift is taxable, you check for exceptions, credits, or exclusions that can help make part or all of the gift tax-free.

4. You keep track of your gifts and at some point compare those amounts against the limitations the government set for gift and estate taxes, as part of your overall estate planning.

This chapter discusses the federal gift tax system. A few states also impose a state gift tax. Check to see if your state has a state gift tax before deciding the potential gift tax liability from gifting.

There are gifts — and there are taxable gifts

In the world of estate planning, gifts are more complex than the presents you give and receive on birthdays and at other holidays. Don't think in general terms of a gift, but rather in terms of *taxable gifts of property* from your estate.

Property can be real property, such as your house, tangible personal property, such as an antique painting, or intangible personal property, such as shares of a mutual fund. (See Chapter 1 for more information on property types.)

So how can you tell when a gift is taxable and subject to a gift tax? The most common situation you'll run into is giving property (including money) that exceeds the annual exclusion (in 2002, the annual exclusion is $11,000, as we discuss in a moment) and doesn't qualify for any of the deductions — marital, educational, and so on — that we discuss later.

If your gift qualifies under the preceding definition and you don't receive anything of value for the amount above the exclusion, you have made a taxable gift for the amount above that exclusion. For example, if you give your son $14,000 in cash and expect nothing in return, the portion exceeding the annual exclusion amount is a taxable gift. But if you give your son $14,000 in cash and receive $14,000 worth of gold in exchange, the cash isn't a gift.

Before you add the kids to your checking account . . .

Many elderly people decide to add their adult children to their bank accounts so that their children can help them pay bills. Most states' signature cards for these accounts treat the addition of the child to the bank account as a joint tenant with right of survivorship (see Chapter 6). Either party — the parent or child — can then withdraw funds.

If the child just signs his or her name to the checks for bill paying, no taxable property transfer occurs. But if the child withdraws money for his or her own use and hasn't contributed to the account, the gift tax law treats those amounts as taxable gifts.

Additionally, to be considered a completed property transfer and therefore a gift, you must give up all control of the property.

A little bit of good news, though, is that each year, you have a certain amount called an *annual exclusion* that works in your favor. The annual exclusion is very simple. For every person to whom you give a gift, you basically have a limit on the amount you can give. For example, in 2002 the annual exclusion is $11,000, so that any gifts you give to someone up to a total value of $11,000 aren't subject to the gift tax for that year. (We discuss more about the annual exclusion, including how it applies when you give gifts to more than one person, later in this chapter.)

The tax guys didn't stop at simply applying gift taxes to transfers of valuable property. You may also make a taxable gift if you:

- ✔ Sell property for less than its fair market value. (We discuss this topic more in the section, "Valuing Gifts.")
- ✔ Make a reduced interest rate loan.
- ✔ Make an interest-free loan.

The person who gives a gift is called a *donor,* while the person receiving the gift is called a *donee.* An easy way to remember these terms is to think about an organ donor — he or she gives away an organ just like a donor gives a gift. The *transfer date* is the date that the property actually transfers from the donor to the donee. The gift's value on the transfer date is called the *transfer value.*

Not all gifts are taxable

Even if the gift's value exceeds the annual exclusion, certain gifts are excepted. These exceptions include gifts to:

- ✔ Your spouse (because of the marital deduction)
- ✔ Most charities (because of the charitable deduction)
- ✔ Political organizations (because of the political exclusion)
- ✔ Tuition (because of the educational exclusion)
- ✔ Medical expenses (because of the medical exclusion)

The marital deduction

You can transfer an unlimited amount of property to your spouse. For example, if you give your spouse $1 million, you have made a taxable gift. But due to the marital deduction, you don't owe any gift tax.

However, you need to meet certain qualifications in order for the marital deduction to be unlimited and tax-free.

- ✔ You and your spouse are married at the time that gift is completed.
- ✔ The spouse receiving the gift is a U.S. citizen.
- ✔ The spouse receiving the gift doesn't have a *terminable interest,* which means that your spouse's interest in the property being transferred as a gift ends when "something" happens in the future (such as a certain date arriving, or maybe your mother-in-law moving in with you).

The charitable deduction

One of the most common forms of estate planning to avoid gift taxes is charitable giving. As with the marital deduction, the amount you give to a charity tax-free is unlimited. You can give any type of property as a charitable gift. So if you're very wealthy and want to be remembered as a great philanthropist, you can gift your favorite charity $10 million and not deal with gift taxes!

Generally, you must give your entire interest in the property as part of your gift to be eligible for the charitable deduction; the technical term used is a *total interest charitable gift.*

The amount of your charitable deduction depends on which of the following four types of gifts you give. All are considered to be total interest charitable gifts:

✓ **Total charitable gift.** The most common type of charitable gifting, when you give the property (including cash) to the charity and receive a charitable deduction. You make this type of charitable gift and expect nothing in return.

✓ **Charitable bargain sale.** You sell property to the charity at less than fair market value (see the section, "Valuing Gifts" later in this chapter) and then receive a charitable deduction on the difference between the property's sale price and property's fair market value. You can use bargain sales for small value property where you want to give a gift but also want something in return.

✓ **Charitable stock bailout.** These types of gifts enable you to give closely held stock and receive a charitable deduction equal to the stock's fair market value. You receive a charitable deduction by giving shares; and at the same time you avoid paying the income tax or capital gains tax that you otherwise would have owed had you redeemed or sold those shares. This strategy may make sense as part of your overall tax planning.

✓ **Charitable gift annuity.** You transfer property to a charity that agrees to pay someone a specified amount for the remainder of that person's lifetime. As a result, the charity keeps the remaining amount of the annuity after you die. The amount of charitable deduction is based on who is named as the lifetime donor.

The charity must be considered a *qualified* charity to avoid gift taxes. The IRS publishes a list of qualified charities. Most public charities qualify, but double-check before writing that very large check!

Political exclusions

If you're really passionate about politics and want to put your money where your vote is, we have good news: Gifts to political organizations are exempt from gift tax. (So you can try to buy political influence and avoid gift taxes too — what a country!)

Educational exclusions

On the education front, to qualify for an educational exclusion, a gift must be:

✓ Earmarked for tuition or training

✓ Paid directly to the educational institution

So your check payable to the University of Knowledge for tuition qualifies for an education exclusion, but what about if you give your nephew a check to be used for his tuition? Sorry, you can only use the education exclusion if you make the check payable directly to the educational institution. (Maybe the tax law writers figured that unless the gift check goes directly to a school, students might use the money for other purposes, such as a winter skiing trip to Aspen, a spring break trip to Cancun, or yet another trip to Europe in the summer.)

Medical exclusions

Medical exclusions apply for payments made to a medical care facility for costs (such as diagnosis and treatment), as well as payments for a person's medical insurance. Make payments directly to the medical institution to qualify for the medical exclusion.

Looking Inside Three Common Gift Tax Situations

To see how the gift tax may affect you, we examine three examples.

Example No. 1: $5,000 to darling daughter

Suppose that you have never given any taxable gifts previously, and in 2002, you decide to give a cash gift of $5,000 to your oldest daughter. In 2003, when you file your tax returns you aren't subject to the gift tax.

You aren't subject to gift tax because the gift amount ($5,000 in this case) is lower than the annual exclusion amount. In 2002, the annual exclusion amount was $11,000.

Every year the federal government resets the annual exclusion indexed for inflation. So if in 2003, the annual exclusion amount is also $11,000, you can give your daughter a gift of $11,000 and that entire gift is free of gift taxes. Each year you must check with your accountant to discover if the exclusion amount has increased before you give any gifts.

Example No. 2: $5,000 each to all three adorable kids

Suppose that you still have never given any taxable gifts previously, and you decide to give $5,000 to each of your three children for a total of $15,000. Even though the annual exclusion is $11,000, you don't owe any gift tax. The annual exclusion amount applies to each person to whom you give a gift. So because no single gift was more than $11,000, each of your gifts — all $15,000 — is not subject to the gift tax.

Think of the annual exclusion as actually being a collection of annual exclusion amounts, one for each person to whom you give a gift. Nobody's annual exclusion spills over into anybody else's, giving you flexibility in how you decide to divide gifts among various recipients. So basically, if you have 15 (gasp!) children, you can give each child up to $11,000 worth of gifts and not have to pay any gift tax.

To be eligible for the annual exclusion, gifts must be for *present interest,* meaning that the person receiving a gift must enjoy and use the property now. Gifts of *future interest* — meaning the donee's use of the gift doesn't begin until some future date or is, in the lingo of estate planning, "otherwise incomplete" — don't qualify for the annual exclusion.

Example No. 3: $21,000 to the fairest of them all

Suppose you've never given any taxable gifts and you give a gift of $21,000 to your oldest daughter. In this case, you do have a gift-tax situation and do have to pay a gift tax, because the $21,000 amount has exceeded the $11,000 annual exclusion by $10,000. So you owe a gift tax on $10,000 (not the entire $21,000).

But the situation can be complicated. By using the current tax rates (remember, though, that tax rates change often, so double-check the current rates with your accountant or tax attorney), the gift tax owed is $1,800 based on an 18 percent tax rate. But you may not have to actually pay $1,800 in taxes out of your pocket — at least right now.

The reason you may not have to actually pay $1,800 is because of how the gift tax and the federal estate tax are linked. You have a *magic number* that determines whether or not estate taxes apply to your estate after you die. In 2002 and 2003, this magic number is a nice even $1 million. The magic numbers (you may see either of the following more formal terms used: *exemption equivalents* or *exclusion amounts*) for other years are shown in Table 11-1.

The federal tax law gives you a *unified credit* amount that represents the taxes that apply to each year's magic numbers. Think of the unified credit as a running total of taxes you don't have to pay on property transfers you make while you're alive (through gifts) and after you die (property transferred from your estate that would be subject to estate taxes). As with the exemption equivalent magic numbers, the unified credit amounts are scheduled to change, as shown in Table 11-1.

Table 11-1	Unified Credits and Exclusion Amounts (2001 Tax Law)			
Year	*Unified Credit (Gift Taxes)*	*Exclusion Amt. (Gift Taxes)*	*Unified Credit (Estate Taxes)*	*Exclusion Amt. (Estate Taxes)*
2002–2003	345,800	1,000,000	345,800	1,000,000
2004–2005	345,800	1,000,000	555,800	1,500,000
2006–2008	345,800	1,000,000	780,800	2,000,000
2009	345,800	1,000,000	1,455,800	3,500,000

Source: www.irs.gov

Notice in Table 11-1 that in 2002 and 2003, the unified credit and exclusion amount numbers shown for gift and estate tax purposes are identical to each other, but beginning in 2004, you actually have two sets of numbers to work with. We explain the difference in the section "Smoothing over the 2004 wrinkle."

Entering the Twilight Zone of Credits and Exclusions

We think you'd rather spend your twilight years doing happier things than keeping track of your unified credits and exclusion amounts. So we're handing you a free pass to assign this whole section to your estate-planning team!

You've decided to stick with it? Okay, we warned you, so here goes, beginning with the example we cite earlier in the chapter, where you gave $21,000 to your eldest daughter. In that case, you can subtract the $1,800 in gift taxes from the unified credit amount. Assume that you gave the gift to your daughter in 2002, which means that the unified credit amount for that year is $345,800 (see Table 11-1); you now have $344,000 remaining on your unified credit. So instead of actually paying $1,800 in taxes to the IRS, you are essentially deciding that the portion of your estate free of estate taxes after you die will be slightly lower because you gave away some of your property now as a taxable gift. You can take this action because the gift and estate taxes are part of the same system (thus the reference to a "unified" credit that applies to both gift and estate taxes).

Feeling a bit confused? Don't worry, you're not alone. Part of the confusion that surrounds gift taxes — even before we get into more complicated aspects, such as gifts over multiple years and what happens in 2004 under the new tax law (both of which we discuss in the next section) — is that the unified credit deals with running totals of taxes you don't have to pay. You can easily lose the big picture as you continually calculate tax amounts, subtract those tax amounts from what's left of your unified credit, and worry about how that amount eventually balances against another tax amount: your estate tax.

Before you worry about the record keeping, concentrate on another more direct, easier-to-understand running total: the value of gifts you give plus what's left in your estate. Even though you eventually do have to get around to tax calculations and unified credit amounts, you probably are more comfortable using the exclusion amount magic numbers shown in Table 11-1 to indicate how much you have left on your gift-giving account as you plan ahead. So in Example No.3, in 2003 you now have $990,000 left to give to others through taxable gifts and your estate before taxes kick in.

Hold on — more complications ahead!

So far, the gift tax doesn't sound too bad. In many cases, you can just forget about the gift tax because you give small enough gifts that are within the annual exclusion amounts. And even when you give taxable gifts, you can counter-balance any applicable gift tax against future estate taxes, and not have to actually pay any gift tax out of your pocket. So what's the big deal?

You need to be aware of two complications for gifts and gift taxes:

- Complicated calculations when you give gifts in more than one year
- The "new wrinkle" in the relationship between gift and estate taxes beginning in 2004

You may notice that we start off each of the three examples of gift giving earlier in this chapter by supposing that you had not previously given any taxable gifts. The tax calculations get somewhat more complicated if you have previously given any taxable gifts and used part of your unified credit.

Without getting overly complicated, the tax rates that apply to gift and estate taxes are *progressive,* meaning that as the taxable amount increases, so does the tax rate when you move into a new tax bracket.

If you've given taxable gifts in the past, you have to take a couple of additional steps when you give new gifts to figure out your new tax. Subtract the new tax amount from your unified credit to determine how much of your unified credit you've used up and how much is left. Take the following steps:

1. Figure out how much in taxable gifts you're dealing with in the current year, after all annual exclusions, marital exclusions, educational exclusions, and so on. (We talk about those exclusions earlier in this chapter.)

2. Add in the total of taxable gifts you've given in previous years.

3. Using the current gift tax tables, figure out the gift tax on the total amount of taxable gifts: the new gifts for this year and all the gifts you have given in the past. (Don't worry, you won't be double-paying gift taxes on your previous gifts; the next step takes care of that.)

4. Take your previous figure for gift taxes and subtract it from the number you calculated in Step 3.

You now have a new total gift tax figure based on the progressive gift tax rates to work with against the applicable unified credit amount for that year.

IRS Form 709 gives you a step-by-step guide, but double-check your math!

Smoothing over the 2004 wrinkle

Notice in Table 11-1 that in 2002 and 2003, the unified credit and exclusion amount for gift and estate tax considerations are identical to each other. But in 2004 and 2005, the table shows different amounts for gift tax considerations and estate tax considerations. The gift tax amounts stay the same as in 2002 and 2003, but for estate taxes the unified credit increases. Then, in 2006, the estate tax figures increases again, and finally once more in 2009. So what's the deal here?

Under the old (pre-2001) tax law, the unified system for gift and estate taxes was truly unified in all aspects, including identical amounts for exclusion amounts and the resulting unified credit. This philosophy carried over into the new tax law, but only for 2002 and 2003. Basically, when you have the same numbers to deal with for estate and gift tax considerations, you can use your exclusion amounts (and the resulting unified credit) in a mix-and-match sense — for gifts, what's left in your estate, or any combination of the two.

For example, consider the figures for 2003 in Table 11-1: $1 million exclusion amounts. (Don't worry about the unified credit, as that only complicates the explanation for a very complex topic!) With $1 million to work with, you may:

✔ Give a total of $1 million in taxable gifts without having to actually pay any taxes, but then you have no exclusion left at all for your estate after you die.

✔ Never give any taxable gifts to anyone, which means that up to $1 million of your otherwise taxable estate will be free of estate taxes.

✔ Give a total of $500,000 in taxable gifts, which leaves up to $500,000 in your estate free of taxes.

✔ Give a total of $200,000 in taxable gifts, which leaves up to $800,000 in your estate free of taxes.

Of course, many other combinations of numbers for gifts and your estate apply, but you get the idea.

So what happens in 2004 when the numbers for estate taxes diverge from gift taxes, which stay constant? Basically, you can no longer use your mix-and-match options to give all the allowable exclusion amount away through gifts. So with the 2004 and 2005 numbers (see Table 11-1) you can, for example:

✔ Give a total of $1 million in taxable gifts, which leaves up to $500,000 of your otherwise taxable estate that will be free of federal estate taxes.

✔ Never give any taxable gifts to anyone, which means that up to $1.5 million of your otherwise taxable estate will be free of federal estate taxes.

✔ Give a total of $500,000 in taxable gifts, which leaves up to $1 million in your estate free of federal estate taxes.

Again, you have many other combinations to work with, but remember that you can give at most $1 million in taxable gifts (make sure you're looking at the column headed "Exclusion Amt. "Gift Taxes"), even though the estate tax exclusion amount has increased to $1.5 million.

Looking ahead to 2006, when the estate tax exclusion amount increases to $2 million, think of your options this way: The most you can give away of your estate through gifts is 50 percent of that $2 million exclusion amount (not 50 percent of your estate). Then, in 2009, with an estate tax exclusion amount of $3.5 million but with the gift tax exclusion amount still stuck at $1 million, the percentage of your estate that you can give through gifts goes down even more (less than 30 percent of the $3.5 million exclusion amount).

So what happens in 2010, when the estate tax disappears for one year but then comes back in 2011? (We discuss this peculiar situation in Chapter 10.) Remember that the gift tax isn't repealed in 2010, as the estate tax and Generation Skipping Transfer Tax (Chapter 12) are. Actually, because you still only have $1 million to work with for your gift tax exclusion amount, if you have a particularly valuable estate, your options may still be rather limited. You can give away only up to $1 million in gifts before gift taxes come into play.

If you were to die in 2010 when the estate tax is MIA, then anything left in your estate after you've given away up to $1 million is tax-free. However, if the estate tax's repeal disappears in 2011 and the estate tax returns — and, if as is currently scheduled, the unified credit and exclusion amount for estate tax purposes goes back to the 2002-2003 levels — then the "2004 wrinkle" will disappear, because the key figures will once again be the same for gift tax and estate tax purposes!

Congress may vote to change the tax code between now and 2010 and 2011. Your best bet is to maximize the amount of your estate that you give away through gifts, whether or not the $1 million cap changes between now and 2010 and 2011. Hopefully, the estate tax repeal will hang around past 2010. Even if the estate tax returns, you'll at least have sheltered as much as possible from estate taxes by giving it away through gifts and taking advantage of the gift tax exclusion amount and unified credit.

Old, out-of-date tables of unified credit amounts and exclusion amounts abound on the Internet and in printed material (such as books and articles) that predates the 2001 tax law. Make sure that you're working with the current figures when you're doing your estate planning, particularly when planning gifts and your gift tax strategy.

The Internal Revenue Service's Web site at www.irs.gov is a good place to get the current figures, especially the next time tax law changes affect estate and gift taxes (and you can be fairly certain that'll happen again!).

Gift Splitting

The old adage says that in marriage you share and share alike — which in the world of gifts is good, because *gift splitting* essentially allows you to double the annual exclusion amount. You and your spouse can share a gift by considering that you give one-half of the gift and your spouse gives one-half of the gift. For example, in 2002 you and your spouse could give $22,000 (the $11,000 annual exclusion × 2) to anyone annually without making a taxable gift.

Suppose you and your spouse give $15,000 to your nephew and $20,000 to your spouse's niece in 2002. By gift splitting, you and your spouse are considering to each be giving $7,500 ($15,000 ÷ 2) to your nephew and $10,000 ($20,000 ÷ 2) to your spouse's niece. Even though the total gift value to each recipient is more than the annual exclusion amount of $11,000, gift splitting enables you to make both gifts nontaxable. Neither of those gifts counts against your unified credit.

You need to follow a few simple rules when it comes to gift splitting to prove that both you and your spouse are in agreement on the gift splitting that you're doing in any particular year. Make sure you check with your accountant to see what tax return forms you need to file, and when.

Valuing Gifts

Remember, we discuss ways you can value the various types of property in your estate in Chapter 2.

If you're trying to get a general idea of what your estate is worth so you can decide to whom you want to leave various property, you don't need to worry about being precise. For example, whether your house is worth $187,000 or $187,500 — or even $190,000 — doesn't make a whole lot of difference when you're doing your basic estate planning.

But in order to determine if a gift tax may be owed on a gift, you need to precisely determine the gift's value. Sound easy? Well, sometimes it is and sometimes it isn't. When you buy a gift for someone, you think of the gift's value as the price you just paid for the item. If you buy a $1000 painting as a gift, your gift's value is $1000. But what if the painting doesn't have a price tag? How can you determine value? And how do you standardize your gift's value so that all the same gifts have the same value?

Valuation is an important part in the calculation of gift tax. If your gift is determined to be a taxable gift subject to gift tax, you need to know the gift's value in order to determine the tax amount. Some common methods are covered in the following sections, and by all means, work with your accountant to make sure you correctly and accurately determine the value of gifts correctly.

Fair market value

The most common valuation technique in the federal gift tax is *fair market value*. The fair market value of property is determined by what the property receives in value in a market comprised of (to use some terminology from basic economics) willing and able buyers and sellers.

For fair market value, buyers and sellers under United States Treasury regulations enter into the market with "neither being under any compulsion to buy or sell." So the free market exchange between buyers and sellers determines fair market value.

How important is fair market value? If you believe that you don't need to file a gift tax return that we discuss later in the chapter because the property's fair market value is less than the annual exclusion, the IRS can challenge and contest the fair market value at any time in the future — even on the donor's estate tax return submitted after death! But if you do file a gift tax return, the IRS has three years to challenge and contest the property's fair market value. You (or your estate) must prove the fair market value. If you can't, the IRS will establish that value.

If the determination of a gift tax depends on identifying fair market value, how do you actually figure out the fair market value? After all, you know the old saying, "All is fair in love and in market value." You determine fair market value differently depending on the type of property, as we discuss in the following sections.

Real property

For gifting purposes, real property, such as your house, vacation home, or investment income-producing property is valued in the same manner we discuss in Chapter 2.

In order to get an independent valuation on real property, you may need to hire an appraiser. Your real property's fair market value is most likely not the price you paid for it because real estate prices change — hopefully increasing rather than decreasing! Fair market value is the amount your property is worth today.

The appraisal looks at factors, such as:

- Recent sales prices of comparable properties
- Property's replacement cost
- Income value from income-producing property
- Property's location and condition

Publicly traded stocks and bonds

Unlike real property, a readily available price tag is attached to publicly traded stocks and bonds. For example, if a share of XYZ Company stock is $44 on Tuesday, the fair market value of a share is $44; if the share price increases to $45 on Wednesday, the fair market value of a share changes to

$45. In fact, throughout days when the stock market is open, you can get real-time prices for stocks.

Because of the ease of obtaining the fair market value of publicly traded stocks and bonds, the calculation of fair market value for purposes of gift taxes is straightforward; however, you should be aware that the fair market value for gift tax purposes is the *mean* of the highest and lowest sales price on the date of valuation.

You always wondered if math skills and statistics would ever come in handy. Now's your chance! A mean is the same as an average and is calculated by adding the set of numbers and dividing it by the amount of numbers in the set. For example, if the XYZ Company shares on the date of valuation reached a high of $48 and a low of $42, the mean valuation is $45 ($48+$42= $90 ÷ 2 = $45).

Closely held stock

Unlike publicly traded stock, which can have thousands or millions of owners, only a few individuals hold closely held stock. Typically, family businesses may have only a few family members as owners of all the shares of stock, so the business is deemed to be *closely held.*

If fair market value is determined in a market with buyers and sellers, how do you value closely held stock that has no sellers and in essence no buyers but possibly the other co-owners?

Factors in determining fair market value for closely held stock include:

✔ Business type

✔ Industry outlook

✔ Financial capabilities of business

✔ Fair market value of comparable publicly traded stock

Even after you determine the fair market value of closely held stock, you still have a situation where your stock isn't part of the free market exchange that is an essential part of fair market value. The IRS sometimes allows special discount techniques that reduce the value of closely held stock to less than fair market value in determining the value of gifted closely held stock for gift tax purposes. The lower the fair market value, the less you potentially owe in gift tax.

Special valuation techniques other than fair market value available for closely held stock are:

✔ Minority discount

✔ Lack of marketability discount

If you own less than 50 percent of a closely held business, you have a minority ownership in the business. Consequently, you probably don't have the ability to set or change policy in a closely held business because of your minority ownership position. Due to the many regulations regarding minority discounts, check the requirements before using a minority discount for closely held stock.

A *lack of marketability discount* acknowledges that you may have difficulty finding a buyer for a closely held business, such as a partnership or corporation. In addition to not having the exposure to buyers as you do with publicly traded stock, the closely held business may have restrictions on who can even buy your stock.

Savings bonds

You probably have some good old savings bonds laying around somewhere that a relative gave you or that you purchased through a payroll deduction plan at work.

You can determine the transfer value of savings bonds by knowing the amount that you can redeem the bond for on the transfer dates, which is called its *redemption value.* Remember, a bond cashed in prior to its maturity date receives a discounted value. So a savings bond with a face value of $20,000 gifted prior to its maturity date has a transfer value that is less than $20,000. Tables published by the government provide redemption values for bonds.

Co-ownership property

We discuss in Chapter 6 several ways that you and others can co-own property: joint tenants with right of survivorship, tenants by the entirety, and tenants in common. Tenants by the entirety and community property are forms of ownership only for spouses, while anyone can use tenants in common and joint tenancy. Additionally, we discuss community property in Chapter 4 as another way of co-owning property.

If you co-own something, you only own a part of it and therefore only have a partial interest in the property. So how do you figure out the fair market value of part of a property for gift tax purposes? Your figure depends on which form of co-ownership you have.

For example, with tenants in common, the gift's value is the fair market value of the percentage owned on the transfer date. So if you own 35 percent of the property you gift, the transfer value is 35 percent of the property's fair market value.

In the case of joint tenancy with right of survivorship, because all joint tenants own equal shares the gift's value is proportionate to your ownership.

Thus if you are one of four joint tenants, for example, the transfer value is 25 percent of the property's fair market value.

To find out the specifics about fair market value and co-owning property, ask your accountant or tax attorney. Also, ask those estate-planning professionals about specific concerns for gifting partial interest in real estate to family members, such as when an elderly parent adds a child to the deed for the parent's home.

Filing Gift Tax Forms

As if dealing with a tax on gifts isn't enough, as a donor you get the pleasure of filing a tax form associated with the gift tax. After all, taxes and forms go together!

The gift tax return is known as IRS Form 709. You must send in Form 709 by April 15 of the following year that you made the gift. If you owe a gift tax, you must pay it no later than April 15 (though most people will pay the tax at the same time that the return is filed, even if that date is before April 15).

 If you file for an extension on your income taxes, you automatically receive an extension for your gift tax return because both are due on April 15. Just check the box on the income tax extension form indicating your intention to also extend the gift tax return date. *Note:* If someone dies more than nine months prior to April 15, the gift tax form needs to be filed at the same time as the estate tax return.

Even if you've become very comfortable in doing your own income taxes each year, you may want to work with your accountant on gift tax returns, especially if you've previously given taxable gifts and now have to use prior years' figures for total gifts and gift taxes (as we discuss earlier in this chapter). You don't want to unwittingly make a mistake that can eventually cause more estate taxes to be paid after you die. Basically, if you make mistakes on your gift tax form that cause you to show more of your unified credit used than is actually the case, the consequences for your eventual estate tax return can be a whole lot of trouble for your personal representative to straighten out.

You must file a gift tax return using IRS Form 709 if:

- ✔ You give anyone (except your spouse) more than the annual exclusion amount in a calendar year.

- ✔ You give anyone (except your spouse) a gift of a future interest rather than a present interest.

✔ You give your spouse a gift that terminates in the future and thus doesn't qualify for a marital deduction.

✔ You give a charitable gift exceeding the annual exclusion amount and the gift does not qualify for a charitable deduction.

✔ You give a charitable gift exceeding the annual exclusion amount that qualifies for a charitable deduction, but you give less than your entire interest in the property.

If the only reason you're filing a gift tax return is because of gift splitting and not because your gift exceeds the annual exclusion, you may be able to use Form 709-A, which is a simpler form. Check the other requirements listed on this form to make sure you can use it.

Now the big question — who is responsible for paying the gift tax owed? The answer is usually the donor. If you gift split with your spouse, each of you is responsible for paying the gift tax associated with your own return.

Chapter 12

Skipping Around the Generation Skipping Transfer Tax

The Generation Skipping Transfer Tax (GSTT) is the most complex estate-related tax you will come across, and the most difficult to understand. Congress introduced the GSTT as a way to prevent well-to-do families from sheltering large amounts of wealth from federal estate taxes by skipping over a generation within a family and giving gifts, setting up trusts, or leaving large amounts of money to "lower" generations within a family: grandchildren instead of children, for example.

The good news, though, is that most likely the GSTT won't apply to you (we explain why). But you still should understand the basics of the GSTT so that you won't stumble into a "tax trap" by thinking that you're cleverly avoiding down-the-road estate taxes if you do someday transfer large amounts of money to your grandchildren instead of your children, for example. Instead of being one step ahead of the taxman, you may only wind up leaving behind a large headache — and a large GSTT tax bill — for everyone instead!

The GSTT: A Parable

Because the GSTT is so complex to understand, we help you out by explaining how it works.

Imagine that your name is Rockefeller Vanderbilt Carnegie I (your friends call you "Rocky One"), and you're by far the wealthiest person in your town of Hard Coal, Pennsylvania. You're now 75 years old and many years earlier you began your career as a coal baron. You retired from the mining business many years ago and now your only son, Rockefeller Vanderbilt Carnegie II ("Rocky Two"), runs the family business, and he's been so successful that he's the second wealthiest person in Hard Coal.

You and Rocky Two each have the same "problem" from the standpoint of estate planning and estate taxes: too much money! More specifically, you're both worried about the tax bite on your estate when you die and you leave most of your estate to Rocky Two, and then what will happen when Rocky Two dies and tries to pass his estate on to his two children: his son Rockefeller Vanderbilt Carnegie III ("Rocky Three") and his daughter Adrienne.

You both worry about the inevitable "double taxation" of a significant portion of your estate that eventually will make its way to Rocky Three and Adrienne. When you die, you'll face a pretty big estate tax bill, even though you've been using gift giving (see Chapter 11), will substitutes (see Chapter 6), trusts (see Chapters 7-9), and other estate-planning strategies to reduce the amount of your taxable estate. Regardless, you expect estate taxes to be significant.

But because Rocky Two's estate is worth so much, whatever he gets from your estate after you die will most likely be subject to estate taxes *again* after he dies and leaves much of his estate to Rocky Three and Adrienne. Basically, property that you pass to the next generation in your family (Rocky Two) that he in turn passes on to the next generation (Rocky Three and Adrienne) gets taxed each time that property gets passed down. And when Rocky Three and Adrienne pass their respective property on to their children, yet another tax hit will happen, and more of what started off as your estate will disappear into the clutches of the taxman. (As Rocky Three puts it, "Yo, Adrienne! All this tax packs quite a punch!")

So Rocky Two, always the clear-thinking businessman, comes to you and says, "You know what, Dad, I have lots of my own money. Why don't you just leave whatever you were going to set aside for me in your will to Rocky Three and Adrienne instead of me? I'm just going to leave that property to them anyway, so this way, the property will only be taxed once."

You think Rocky Two's plan is a pretty good idea to save on taxes, but guess who else thinks Rocky Two is onto something? The federal tax guys! And because the tax guys get to make the rules of this game (helped by the U.S. Congress, who actually creates the laws), they've come up with a "special tax" called the *Generation Skipping Transfer Tax* (GSTT) to counteract and negate the "skipping over" of one generation in a family and passing property to yet another generation to try and save on estate taxes.

Taking Comfort from the Exemption: A Cool Million and Rising

Your first step in dealing with the GSTT is seeing if you can sneak through the escape clause — figuring out if your estate is exempt. And on this front, we have good news: Your estate probably is.

In fact, if you read through this section and decide that based on your financial situation you see no chance that the GSTT will ever apply to you, then you may want to just skip over (pun intended) the rest of this chapter. After all, if you later become very wealthy and have to then worry about generation-skipping transfers and the tax impact, you can always come back to the rest of our GSTT discussion!

Before we specifically determine what the GSTT is, we discuss whether it even applies to you. (If it doesn't, please feel free to read another more relevant chapter.) As with the gift and federal estate taxes (see Chapters 11 and 13), the GSTT has an *exemption amount* that you can think of as a magic number for tax-savings purposes. Under the 2001 tax law, you have a lifetime exemption for generation-skipping transfers under a specified dollar amount — basically, a free pass up to a certain amount of generation-skipping transfers without having to worry about the GSTT.

And, as with the federal estate tax, the amount of the lifetime exemption amount actually increases throughout the decade until 2009, as in Table 12-1.

Table 12-1	Generation Skipping Transfer Tax Exemption Amount
Year	*Exemption Amount*
2002–2003	$1.1 million
2004–2005	$1.5 million
2006–2008	$2 million
2009	$3.5 million

So according to the figures we show in Table 12-1, in 2009 you can make generation-skipping gifts up to $3.5 million, a hefty increase from the 2002-2003 figure.

And we have even more good news! As with the federal estate tax, the GSTT disappears in 2010, meaning that you don't have to worry about the GSTT, but (to temper the good news with a bit of bad news) only for one year. Why?

Unless Congress acts, the GSTT reappears in 2011 when the 2001 tax law *sunsets* (basically, goes away). So in 2011, the GSTT exemption amount could reappear and drop back to $1 million, way down from the $3.5 million in 2009. So you definitely need to work with your accountant and attorney to understand the implications of what may happen if the GSTT not only reappears, but also with dramatically lower exemption amounts than only two years earlier.

The exemption amount in Table 12-1 can be applied to any combination of lifetime generation-skipping gifts and generation-skipping transfers at death. As a result, you can use a mix-and-match approach to direct transfers (that is, gifts) while you're alive and what you leave behind through trusts after you die.

The GSTT lifetime exemption amounts in Table 12-1 apply to each person, which means that if you're married, you and your spouse have twice as much to work with for generation-skipping property transfers.

Some trusts created before 1985 and most gifts exempt from gift tax are also exempt from generation-skipping transfer taxes; you don't need to count those amounts against your GSTT exemption.

Playing Hopscotch: Understanding Generation-Skipping Transfers

You need to understand how the GSTT works and what you can do to minimize its effects if you plan on making generation-skipping transfers. We assume that you know how to reduce your taxable estate by gift giving (see Chapter 11), will substitutes (see Chapter 6), and trusts (see Chapters 7-9). Though all the details of the GSTT can get very complicated, its most basic aspects are fairly easy to understand. Typically, the GSTT can come into play in three kinds of situations:

> ✔ You directly transfer property to someone and in doing so, you skip at least one generation (we explain what we mean in a moment). The most common kind of direct property transfer that fits this category is to transfer property to your grandchildren or great-grandchildren (or, on the flip side, if you were to receive property directly from one of your own grandparents or great-grandparents).

✔ You establish a trust for your child's lifetime, with the remainder of that trust going to your grandchildren after your child dies.

✔ You place property in trust to benefit someone and in doing so, you also skip at least one generation. Again, a common generation-skipping trust situation is when you create a trust to benefit your grandchildren, great-grandchildren, or both.

So no matter whether you transfer property directly to someone or do so through a trust, certain rules come into play to determine if you're skipping generations and therefore need to worry about the GSTT.

Knowing the rules for skipping generations (so you don't break 'em)

A *generation-skipping transfer* occurs — and your potential exposure to the GSTT begins — when:

✔ You transfer property to someone two or more generations lower than your own.

✔ You transfer property to someone more than 37 ½ years younger than you.

Generation-skipping transfers typically occur within families, so according to the first rule — two or more generations lower than your own — the following are common examples of generation-skipping transfers:

✔ You transfer property to your grandchild.

✔ You transfer property to your great-grandchild.

✔ You transfer property to your sister's grandchild (your great-grand-niece).

Our regular dose of legal-speak

We discuss in Chapter 6 the pattern in legal terminology where words ending in *or* are the persons controlling the property whereas words ending in *ee* are the persons receiving something from the *or*. With generation-skipping transfer tax lingo, the same holds true. The *transferor* transfers the property to the *transferee*.

Imagine any family tree — perhaps your own family's — and think about how you have some old-timers (maybe the family's great-great-grandparents, who first came to the United States many years ago) at the top of the chart, their children one level below them, their children's children below them, and so on. Any time you move down the family tree at least two levels between any two people, you're skipping a generation.

Generation-skipping transfers can also occur outside of your family! The second rule — someone more than 37 ½ years younger than you — comes into play if, for example, you transfer property to your lifelong best friend's oldest daughter. If you're 45 years old and you transfer money to your best friend's oldest daughter, who is 6 years old, you made a generation-skipping transfer.

Clarifying the generations and confusing complications

Figuring out who is in which generation within your family is usually straight-forward. However, be aware of two minor considerations:

- The same-generation treatment for spouses and former spouses, regard-less of the age difference
- The *deceased ancestor skip rule* when you skip up a generation

If you transfer property to a spouse — or even your ex-spouse — even if he or she is 37 ½ years of age older or younger, the transfer isn't considered to be generation skipping.

The second consideration — the *deceased ancestor skip rule* — allows trans-ferees (people receiving property) to move up (or skip up) a generation and avoid a generation-skipping transfer. The rules are as follows:

- You and the other person must be blood relatives.
- The transferee (again, the person receiving property) must be a *lineal descendant* of the transferor (the person giving the property). Lineal descendants are family members in a vertical line on a family tree like children, grandchildren, great-grandchildren, and so on. (A more common, but less official term, is *direct descendant.*)
- The transferee's parent must be dead at the time of the property transfer.

For example, if in your elderly years, you transfer property to a grandchild, your transfer is usually considered generation skipping. However, if your grandchild's parent (your own child) has already died, then the transfer isn't considered to be generation skipping. Why? Because of your child's death, your grandchild has moved up (or, again, skipped up) one generation and for estate transfer purposes, now is considered in the same manner that your child once was, only one generation removed from you.

Making Sense of GSTT Tax Rates

Once you use up your lifetime exemption amount, you need to worry about the GSTT. As you can see in Table 12-2, the tax rates are pretty steep! Even with the gradual reduction in GSTT rates through 2009, as specified by the 2001 tax law, you're still looking at least at a 45 percent tax on generation-skipping property transfers. And if the GSTT reappears in 2011, the GSTT rate goes back up to its 2001 amount of 55 percent!

Table 12-2	Generation Skipping Transfer Tax Flat Rate
Year	Tax Rate
2001	55 percent
2002	50 percent
2003	49 percent
2004	48 percent
2005	47 percent
2006	46 percent
2007	45 percent
2008	45 percent
2009	45 percent
2010	0 percent
2011 +	55 percent

As we note earlier in this chapter, Generation Skipping Transfer Taxes can occur either while you're alive through property transfers as gifts or at your death through your estate's property transfers. Keep this very important point in mind: Your property transfers may be subject to the GSTT in addition to any gift tax or estate tax that you owe! You can't offset the Generation

Skipping Transfer Tax against your unified credit (see Chapters 10, 11, and 13) as you can the gift tax and estate tax. So whereas the payment of a gift tax or estate tax may actually offset against your allowable unified credit, you actually have to pay the Generation Skipping Transfer Tax if due.

Looking Deeper into Generation-Skipping Transfers and the GSTT

Don't say we didn't warn you! Generation-skipping transfers and the GSTT are among the most complex estate planning subjects. As we note earlier, if you don't see yourself giving millions of dollars to your grandchildren or setting up multimillion dollar trusts to benefit your great-grandchildren, you may just want to quickly skim or even skip the rest of this chapter.

To understand the GSTT, you need to look at:

✔ Different types of skips — direct or indirect

✔ The impact of the skip type on your potential tax liability

✔ The importance of the skip valuation date for different types of skips

Scanning over the skip types

The word *skip* sometimes brings back carefree memories of summer days in childhood, but in the world of the GSTT, the word is anything but carefree. In fact, different types of skips have very different tax impacts.

You need to make a distinction between two different types of people: the *skip person* and the *nonskip person*. If a transferee (the person receiving property) is two or more generations removed from the transferor (the person transferring property), the transferee is called a *skip person*. For example, your oldest grandchild is a skip person in relation to you because he is two generations removed from you. However, your oldest daughter, who is your oldest grandchild's mother, is called a *nonskip person* because she's only one generation removed.

Based on the distinctions between skip persons and nonskip persons, you have two types of skips to look at:

✔ Direct skips

✔ Nondirect skips

Before proceeding, we want to answer the question you're about to ask: Why do I need to understand skips? The answer is that skips have to do with money:

- ✔ When the generation skipping transfer tax is reported and owed

- ✔ How the generation skipping transfer tax is calculated

Direct skips

A generation-skipping transfer is considered to be a *direct skip* if the property transfer's interest is only with a skip person. Think of a direct skip as a transfer that totally bypasses the middle generation (the nonskip person) and goes directly to a skip person who is two or more generations removed. For example:

- ✔ Your grandmother gives your brother and you $25,000 each.

- ✔ Your great-grandfather names your father as the sole beneficiary of an irrevocable trust.

In these simple examples, the only people with an interest in the property after the transfer are skip persons — those who are two or more generations lower than the transferor — which means that these generation-skipping transfers are considered direct skips.

Indirect skips

An *indirect skip* is a generation-skipping transfer where both a skip person and a nonskip person hold interest in the transferred property. With indirect skips, the property transfer doesn't go directly to a skip person because a nonskip person is also involved in the transfer. For example:

- ✔ Your grandmother sets up a $300,000 irrevocable trust with income paid to your father for his lifetime and the remainder paid to your brother and you at your father's death.

- ✔ Your great-uncle who is close to your brother places his beach house in a *life estate* for your mother with a *remainder interest* in the beach house to your brother, meaning that your brother receives the house upon your mother's death.

In the first example, your father is a nonskip person (one generation removed from his own mother) and your brother and you are both skip persons (two generations removed from your grandmother, who is the transferor). In the second example, your mother is a nonskip person and your brother a skip person. Because these two examples of generation-skipping transfers involve both skip and nonskip persons, the transfers are indirect skips.

For direct skips, the rules that affect the when and how are fairly straightforward. Generation Skipping Transfer Tax is reported and owed depending on whether the transfer occurred during the transferor's lifetime or at that person's death. The party filing the gift tax return pays any tax and reports it by April 15 of the year following the transfer. Direct skips made at the transferor's death are reported and paid with the estate tax return, which is due nine months after the date of death.

If the applicable dates we describe look familiar, you may recognize them as the same dates for the gift tax return, as we discuss in Chapter 11. Coincidence? Not really. The form required for a generation-skipping transfer is the same Form 709 as the Federal Gift Tax return form.

The person who files the estate tax return — such as the personal representative — is also responsible for reporting the direct generation-skipping transfer and paying any associated Generation Skipping Transfer Taxes due.

For indirect skips, the reporting requirements aren't as well defined as they are for direct skips. Why? Because with an indirect skip, both skip persons and nonskip persons have an interest in the property transferred: Part of the property goes to the nonskip person and part of the property to the skip person. Because only the part of the property transfer that goes to the skip person is subject to the Generation Skipping Transfer Tax, the tax can't be determined right away.

Chapter 13

Paying or Not Paying the Death Tax: That's the Question

You know Ben Franklin's saying: "The only two certainties in life are death and taxes." Today, those two items come together in the federal estate tax.

At the most basic level, the federal estate tax is fairly simple. You add up your estate's total value when you die (actually, someone else does the tallying, considering you're dead) and subtract out certain exclusions. If the remaining value is greater than a particular amount, your estate owes a percentage of that remaining value for federal estate taxes.

But don't worry — most people can escape the federal estate tax by planning right. In this chapter, we tell you how.

Discovering Federal Estate Tax Basics

You can understand the federal estate tax by focusing your attention on four main items:

✔ Understanding what the federal estate tax is and when it comes into play

✔ Remembering the exemption amount magic number and why you may not ever have to worry about federal estate taxes

✔ Knowing the estate tax bracket rates, specifically the top rates

✔ Identifying the complications of the moving target situation between now and 2011

We discuss each of the preceding topics in the following sections.

Figuring out how the federal estate tax works

The simplest straight-to-the-point definition of the federal estate tax is "a tax on the transfer of property from your estate to others." Basically, if you own something today and somebody else owns it after you die, the federal estate tax comes into play for that transfer of ownership.

Don't panic, though! Even though the federal estate tax technically applies to every single transfer of ownership, your estate may not actually owe any taxes. The potential tax depends on your estate's total value and how that total compares to the exemption amount magic number that we discuss later in this chapter.

As we discuss in Chapters 10 and 11, the federal estate tax is part of a unified tax system along with the gift tax. Essentially, between the gift tax and the federal estate tax, everything you own is at least considered for taxation when you transfer ownership, either while you're alive or after you die. "Everything you own" includes property that:

✔ Is mentioned in your will (see Chapter 3)

✔ Is covered by a *will substitute,* such as joint tenancy or a living trust (see Chapter 6)

✔ Is covered by your state's *intestate laws* if you don't have a completely valid will and therefore die either intestate or partially intestate (see Chapter 3)

So when we say the federal estate tax applies to everything you own at the time of your death, we mean everything! So don't think that "if I leave something out of my will" (or if you don't even have a will) the estate tax won't catch up with you. As we discuss later in this chapter about how to calculate your estate's value for tax purposes, completeness is the name of the game!

Using your exemption to sidestep the government

The sort-of-good news about federal estate taxes that we briefly mention in the previous section is that even though everything you own is subject to the tax, the federal estate tax comes with a built-in magic number — more formally, an *exemption amount.* If your estate's total value is below the exemption amount, your estate doesn't owe any taxes.

The exemption amount magic number actually applies to property you give away in the form of gifts, as well as property you leave to others upon your death, as we discuss in Chapter 11.

As you can see in Table 13-1, the exemption amount changes every two or three years throughout the decade until 2009. And in 2010, something wonderful happens! (But more on that in a moment.)

When looking up tax law tables on the Internet, make sure you're looking at current information from the 2001 tax law and not old numbers. Use Table 13-1 for current figures.

Table 13-1	Federal Estate Tax Exemption Amounts, 2002–2009 (2001 Tax Law)
Year	*Exemption Amount*
2002–2003	$1 million
2004–2005	$1.5 million
2006–2008	$2 million
2009	$3.5 million

What do the amounts in Table 13-1 mean? If you were to die in 2003, up to $1 million of your otherwise taxable estate (we discuss the applicable calculations in "Digging Down to the Bottom Line," later in this chapter) is free of federal estate taxes upon your death. (For ease of understanding, assume that you haven't previously given any taxable gifts that have been applied against your unified credit, as we discuss in Chapter 11.) So if your taxable estate is $1 million or less, then congratulations (sort of, considering we're talking about your death), your estate doesn't owe any taxes.

What if you die in 2003 and the value of your taxable estate is $1.5 million? Basically, you subtract the magic number of $1 million, which leaves $500,000 subject to estate taxes. Simple enough, right?

But suppose that you die in 2004 or 2005 rather than 2003, and the value of your taxable estate is still $1.5 million? Now, your estate doesn't owe any federal estate taxes, because the exemption amount (again, think of the exemption amount as a magic number) is now $1.5 million, the same as the your taxable estate's value, which means that your entire estate can be transferred to others free of federal estate taxes.

The same model happens again in 2006, when the exemption amount increases to $2 million, and then again in 2009 when the exemption amount goes up to $3.5 million. Consider the significance: If your taxable estate is worth $3.5 million and you die in 2003 when the exemption amount is $1 million, your estate owes federal estate taxes on $2.5 million (the $3.5 million value of your estate minus the $1 million exemption amount). And, as we discuss in the next section, we're not talking small change when we're talking about federal estate tax rates, either!

But if you live a mere six years longer and were to die in 2009 — and assuming that your taxable estate's value stays exactly the same, at $3.5 million — your estate won't owe any federal estate taxes at all!

And if you think that's good news, wait until 2010 when the exemption amount magic number and federal estate tax disappears completely! So for example, if you have been very successful financially during your life and you have a taxable estate valued at, say, $10 million, and if you were to die in 2009, your estate would owe taxes on $6.5 million ($10 million minus the $3.5 million exemption amount). But if you died in 2010, everything in your estate is free of federal estate taxes, no matter what the value!

But before you start celebrating, consider what happens in 2011. The death tax comes back from the dead (sorry, we had to work that one into this discussion somehow!). More formally, the 2001 tax law is *sunsetted* — a commonly used term in business, law, and technology that basically means "goes away." Essentially, the repeal of the federal estate tax that takes place in 2010 is itself repealed, meaning that — you guessed it — the federal estate tax comes back.

And not only does the federal estate tax come back, it also comes back with a vengeance! Take a look at the exemption amounts shown in Table 13-1. See how the amounts go up through the decade? Well guess what? In 2011, the exemption amount goes back to the same $1 million that it was in 2002 and 2003. Essentially — and we know this statement sounds morbid, but critics of the 2001 tax law have repeatedly said — from a federal estate tax standpoint, you're penalized for living past 2010! Remember that $3.5 million taxable estate that is free of federal estate taxes in 2009 (as well as in 2010, when the estate tax disappears for a year)? Well, if you were to die in 2011, the federal estate tax whacks $2.5 million of your taxable estate ($3.5 million minus the exemption amount of $1 million for 2011).

If this whole business of what will happen in 2009, 2010, and 2011 sounds pretty weird to you, you're not alone! Many accountants, attorneys, and editorial columnists and broadcasters have mentioned that this "repeal-the-repeal-and-stick-it-to-the-taxpayers" business is one of the dumbest (not to mention financially damaging) sequences of events in the history of the federal tax code.

In the next section, we discuss how in addition to the exemption amounts, the top federal estate tax rate changes over time.

Looking at federal estate rates (specifically the highest rates)

As with the exemption amounts, the 2001 tax law gives you a break throughout the decade in the form of the top (highest) rate applicable to estate tax calculations. First, though, you need to understand that just like with your income taxes, the federal estate tax is actually constructed from a series of *brackets*, or amounts, with a steadily increasing applicable tax rate. Under the 2001 tax law, the tax rates start at 18 percent and steadily increase, up to a top tax rate that changes throughout the decade.

 Rather than include the entire schedule of federal estate tax brackets and applicable tax rates — specifically because the top rate moves frequently — we suggest that you get the latest and greatest information from a source, such as your tax accountant or the Internal Revenue Service (www.irs.gov).

Table 13-2 shows how the top rate changes under the 2001 tax law throughout the decade. By comparison, the old top tax rate before the new tax law was 55 percent. (Remember that number, because we come back to it in a moment!)

Table 13-2	Federal Estate Tax Top Rate, 2002–2009 (2001 Tax Law)
Year	*Top Tax Rate*
2002	50 percent
2003	49 percent
2004	48 percent
2005	47 percent
2006	46 percent
2007	45 percent
2008	45 percent
2009	45 percent

If you look back to Table 13-1, you notice that the exemption amounts change every two or three years — but not every year — whereas the top tax rate does change annually (specifically, going down 1 percent) every year until 2007, when the top tax rate stays at 45 percent.

So what happens in 2010? Because the federal estate tax is repealed for that year, no top tax rate exists (just like no exemption amount), because no federal estate tax exists! Great news!

But come 2011 — you guessed it — not only does the federal estate tax's return bring back a top tax rate, it also brings back the 55 percent top rate that existed before the 2001 tax law. The rate is higher than any of the top tax rates for the years 2002–2009 under the 2001 tax law.

With the highest tax rate, each year through 2009 increasingly less of your estate is likely to be lost to federal estate taxes, and then in 2010 you essentially have a tax holiday — though quite possibly only for one year. Then, in 2011, the top tax rate increases to significantly more than what it was only two years earlier, not to mention that much more of your estate is likely to be subject to estate taxes because of the dramatically lower exemption amount.

Tracking a moving target

Nobody really knows what will happen to the federal estate tax in 2011 — whether the tax will come roaring back to life or sink forever into the sunset. So what can you do in this climate of tremendous uncertainty?

If your estate is in what we call the *swing range* — somewhere between $1 million and $3.5 million for the low and high exemption amounts — work with your accountant, your attorney, and the other members of your estate-planning team to develop a prudent and reasonable strategy to keep as much of your estate as possible safe from taxes. See Chapter 14 for details of how to plan to minimize the bite the federal estate tax takes on your estate.

If you're very rich, then other than planning to die in 2010 during that brief year when under the current law the federal estate tax is repealed, you pretty much need to take the same action as people in the swing range. Develop a prudent plan with your estate-planning advisers that includes a variety of trusts and other tax-advantaged investment vehicles and the pointers we present in Chapter 14.

Digging Down to the Bottom Line

You probably aren't surprised to discover that you can determine your taxable estate's value — that is, the bottom line of your estate after all allowable deductions are included — in several different ways to then tell if you owe any federal estate taxes and if so, how much.

In this section, we help you through this maze by showing you the shortcut — the most basic steps that apply to most peoples' estates. Where applicable, we provide you with additional information for which you may wish to work with your estate-planning team.

To be as precise as possible, though, the official formula for calculating estate taxes is as follows:

```
(gross estate - deductions) = net estate + taxable post-1976
lifetime gift transfers = taxable estate x applicable estate
tax rate = tentative estate tax - credits = estate tax due
```

Wow! The good news, though, is that to get a good idea of the potential tax bite, you may very well need to worry about only three things:

- ✔ Figuring out the value of your *gross estate*
- ✔ Calculating deductions from your gross estate to arrive at your *net estate*
- ✔ Comparing the result with the exemption amount magic number to see if you owe any estate taxes and if so, how much

Figuring out your gross estate's value

When figuring out your estate's value for estate tax purposes, you need to know all your stuff's exact value! For purposes of the estate tax calculations, your starting point is your *gross estate,* which for most people includes the following:

- ✔ Your probate estate (as we discuss in Chapter 5) — everything that passes through probate
- ✔ Your ownership share(s) of property held in some form of will substitute (see Chapter 6), such as joint tenancy with right of survivorship
- ✔ Your life insurance's value, depending on certain factors (see Chapter 17)

Regardless of whether you're dealing with probate or nonprobate property, you need to include your ownership percentage of each item of property. For example, your one-third-ownership share of a real estate investment that you and two other people own needs to be included. However, when dealing with partial ownership, you come across various rules that apply depending on

- ✔ The form of ownership
- ✔ Your contributions relative to other co-owners

The downside of winning the lottery

Remember the last time you heard that some woman won $60 million in the lottery? Besides being a tad envious, did you think she was free from financial worries? She may be set for her lifetime, but her estate may face some major taxation if she doesn't take immediate action.

When determining your estate's value, you may need to know about *deferred income,* or income that technically isn't owned (that is, shows up in a bank account) upon death but rather is guaranteed to be received in the future.

Perhaps the most stunning example: Instead of choosing to receive a lump sum payment, the woman who won the lottery elects to receive a larger amount paid out over an extended period of time, such as 20 or 25 years. (When most state lotteries began in the 1980s, few if any had a lump sum option, forcing winners to accept the extended annuity option.)

Guess what? If you were to win tens of millions of dollars in the lottery and elect an annuity option and then were to die a year or two after your lucky winning day, your estate gets whacked by federal estate taxes, because the value of your lottery winnings is included in your estate, even though you don't receive most of the money for years!

Technically, a lower number represents the present value of the annuity stream and not the entire "face value" of your annuity winnings — say, $2 million each year for 18 more years after you die, or a total of $36 million. Anyone who has taken a college finance class is familiar with present value calculations, which use a discount rate to figure out what that annuity stream is worth today. For the sake of simplicity, all you need to realize is that even using present value calculations, your estate is still taxed on assets that technically aren't even part of the estate because money hasn't yet been received.

Other examples of *income in respect of a decedent* (the technical term) include certain bonuses to be paid in future years, deferred compensation, and royalties. If any of these situations apply to you and your estate, you must work with your estate-planning team to develop a strategy to pay any estate taxes. For example, you may purchase a life insurance policy that covers the estate taxes if you die before the entire stream of future income is received.

Rather than going through all the various combinations, we suggest that you work with your attorney and accountant to make sure that you correctly value your ownership portions of any jointly owned property (including property you own with your spouse) so that you're neither over-counting nor under-counting your estate's value.

Calculating deductions from your gross estate

As we note in Chapter 1, when it comes to federal estate taxes and your estate's value, more is definitely not better! Sure, you may have a few moments of satisfaction when you add up your property's value and realize that you're actually worth much more than you thought, but when you realize that estate taxes can grab a pretty hefty bite out of your estate, you may think differently.

The good news: You have several deductions to work with to reduce your estate's value before making any tax calculations. Essentially, you use these deductions to reduce your gross estate and determine your *net estate*.

Just as with your federal income taxes, you want to use deductions to the greatest extent possible to come up with the lowest possible net number no matter how high your starting gross number was. So whether you're dealing with gross income or gross estate, and net income or net estate, your strategy is the same: Maximize those deductions!

For most people, the main deductions for estate taxes are:

- ✔ The marital deduction
- ✔ The charitable deduction
- ✔ Deductions for debts on your property
- ✔ Cost-of-dying deductions (In value terms, the amount of cost-of-dying deductions are far less than either marital or charitable deductions [unless you're planning on one heck of an expensive funeral, worthy of a head of state or perhaps the famously ostentatious Rudolph Valentino funeral in 1927!].)

The marital deduction

You can use the marital deduction to shelter every single dollar of your estate from taxes — no matter how much your estate is worth, and no matter what the exemption amount magic number is in the year you die — by simply leaving everything you own to your spouse.

Or, if you wish, you can leave part of your estate to your spouse and other portions of your estate to your children or others; whatever you leave to your spouse is free of estate taxes.

The marital deduction applies to any property, no matter what form of ownership applies: community property, joint tenancy with right of survivorship, and so on. However, the marital deduction only applies if your spouse is a U.S. citizen! (If you're married to a non-U.S. citizen, check with your accountant and attorney about special rules governing gifts, as well as special trusts you can use, to shelter property transfers from some gift and estate taxes, at least for a while.) However, if you aren't a U.S. citizen and your spouse is, your spouse is eligible for the marital deduction. Again, if the marital deduction applies to you, work with your accountant and attorney to figure out the best plan.

The marital deduction only applies to legally married, man-woman couples. Same-sex or opposite-sex unmarried couples, regardless of any state domestic partner statutes, aren't eligible for the marital deduction from federal estate taxes (just as with being able to claim "married" status when filing federal income taxes).

So you've found the perfect way to beat Uncle Sam: Just leave everything to your spouse, and you have no estate tax worries, right?

Not so fast! Depending on your financial situation and that of your spouse, you may be better off not taking advantage of the marital deduction! Basically, you and your spouse may benefit more by dividing up the property you've accumulated over the years more or less evenly, with each of you trying to stay beneath the exemption amount magic number for your respective property.

By not leaving your respective estates to each other (and therefore taking advantage of the marital deduction), you can still avoid federal estate taxes — assuming that you've each stayed beneath the exemption amount — by leaving your respective estates to other people (for example, divided among your children).

If, however, you were to die first in 2006 and leave your entire estate of, say, $2 million to your wife — and therefore take advantage of the marital deduction so you don't owe any federal estate taxes — and if your wife, who has her own estate of $2 million, were to die in 2008 when the exemption amount is still $2 million, she would die with an estate of approximately $4 million. (Assume that she didn't make any poor investments or otherwise have to use a significant portion of her estate for something like nursing home.) If she dies with an estate of $4 million, then approximately $2 million (after subtracting other deductions such as funeral expenses, and assuming that a significant portion of her estate didn't need to be used for something like nursing home care) would be subject to federal estate taxes!

However, if you had simply left your $2 million estate to your children, the entire $2 million would have been transferred tax-free, and your wife could do the same thing in 2008, also tax-free. Essentially, from a $4 million estate for you and your spouse, neither you nor your spouse would have owed estate taxes if you hadn't taken advantage of the marital deduction.

(As we discuss earlier in this chapter, the exemption amount is a moving target throughout the decade and could conceivably come back at a lower amount in 2011. For example, if your spouse were to die in 2009 when the exemption amount is $3.5 million instead of 2008's $2 million, only $500,000 is exposed to federal estate taxes instead of $2 million a year. However, if you and your spouse have worked to stay beneath the exemption amount and your spouse dies in 2011, remember that the estate tax comes back in 2011 with a $1-million exemption amount.)

Picking a date to value all your stuff

Within the world of estate taxes, your property is valued at its *fair market value.* As we discuss in Chapters 1 and 2, fair market value is essentially the value that a willing buyer and seller determine is the value in the market.

Your property is valued on the date of your death. However, another date, which is called the *alternative valuation date,* can also be used to determine the date that fair market value is set. Specifically, the alternative valuation date is six months after the date of your death. So why two different dates to choose from for determining fair market value?

If property decreases in value between the date of death and the alternative valuation date, choosing the latter may result in a lower value of the gross estate due to a decrease in the fair market value, and thus lower estate taxes. Basically, if your property's value decreases dramatically shortly after you die, why should your estate have to pay significantly higher taxes on out-of-date valuations, essentially taking that money away from your beneficiaries? (Think "stock market, post-2000.")

However, you (or, more accurately, your personal representative) can't pick different valuation dates for different property within your estate. Basically, when you select to use the alternative valuation date, all property in the gross estate must use this same date.

The preceding example is based solely on tax considerations for families with a reasonably large amount of assets, and may very well not be the best strategy for you! For example, if you and your spouse both have modest incomes and modest estates with a combined value well beneath even the lowest exemption amount of $1 million, then you really don't have to worry about pursuing a strategy to avoid federal estate taxes, because those taxes will likely never apply to you. In fact, if you die first and not leave your property to your spouse (and technically take advantage of the marital deduction, even though doing so isn't really necessary because no estate taxes would be due anyway), you may cause problems for your family if your property isn't available to your spouse to use or sell. So by all means, don't get too clever and actually cause problems for your family by trying to avoid taxes that you wouldn't have to pay anyway!

The charitable deduction

In Chapter 11, we discuss how gifts to qualified charities are exempt from gift taxes. The same is true for property you leave behind after you die that is designated to go to a qualified charity.

Depending on your situation — married or not, children or none, family well off on their own or not, and so on — you may want to consider leaving some or all your very valuable, in-the-estate-tax-zone estate to one or more charities. After all, if you decide that your estate isn't going to go to your family because they don't need it (or if you have no family for your estate to go to), why not leave your property to your favorite charity or charities via the charitable deduction rather than the government through estate taxes?

Deducting debts

If you have a home worth $1 million, your gross estate reflects that complete value. However, suppose you still owe a mortgage of $700,000? Why should your estate pay taxes on the complete value of your home when you technically own only $300,000 of that property?

You get to deduct all debts, such as mortgages, credit card debts, personal loans, and everything else that we discuss in Chapters 1 and 2 as negative balance amounts in determining your estate's value. So essentially, the calculations work out correctly: Your net estate factors out your debts from what you own.

Deducting the cost of dying

The costs of your funeral and expenses to your estate, such as probate fees and appraisal fees, are also deductible from your gross estate before arriving at a bottom line number upon which to figure out taxes due (if any). Make sure that your personal representative works with your accountant or attorney (or better yet, lets one of those professionals fill out the estate tax return) to take advantage of permissible costs in the year in which you die.

Going for extra credit

After you add up all your property and then reduce your property's value as much as you can, you figure out what (if any) tax liability your estate has. Part of the what-do-you-owe calculations includes applying certain credit, such as foreign estate tax credits or out-of-pocket gift tax credits, against the number you come up with.

However, because estate tax credits get complicated and are a moving target as a result of tax law changes, we recommend consulting with your accountant and attorney.

Choosing How to Pay Estate Taxes

In Chapter 3, we mention how you can choose to include a *tax clause* in your will that specifically identifies the manner in which any estate taxes are paid (for example, from a specific bank account or from the proceeds of selling a particular portion of real estate). Alternatively, you can use the default approach, which is having any estate taxes paid out of property covered by your will's residuary clause.

Whichever approach you choose, you need to periodically make sure that your selected means of paying estate taxes is still aligned with your estate's status. For example, if you have specifically designated the proceeds from the sale of stock or real estate to be used, make sure that the equation still works. Double-check that the proceeds are adequate to cover anticipated estate taxes, and that your estate's overall value has neither increased nor decreased too much.

Or, if you're going to rely on a residuary clause, make sure that the value of property covered by the residuary clause is still adequate to cover taxes. You also don't want any of your beneficiaries that you're taking care of through residuary property to be shortchanged if most or all of your residue is needed for a larger amount of taxes than you had anticipated.

Filing the Estate Tax Return

The federal estate tax return on Form 706 is due within nine months of the death date, unless an extension has been granted.

Many personal representatives decide to file the estate tax return along with the final income tax return, but if you were to die between April 15 and July 15, then your estate tax return needs to be filed prior to your final income tax return the following April 15 to meet the nine-month deadline.

If your *gross estate* exceeds the exemption amount in the year you die, your personal representative must file an estate tax return, even if after taking all permissible deductions, your net estate falls below the tax radar and no tax is due.

Once of the responsibilities of your personal representative as we discuss in Chapter 5 is to file your estate tax return in a timely manner. However, you need to realize that your beneficiaries can be liable for estate taxes where they have received property and estate tax hasn't been paid.

Stepping Up to the Plate and Filling the Bases (Basis)

In Chapter 14, we discuss various "give-and-take" decisions you need to make when managing your estate's tax considerations. We now discuss one of those items — adjustments to the basis of property you transfer to others upon your death.

According to tax law, property has a basis that is (to oversimplify a bit) calculated as the cost of the property plus improvements you make. Think about the calculations you make when selling your home, or figuring out what the gain (or loss) on rental real estate you own will be. You start with your purchase price, and then add in the cost of that new kitchen and how much that new roof cost you. So if you bought a rental property for $100,000 and put another $35,000 worth of improvements into the house, your basis is $135,000. Later, if you sell that property for $200,000, your gain is $65,000 ($200,000 minus your $135,000 basis).

Suppose, though, that you never sell that rental property, and when you die the house is worth the same $200,000 that we mention above. And suppose that you leave that house to your sister in your will. Under current tax law, your sister's basis in this property that she now owns isn't the same $135,000 that yours was, but rather $200,000 — the house's current fair market value.

When property is passed to someone else through inheritance, the basis is *stepped up* to the current fair market value, which eventually saves the property's recipient (your sister, in this example) money on taxes. Suppose that five years later, your sister sells the house for $235,000. Her taxable gain will be $35,000 ($235,000 minus her $200,000 stepped-up basis), which is far better than a taxable gain of $100,000 ($235,000 minus what your basis had been — $135,000). Your sister still gets the same amount of money from the sale of the rental house; she just owes much less in taxes.

So what does stepping up the basis of property have to do with your (or anyone else's) estate taxes? Technically nothing, because your property is still valued as part of your gross estate according to its fair market value. However, as part of your overall estate planning, you need to be aware of a very important distinction. The basis of property isn't stepped up when you give the property to someone as a gift while you're still alive, compared to the stepped-up basis for inherited property. So even though gift taxes and estate taxes are part of the same unified system, post-transfer rules regarding whether or not the basis of property is adjusted can make a big difference in eventual taxes to your beneficiaries.

Chapter 14

Planning to Minimize All Your Estate-Related Taxes

*I*f you enjoy games and puzzles like chess and the good old Rubik's Cube, then you may feel at home when it comes to planning for estate-related taxes. But if you always lose at chess and were never able to solve a Rubik's Cube, and if you prefer a jigsaw puzzle that comes with a label that states "suitable for ages five and up," then don't worry, we've boiled down the steps you need to take for estate-related tax planning into a concise, comprehensive action plan.

Notice that in this chapter we use the phrase "estate-related" taxes, and not "estate tax," "federal estate tax," or even the slang term "death tax." Just as you do when you play your annual income tax fun and games, you likely find yourself dealing with more than one type of tax. You run into the federal income tax, state income taxes, local income taxes, property taxes, as well as state inheritance and estate taxes. As a result, when dealing with estate planning, you need to think about *estate-related* taxes, not just the federal estate tax.

In this chapter, we help you to focus on the estate-related taxes that will most likely impact your estate — and to not worry about taxes that don't.

Figuring Out Where You Are Today

Your first step in minimizing your estate-related taxes is to conduct a snapshot analysis of your current situation. Ask yourself: "Would I have any estate-related tax liability if I died today?"

In order to determine your estate-related tax liability, you need to perform the following activities:

- Determine your estate's value
- Conduct an inventory of what estate-planning steps you've already taken
- Consult the appropriate tables and charts to understand preliminary federal and state tax liability
- Look for tax traps that may unnecessarily cost you money

After completing the preceding list of activities (we show you how in this section), you have a good idea of which of the following categories you fall into with regards to estate-related taxes. The categories are:

- Significant tax-related concerns, which means that you have a lot of work to do with your estate-planning team
- Modest tax-related concerns, meaning that you have some exposure, but with some fairly simple tactics, you can minimize your estate-related tax liability — or perhaps make that liability disappear altogether
- No tax-related concerns, meaning that your estate's value is so far below the tax radar and you live in a state without any estate or inheritance taxes, that you don't need to worry at all about estate-related taxes

Determining your estate's value

In Chapter 2, we describe how you need to have a good idea of your estate's value, and the tasks and steps you need to assess that value. In other chapters, such as Chapter 15 with regards to family businesses, we further discuss ways you can determine your estate's value.

So if you haven't completed this estate valuation activity, get to it! In this section, purely for example, we assume that your estate right now is worth $900,000 after subtracting out liabilities such as the remaining mortgage on your home, an automobile loan, and credit card debt.

Totaling your gifts to date

In Chapter 11, we discuss how the federal estate tax and gift tax are part of a unified tax system. In that system, you have a set of magic numbers that you can use in a mix-and-match manner to transfer property from your estate to others. Beyond non-taxable gifts such as those with amounts lower than the annual exclusion amount or that are otherwise free of gift tax (see Chapter 11 for the details), your taxable gifts reduce the amount of property that you can leave to others free of federal estate taxes after you die.

You need to compile a comprehensive list of any gift giving, as well as the tax impact of those gifts. Take that amount and set it aside (you use it in the next section). Also, write down your estate's value. You use the two figures to get an idea of estate-related tax liability if you were to die today.

For example, suppose that you're generous, and have given $250,000 worth of taxable gifts through the years, and haven't paid gift taxes along the way. Rather than paying the gift taxes, you filed your gift tax returns as required and are holding off on gift taxes until those amounts are settled up against federal estate taxes after you die.

Checking the tax tables

Take a look at the various tables for estate-related taxes — particularly Table 13-1 in Chapter 13 — and assume that you were to die today. You want to compare the exemption amount magic numbers for this year (that is, the year in which you're doing your estate-related tax planning) with the answers to the questions you've asked according to the steps we describe in the preceding section ("How much is my estate worth?" and "What have I done so far?").

Make sure that you use official tax table sources, such as those available on the Internal Revenue Service Web site at www.irs.gov and the tax-related pages you will find on the Web site for your state.

Suppose that you're doing your estate tax planning in 2003, when the exemption amount magic number is $1 million. From the previous example, if your estate is worth $900,000, then you don't have to worry about federal estate taxes, right?

Wrong! Because (again, according to the previous example) you've already used up $250,000 of your exemption amount through taxable gift giving. Therefore, you have a potential federal tax liability. Specifically, you may have to pay estate taxes on $150,000, calculated as follows:

1. **Take the $1 million exemption amount for 2003.**

2. **Subtract out the $250,000 you've already used up through gift giving. You have $750,000 left.**

3. **Take the $900,000 value of your estate and subtract the $750,000, leaving approximately $150,000 of your estate that may be subject to federal estate taxes.**

Why did we write "approximately" when giving the answer of $150,000 of your estate that may be subject to federal estate taxes? As we discuss in Chapter 13, you have several available deductions to further reduce your estate's value when it comes to tax liability, such as probate costs, funeral expenses, and appraisal fees. So that $150,000 figure may be further reduced before applying any tax rate calculations.

Even more important, regardless of your estate's value, you can make two deductions that enable you to avoid having to pay any federal estate taxes. Specifically, you can use the marital deduction and charitable deduction (see Chapter 13) to transfer significant amounts of property to your spouse or your favorite charities free of taxes. So if you leave most or all your estate to your spouse or to one or more charities, then at least from a federal estate tax perspective, you don't have any concerns right now.

Even rather modestly valued estates that are way beneath the amounts at which federal estate taxes become applicable may face significant tax liability in certain states that have fairly high estate or inheritance tax rates! So don't forget to check your state's tax rates.

In some states, the estate and inheritance tax system has different rates that apply to different people to whom you leave property. Those rates vary by the relationship of those people to you: a relatively low rate for your children, for example, but a fairly high rate for someone unrelated to you. Additionally, your state may have various rates that increase the more your estate is worth (in technical terms, a *graduated* tax system).

Therefore, you need to take a look at the answer to yet one more question — "Who gets what?" — as you've specified in your will and as set up in various will substitutes (see Chapter 6), such as joint tenancy with right of survivorship, or payable on death bank accounts. The answer to this "who-gets-what?" question, in concert with "What is my estate worth?" and "What have I done so far?" helps you obtain an accurate picture of your total estate-related tax liability if you were to die today.

Looking out for tax traps

To assess your current estate-related tax liability, look for tax traps in how your estate is structured. One of the most common tax traps that can whack even the most modest estate with unanticipated and unnecessary tax liability is your life insurance policy.

As we discuss in Chapter 17, depending on how you've structured your life insurance — specifically, who owns your life insurance policy — the insurance's death benefit (that is, the amount of money that will be paid to one or more beneficiaries upon your death) may be added on top of your estate's value for federal estate tax calculation purposes.

For example, suppose that your estate is valued at $500,000 and you live in a state that has neither an estate nor inheritance tax, and you've never given any taxable gifts before. Most likely, you have no estate-related tax liabilities — or so you hope. But suppose the following three items occur:

- ✔ You have a term life insurance policy (we define various types of life insurance in Chapter 17) with a death benefit of $2 million.

- ✔ You haven't taken steps to negate the federal estate tax bite, such as setting up a *life insurance trust* (see Chapters 8 and 17).

- ✔ You die in 2003, when the federal exemption amount for estate taxes is $1 million.

Guess what. You essentially have died with $1.5 million subject to federal estate taxes (the $500,000 value of your estate plus the $2 million life insurance death benefit minus the $1 million exemption amount) — even though your estate is really only worth $500,000 until you die!

So make sure that as you inventory your estate to determine its value, you work with your estate-planning team to look for tax traps in the following area:

- ✔ Life insurance (the previous example can be a painful case in point!)

- ✔ Pensions, particularly any guaranteed future amounts that may be considered part of your estate even if you don't have the right to take distributions right now

- ✔ Other guaranteed future payments that may be considered part of your estate, such as future payments on deferred compensation, royalties, patents, monthly payments and balloon payments on money you've loaned out, and so on

Fortune Telling: Picturing the Future as Best You Can

Taking a snapshot of where you are today is fairly easy if you follow our suggestions earlier in the chapter. But most estate planning is based on some future scene — your circumstances in 5, 10, 20, 50, or even 100 more years!

Impossible you say? We say that far-out tax planning is much more possible than you may imagine if you take care to:

- ✓ Predict (as best you can) your estate's future value when you die.

- ✓ Cross-reference your lifespan possibilities (that is, various scenarios on how much longer you may live) against future estate-related tax liability, paying special attention to the exclusion (or exemption) amount magic numbers.

- ✓ Understand the tax impact of estate-planning strategies you already have in place.

- ✓ Consider the tax impact of likely or inevitable changes to your family situation.

- ✓ Make your best guess at future estate-related tax exposure.

Predicting the future

No, you didn't suddenly wind up at the state or county fair, walking down the midway and finding yourself beckoned over to the palm-reading booth. But *estate planning* does involve making some educated guesses about what may happen in the future.

Specifically, you need to make a rough guess about how much your estate will be worth when you die. Of course, few people know when they'll die, other than those who have a terminal illness and who have received a medical opinion as to how much longer they have to live.

For most other people, the best course of action is to look ahead to whatever an average life span is and how many years are left between now and then. For example, suppose that you are a 35-year-old female, in fairly good health, and with a family medical history that doesn't have a lot of your relatives dying at relatively young ages. You may reasonably expect to live until 75, 80, or maybe even older, meaning that you can predict the future and settle on one particular target age — say 80 years old.

Hopefully, you already have a general-purpose financial plan (and if you don't, please consult with your accountant to develop one) that takes into account factors, such as:

- ✓ Your property's value

- ✓ Your property's expected future earnings, such as interest on your bank accounts and growth in your stocks, annuities, and mutual funds

- ✓ Your current and anticipated future income

✔ Anticipated significant future family expenses, such as your children's college education or weddings for your three daughters

✔ Additional expenses that are likely, such as caring for your own aging parents and your own anticipated medical expenses (as well as those of your spouse, if applicable)

✔ The age at which you plan to retire

✔ Some rough idea of ordinary living expenses during your retirement years, based on the lifestyle you anticipate and (as we discuss in Chapter 18) your retirement-versus-estate philosophy. (Do you specifically want to leave certain amounts of property behind for your children, grandchildren, or charities, or do you plan to spend as much of your money as possible during your retirement years?)

If you're looking at a span of 30, 40, or more years between now and the age at which you're trying to predict your estate's value, your calculations may be way off. But that's okay, because all you're trying to do is get a rough idea of whether your future estate may be worth, say, $1 million or $10 million when it comes to estate-related tax planning.

If, however, you're close to retirement age — or maybe already in your retirement years — and you have a fairly accurate idea of how much of your estate you already are or soon will be spending during your retirement, then you can predict whether your estate's value will be

✔ About the same as it currently is

✔ More than it currently is (you're earning more in interest and retirement-years income than you're spending, meaning that your estate continues to grow in value)

✔ Less than it currently is because you're gradually drawing down your estate's value to provide retirement-years living expenses

Regardless of your current age and your particular situation, you need to have some idea of your estate's future value so you can perform the next step — tax liability analysis — with some degree of accuracy.

Looking at several scenarios for the federal estate tax

As we discuss in Chapter 13, the 2001 tax law makes tax planning the financial equivalent of skeet shooting. (Good luck trying to hit a moving target!) The exemption amount magic number changes frequently between 2002 and

2009, disappears along with the estate tax in 2010, and then (most likely) comes back at a lower amount in 2011. So how can you possibly do any tax planning in such a volatile environment?

We recommend that you actually set up three different comparison numbers that feed into the steps that follow. Specifically, you want to look at:

- The best-case scenario
- The in-between scenario
- The worst-case scenario

The best-case scenario

You can hope that the repeal of the federal estate tax in 2010 becomes permanent, meaning that no matter how much your estate is worth, you won't have any federal estate tax liability. So if that's the case, why do any tax planning at all?

Don't get complacent! Your state may still have estate or inheritance taxes that don't go away, either temporarily or permanently. Or Congress may decide to keep the federal estate tax repealed, but still apply the gift tax and generation skipping transfer tax (GSTT) (see Chapter 10 for more about these various taxes). Another concern: As we discuss in Chapter 10, if you receive certain government-provided medical care, your estate may get whacked for big dollars under the Estate Recovery Act.

So in the best-case scenario, you can put a big fat zero in the column entitled "federal estate tax I may owe" because you won't have an estate tax or an exemption amount. But don't forget to consider other estate-related taxes and any related exemption amount magic numbers and other details.

The in-between scenario

The second scenario to consider — the in-between scenario — is one in which the federal estate tax reappears in 2011 after its one-year repeal in 2010 (or even never being repealed at all, if Congress decides to make more changes to the 2001 tax law between now and 2010). However, the 2009 federal tax exemption amount of $3.5 million is retained in 2011 instead of the scheduled return to a $1 million exemption amount. (See Chapter 13 for details.)

Under the in-between scenario, you may find yourself having to worry about federal estate taxes, but only if your estate is worth more than $3.5 million.

Again, as with the best-case scenario that has no federal estate tax, don't forget to check your state's estate-related taxes.

The worst-case scenario

The last scenario to consider is, unfortunately, the one that will currently happen unless Congress makes changes to the tax law over the next few years. Specifically, the federal estate tax exemption amount will be lowered back to $1 million in 2011, meaning that if your taxable estate's value exceeds that amount, say hello to federal estate taxes!

We use worst-case scenario because many people may find themselves susceptible to federal estate taxes, simply because of the low exemption amount.

Blending your present strategies into the future

So far, from the preceding steps in this chapter, you have some key pieces of information with regards to estate tax planning and your future. Those keys are:

✔ Your future estate's likely (or at least possible) value

✔ Some raw data with regards to three different taxation scenarios that you can cross-reference against your estate's value to predict future tax liability

Chances are, though, that if you're not a newcomer to estate planning, you already have some of the strategies that we discuss throughout this book, such as:

✔ Taking advantage of below-the-radar tax-free gift giving (see Chapter 11)

✔ Various types of trusts (see Chapters 7-9)

✔ The marital deduction for property you leave behind for your spouse, if doing so makes financial and tax sense

After looking at the items listed above and noting which ones are already part of your estate planning strategy, you can come up with a revised figure — we'll call it an *adjusted future estate value* — that more accurately represents what your estate is likely to be worth in the future, regardless of what it's worth now.

The *adjusted future estate value* figure you come up with is what you use as you move forward to the next few steps as you try to predict future estate-related tax liability.

Considering the impact of death, divorce, and other bum breaks

Significant changes in your life, such as divorce or your spouse's death, can dramatically affect your estate's value.

For example, if your spouse is terminally ill and will almost certainly die before you do, and if your spouse plans to leave his or her property to you under the marital deduction, then your estate's value will increase — perhaps significantly — after your spouse dies.

Similarly, if you expect a significant inheritance in the near future from an elderly relative who is in poor health, factor that inheritance into your calculations.

Or if a divorce is on your horizon, your estate's value will likely be lower if you expect that a significant portion of your estate will be lost as a result of the divorce settlement.

The important point to note is that when you try to figure out your estate's value in the future, you need to look at more than just the regular financially-oriented factors, such as income, expenses, earnings on your investments, and so on, plus estate planning strategies you already have in place. All factors are complicated enough when you look out more than a year or two. To complicate matters, you need to look at significant life changes and try to understand as best you can how they may affect your estate's value.

Carefully comparing, then betting the house and rolling the dice

You now have all the numbers you need: your estate's future value when you die, as well as three sets of tax-related data from the best-case, in-between case, and worst-case scenarios. Now you need to compare the three.

First, look at the best-case scenario: no federal estate tax at all, but possible state inheritance or estate taxes and possibly other liability, such as Estate Recovery Act considerations. Based on what you think your estate will be worth, are you still looking at significant tax liability? Moderate tax liability? No tax liability?

Now look at the in-between scenario: a federal estate tax exemption amount that stays at $3.5 million. Now do the same comparisons, looking to see if you have significant tax liability, moderate tax liability, or no tax liability?

Finally, just like they say in shampoo commercials, "lather, rinse, repeat" — do the same comparisons and come up with the same significant/moderate/ none answer for tax liability under the worst-case scenario of the federal estate tax exemption amount being at $1 million when you die.

The three answers you get for the three possible scenarios tell you how much estate-related tax-planning work you have ahead of you. If, for example, your answer under all three scenarios is "no tax liability," then your estate-planning job is done! (Well, for tax purposes anyway; don't forget you still need to worry about your will, probate, insurance, and so on.)

On the flip side, if your answer under all three scenarios is "significant tax lia-bility," then you have lots of work ahead. You specifically need to spend time with your estate-planning team looking at different tax-saving strategies.

If your answers are somewhere in between — for example, you only have sig-nificant tax liability if the federal estate tax exemption amount is $1 million, but otherwise you have either moderate or no tax liability — then you still need to consult with your estate-planning team. More likely, the basic trade-offs we discuss in the section, "Hmmm . . . Deciding on Strategies and Tradeoffs" will be enough to reduce or eliminate estate-related taxes.

Whatever answers you come up with under the three scenarios, run your results past your estate-planning team at least once just as if you were still in grade school and asking one of your parents to double-check your home-work. Certainly, do most of the planning work on your own, but also get a professional opinion.

Hmmm . . . Deciding on Strategies and Tradeoffs

We have good news for you: Most of the basic tax-savings strategies you can employ as part of your estate planning are very straightforward and simple, and require very little effort and expense on your part!

But we also have some potentially bad news: If you don't plan carefully, you can really mess up your estate planning and wind up with a larger tax bill. And if you really mess up, your beneficiaries may get stuck paying more taxes.

So use the following list as a starting point of tax strategies. Realize that each point has several alternatives available to you and, depending upon various circumstances, may or may not be advantageous to you. Also, you need to plan ahead beyond the most immediate tax consequences and consider down-the-road tax consequences as well.

The most common estate tax-related strategies available to you include:

✔ Whether you should give property to someone as a gift or if you should leave that property in your will

✔ Whether or not you should leave all your property to your spouse

✔ How to structure your life insurance policy or policies

✔ Whether or not you should use gifts below the exclusion amount

✔ How to use double dipping on tax savings from charitable gifts

Gifting versus leaving property as part of your estate

Suppose that you and your spouse have a vacation home that you purchased 20 years ago for $50,000. (Imagine that it was a real fixer-upper!). Over the past 20 years you've put about $100,000 in renovations into the home, and — even better — property values in that area have gone way up. In fact, your vacation home is now valued at $500,000, according to the most recent appraisal.

(For the sake of this example, the home is entirely in your name rather than jointly owned with your spouse, meaning that the $500,000 value is entirely within your estate.)

You decide to give the house to your oldest daughter — a freelance writer who wants to live in a secluded location. You have two options available. You can:

✔ Give the home to your daughter as a gift (being the generous parent you are)

✔ Leave the home to your daughter in your will as part of your estate or through a trust

Suppose that you decide to give the home as a taxable gift. The home's value — $500,000 — becomes the starting point for figuring out any gift tax liability. As we discuss in Chapter 11, in 2002, you have an $11,000 annual exclusion on gifts that reduces the taxable amount to $489,000 ($500,000 minus $11,000).

If, however, you decide to hang onto the home and leave it you daughter as part of your will — the entire $500,000 would potentially be subject to federal estate taxes.

But forget about the $11,000 difference because that's not the point we want to make. So assume that your estate isn't subjected to any federal estate taxes at all because in the year you die, your estate's value is far below that year's exemption amount. In fact, the value is far enough below, that even if you had given the home to your daughter as a taxable gift and therefore used up part of your combined gift-and-estate exemption amount and unified credit (see Chapter 11), you still don't have to worry about federal estate taxes.

For purposes of your estate, either giving the home to your daughter as a gift or leaving the home to her as part of your estate has the same tax impact on your estate: zero. However, from your daughter's perspective, receiving the home as part of your estate likely will cost her much less in eventual taxes if she ever decides to sell that home than if she had received the home as a gift.

Why? The answer lies in how the tax basis of the home is calculated and how for estate purposes — but not for gifting purposes — that tax basis is "stepped up" to the current value of the home at the time it was transferred.

Don't panic! We explain what we mean, step by step. You may recognize the first part of this puzzle — calculating the tax basis — if you have ever owned and sold a home. To overgeneralize a bit, the tax basis of any property (not just real property like a house but any property, even including your stocks and mutual funds) is usually calculated as the price you paid for that property, plus any improvements you've made. (In the case of stocks and mutual funds, those improvements include dividends and capital gains that you reinvest.) In this example, the tax basis of your vacation home is $150,000: your original $50,000 purchase price plus the $100,000 in renovations you put into the home.

As we note earlier in this chapter, if you leave property to someone upon your death as part of your estate, the value of that property is stepped up to the current value. Now your daughter inherits a home worth $500,000, and that same $500,000 figure is her tax basis in that property. Assume that she doesn't make any further improvements, and ten years later she sells that home for $700,000, she would potentially have a taxable gain of $200,000 (the $700,000 she receives minus her $500,000 tax basis).

If, however, you give the home to your daughter as a gift, she doesn't receive a stepped-up basis, and instead receives the same tax basis in the property as you had: $150,000. So if she were to someday sell that home for $700,000, her gain is now a whopping $550,000 ($700,000 minus her $150,000 tax basis) rather than the $200,000 if she had received the property from your estate upon your death.

Depending on the tax laws governing the sale of primary residences, your daughter may never owe any capital gains tax, regardless of the home's value or how low the tax basis is. So for a house, as in this example, the gift-versus-estate consideration may be different than for stock or anything else that doesn't qualify for the primary residence tax break. However, this tax break, the rules for rolling over gains, and the amount of the final tax break have changed occasionally in recent years. As with pretty much everything else in tax planning, you need to look ahead, make some educated guesses, and consult with your estate-planning team!

The two key points to remember are:

✔ For purposes of your estate, the federal tax impact of giving property as a gift is more or less the same as leaving that property as part of your estate.

✔ For the person to whom you give or leave the property, the down-the-road tax impact can be very different depending on which choice you make!

Among the many wild and crazy points in the 2001 tax law are significant changes to the rules for stepping up the tax basis of property in 2010 that are likely to be detrimental to you, and all kinds of uncertainty afterwards. Make sure that you and your accountant stay on top of what will happen — or not happen — to the stepping-up rules.

Imagining the ups and downs of leaving your estate to your spouse

Many married people automatically set up their wills and their overall estate plans to leave their entire estate to their surviving spouses. But they could be walking into a trap!

Suppose that you and your spouse each have estates that are slightly below the federal estate tax exemption amount. Suppose that you die before your spouse does, and you leave all your property to your spouse. Now suppose that your spouse dies shortly after you do, with most of the property that was once yours still unspent and part of your spouse's estate. Guess what? Federal estate taxes probably come into the picture because by leaving your estate to your spouse, you have created a situation where estate taxes kick in. Now your spouse's new, larger estate is higher than the exemption amount.

When deciding whether or not to leave property to your spouse, you need to look ahead and understand if you're creating a tax liability that you can avoid. (You can leave your property to your children or someone else, or place your property into a trust for your spouse.)

Avoiding estate taxes on your life insurance proceeds

In Chapter 17, we discuss the potential federal estate tax impacts on proceeds from your life insurance. Make sure that you structure your life insurance policy or policies to avoid an unpleasant surprise from the estate tax agents.

Using gifts below the exclusion amount

In Chapter 11, we discuss the annual exclusion available to you for giving tax-free gifts. You can give gifts to anyone up to the exclusion amount (currently $11,000, and later adjusted annually for inflation) without having any tax impact at all or even using up your unified credit against down-the-road estate taxes.

If you have cash, investments, or other property that you're certain you'll leave to certain people — your children, for example — and if your estate is valuable enough that federal estate taxes will apply, then why not transfer that property now as gifts in small-enough chunks to stay below the gift tax radar, and therefore lower the value of your taxable estate?

Why not indeed? Go to it!

Double dipping on tax savings from charitable gifts

The charitable deduction for gifts that we discuss in Chapter 11 allows you to give gifts to qualified charities without worrying about gift taxes.

But guess what? You can double dip on the tax savings front and also take an itemized deduction on your federal income taxes for those same gifts! So you not only are skipping out on gift taxes and reducing the amount of future estate taxes, but also you're saving more money on your federal income taxes! And, if your state allows you to itemize deductions on your state income tax and to include charitable deductions, you can save even more!

So why not get two — or even three — tax deductions out of the same charitable gift?

Just like we said above, why not indeed? Go to it!

Putting Together a Comprehensive Estate-Related Tax Plan

What's that? You're still a bit uncertain about where to start? Just follow the steps below and before you know it, the tax portion of your estate planning will be well within your control.

Fixing the holes

You've identified the problem areas in your estate plan that can possibly cause your estate to get hit with unnecessary taxes, so do something about those problems — right now! If, for example, your life insurance is poorly structured so the death benefit amount causes an otherwise non-taxable estate (for federal estate tax purposes) to be taxed, then create a life insurance trust (see Chapter 8) or otherwise change your life insurance policy's ownership, as we discuss in Chapter 17.

Starting on that gift giving

Remember that one way or another, the ownership of every single piece of property in your estate eventually is transferred to someone else, in some way: through your will, through your state's intestacy laws, through a will substitute, such as joint tenancy, through a trust, or through a gift. Because you really can't take your property with you, and if you've already given serious consideration to the many beneficiary decisions when you prepare your will, why not give certain property away now or in the near future, rather than waiting until after your death for that property to be transferred? You not only can smooth out the property transfers in your estate by regularly giving gifts, but also you can keep a substantial amount of the overall property transfer tax-free by keeping the gifts below the annual exclusion amounts.

You can take the complete inventory of your estate that you created (see Chapter 2, as well as our discussion earlier in this chapter) and divide the list into three columns. The columns

- ✔ Identify the intended recipient (person, charity, foundation, and so on) for that property

- ✔ Indicate if you want to give that property as a gift rather than wait for it to be transferred as part of your estate

- ✔ Specify the year or years in which you want to make the gift

You can also split up certain property to keep the gift amounts below the annual exclusion amounts and further reduce any potential tax exposure. For example, if you have 1,000 shares of a stock that's relatively stable in price, and the current price per share is $50 — meaning that you have $50,000 worth of stock — you may decide that you want your oldest daughter to receive that stock to start her own portfolio. Rather than give her the entire 1,000 shares in a single year, which means that part of the gift is taxable, you can give her just enough shares this year, next year, and also the following year (and so on) to stay beneath the annual exclusion radar of $11,000 (or whatever the figure adjusts to each year along with inflation, as we discuss in Chapter 11).

Setting up trusts if necessary

In Chapters 7, 8, and 9, we discuss various types of trusts, many of which you can use to reduce or eliminate tax liability on your estate. Don't go overboard — that is, don't set up all kinds of trusts (and pay lots of fees to your attorney or financial planner) if you don't really need to do so. By all means, set up the trusts you need to help prevent an unnecessary tax bite.

Planning ahead for property transfers upon your death

How much should you plan ahead if you leave all your estate to your spouse? How about part of your estate? Or maybe none of your estate to your spouse? Should your spouse leave his or her estate to you?

Part of your beneficiary decisions you specify in your will or through various types of will substitutes must include estimating the tax impact. If your state has an estate or inheritance tax, pay particular attention, because chances are that even if you can sidestep the federal tax bite, your estate may get hit hard by your state. So the key, just as with every other aspect of estate planning, is to plan ahead!

Schedule a meeting with you estate-planning team to discuss what tax-planning ideas may make sense for you, the pros and cons, and potential pitfalls.

Part V
Estate Planning for Family Businesses

The 5th Wave   By Rich Tennant

"The instructions for the Will say we should name a guardian whose personality is consistent with our children. I'm not sure we know anyone with a Godzilla/Batman/Barney personality."

In this part . . .

*I*f you're involved in a family business, the chapters in this section present you with a concise but thorough discussion of the major issues you need to know for your estate planning. Even if you aren't directly involved in the family business, chances are that someone close to you is, and quite possibly their estate planning — or lack thereof — could eventually affect your own. So use the information in these chapters to help guide the estate planning for anyone involved in a family business, whether small or large.

Chapter 15

Grasping the Basics of Estate Planning for Family Businesses

· ·

· ·

*I*f you're involved in a *family business* — a small retail store, a farm, or perhaps a factory that has been successful over the years — you probably spend most of your time just running the business. That's plenty to keep you busy!

Quite possibly, you've been so consumed with day-to-day operations and general business planning that you haven't had much time to think about estate-planning concerns for your business — like what happens to the business when a key family member dies. Will you have to sell the business to settle the estate?

Other questions need answers, too, like how the legal structure of your business affects estate planning and how much the business is worth in the marketplace. In this chapter and in Chapter 16, we present you with a concise reference on the various topics that are most important for your estate-planning considerations — business valuation, key estate-planning decisions you need to make, succession planning, ownership transfer, and estate taxes.

Defining "Family Business"

The lemonade stand that you and your sister had when you were in the fourth grade is a family business. The music store that your father began and that you and your brother now manage is a family business. Even some global

Fortune 500 businesses started as family businesses! For estate-planning purposes, we focus on the definition of family business that helps you qualify for certain tax breaks. (You need these tax breaks if you want to keep your business in the family.)

- ✔ First and foremost, the family or families involved must own a significant portion of the business. If only one family is involved, that family must own at least 50 percent. If two families are involved, then their combined ownership must be at least 70 percent. And if three families are involved in the business, their combined ownership must be at least 90 percent. Therefore, you can own a business with your family members and with outsiders (that is, people not related to you) and still have your business classified as a family business — and qualify for the pertinent tax breaks.

- ✔ In addition to the ownership requirements, the business must be privately held — that is, not listed on a stock exchange and available for public trading — within the past three years. Check with your accountant or financial planner if you have any questions or concerns in this area.

Another requirement (incidentally, these requirements come to you courtesy of the IRS) for determining whether or not a business is a family business deals with the ever-popular IRS phrase "materially participated." If you fill out any business-related income tax return, such as a Schedule C or (for a farm) Schedule F, you're familiar with this phrase because the IRS wants to know, basically, if you're really in business or just messing around trying to get tax deductions. When it comes to potential estate tax breaks, the person who just died and whose estate is being settled must have "materially participated" (that is, really worked) in the business for at least five of the eight years before he or she died.

Additionally, the person who inherits the business must likewise "materially participate" in the business in the years ahead — specifically (try to follow this, it sounds a bit complicated) during the ten years after the former owner's death, an eight-year period is designated and the inheritor must materially participate in at least five of those eight years. Also, the inheritor must either be a family member or an employee who worked in the business for at least ten years before the owner's death.

Getting a bit complicated, huh? Many more requirements come together to determine whether or not a business is considered a family business. Our advice: Check with your accountant and see if your business meets all the pertinent regulations.

Making the Critical Estate-Related Decisions Upfront

Anyone who owns and manages a family-owned business has thousands of decisions to make in the course of day-to-day operations: whether to turn the restaurant's menu into all-vegetarian, whether or not to expand to a new city, how many new employees to hire — the list goes on and on.

But in this chapter, we focus on a small number of estate-related decisions for your family business, and what areas you need to regularly revisit to see if circumstances have changed. Depending on the decisions you make, some of the estate-related challenges we discuss in the next section may not be problems at all for your family business — or, on the other hand, you may have your hands full trying to head off a full-blown estate-planning problem!

You need to decide the following key points:

- ✔ Whether or not you want to continue your current level of involvement and investment in your family business, and for how long

- ✔ Whether or not the business's ownership picture should change (we discuss your choices later in the section, "How the Form of Business Ownership Affects Your Estate")

- ✔ What your succession plan is (deciding who will take over running your business from you, and under what circumstances), both for you personally and (if applicable) for other family members involved in the business

Choosing to stay or go

We're guessing that you want to stay in the business. After all, you've devoted your life to it! Okay, so how long are you going to stay?

Beyond the obvious career-oriented aspect of this decision, you need to understand how this decision affects your estate's structure and value. Assume that you intend to maintain your current level of involvement in your business for as long as you live, and never intend to sell or give your share to anyone else. If so, then your estate's fate and value are closely aligned with the fate and value of your business.

Even if you have significant assets in your estate that aren't directly related to your business, those assets may still be exposed if your business is a sole ownership or partnership. (See the section, "How the Form of Business Ownership Affects Your Estate" in this chapter.)

If your intention is "to be carried out feet first from behind your desk," then you need to:

✔ Make sure that you have adequate insurance (long-term disability, business interruption, liability, and the other types we discuss in Chapter 17) to protect your business and, by extension, your entire estate.

✔ Spend significant time on estate-tax planning (as we discuss in Chapter 16) to minimize the business and financial impact upon your death and, if possible, to take advantage of the family business-related estate tax breaks.

You may, however, seriously think about ending or at least scaling back your involvement and investment in your business. You're probably getting tired of the long hours, or you see potential troubles on the horizon. (Maybe you see some drastic changes in your industry or some powerful new competitor is planning to move into your area.) Perhaps your business is so significant a portion of your estate that you're worried a business downturn could devastate your estate, and you want to diversify.

If so, consider the points we make in the following section about how your family business ownership picture may change and how you can plan for the impact on your estate.

Adjusting the family business ownership picture

Suppose that you and your three sisters are all equal co-owners of a local restaurant, and you decide that you want to retire. You have a number of options available to you, including:

✔ Having your three sisters buy you out in equal amounts, leaving each of them owning one-third of the business

✔ Having only one of your sisters buy you out, with that sister now owning 50 percent and the others still owning 25 percent

✔ Selling your ownership to another family member — a cousin or maybe your oldest daughter — who then is an equal co-owner with your three sisters

- ✔ Selling your ownership to one person who isn't a family member, who then is an equal co-owner with your three sisters

- ✔ Selling your ownership to several people who all together own 25 percent of the business (each owns a smaller percentage of the overall total business) — they plan to expand the business and anticipate that their ownership shares will increase in value

- ✔ Giving your ownership as a taxable gift (by taking advantage of the gift tax marital deduction we discuss in Chapter 11, no gift taxes apply) to your spouse who is ready to retire from a 30-year government career, and who now is a 25 percent equal co-owner with your three sisters while you find something else to do (including maybe just relax!)

- ✔ Giving your ownership as a taxable gift to your oldest daughter, which reduces your estate's value by your share of the business, but still counts against your combined gift-and-estate tax exemption amount and unified credit (see Chapter 11)

You can probably think of many other possibilities, but for what we want to point out, the preceding list is complete enough. If you look at the various alternatives, some key points jump out:

- ✔ If you sell your ownership and receive full price, your estate's value probably won't initially change much because you're exchanging one type of property — business ownership — for another type of property — cash (more on that in a moment). However, you still owe capital gains taxes on the difference between what you received and your tax basis in the property (*tax basis* is an IRS term for cost — in general, what you paid).

- ✔ If you don't receive all the cash upfront and instead allow the purchaser or purchasers to pay you over time, your estate may include the future guaranteed value of those payments. (If you die before receiving all the payments, the necessary cash to pay federal estate and any state inheritance or estate taxes may not be readily available.)

- ✔ If you sell your ownership in your family business to a larger business and receive stock instead of cash, you need to be aware of possible restrictions you have with the stock. For example, the law may restrict you from selling any stock for at least one year, and the law may limit you from selling certain amounts over the next several years. Aside from the obvious financial diversification and general financial planning, realize that a sudden and dramatic drop in the stocks' value can cause your estate's value to go way down.

- ✔ If you give away your ownership as a gift, your estate's value decreases by the same amount of your ownership. Depending on to whom you give your ownership, gift taxes may or may not apply.

> ✔ If you sell your shares to someone outside your family, you may change the designation of your business as a family business, eligible for some specific estate tax breaks and treatment, to a business that is no longer a family business. The IRS is rather particular about what is and isn't a family business, so any change in ownership may potentially affect how your business is classified and treated.

The main point: If the ownership structure of your family business changes, it can have interesting (and sometimes unwelcome) future effects not only on your estate but also on others' businesses and estates.

Deciding on your succession plan's details

Whether or not you plan to exit your family business over the next several years, upon retirement age (sometime in your early or mid-60s), or upon your death, you need to have a succession plan in place. The *succession plan* determines who takes your place, and under what circumstances.

Beyond the business-operations side of succession planning, you have estate-planning considerations. For example, your succession plan for business operations may be indistinguishable from how you plan to dispose of your ownership in the business. That is, if you give your sole-ownership business to one of your children or sell the business to your brother, or if perhaps you plan to leave the entire business to one of your children as specified in your will, then the family member who receives or inherits the business now is in charge of running the business.

Get the person involved in the day-to-day business operations several years before you anticipate him or her taking over. You want to have ample time to share all the important information about how to run the business.

Alternatively, you may want to put a succession plan in place where someone succeeds you as the day-to-day manager or operator of the business, but you still retain at least a partial ownership. Perhaps the new manager/operator spends at least a couple years on a trial basis before you give or sell the business to him or her.

If your family business isn't a one-person show and you have other relatives as partners or co-owners in a corporation, then you each need to have a succession plan that may or may not include bringing in outsiders versus taking over for each other.

You also need to have temporary succession plans (what happens if you have to take a year or two off because of a serious medical problem?) versus permanent succession plans.

You can probably think of dozens of other possible succession possibilities. Just remember, succession planning is critical to preserving your family business and therefore preserving your estate's value. You may also decide not to have a succession plan, which means when you retire or die, your sole ownership business goes away.

Most likely, though, your business will have at least some value for estate-planning purposes. Whether you like it or not, the business will be part of your estate and subject to estate and inheritance taxes.

So think of succession planning as one more business decision you need to make that affects not only the future of your business, but also your estate's health and value.

How the Form of Business Ownership Affects Your Estate

You can find various legal forms of ownership for family businesses (as well as businesses in general), such as:

- ✔ Sole ownership (also called sole proprietorship)
- ✔ Partnership
- ✔ Corporation
- ✔ Limited partnership
- ✔ Limited liability company (LLC)

Each of these ownership models has its advantages and disadvantages. In the following sections, we briefly introduce each ownership type and point out specific concerns and issues that you need to know for your estate plan.

Sole ownership — everything is mine!

If you own a business, receive all the profits from that business, and are responsible for the business's debts and liabilities, then your business is considered to be a *sole ownership* (or *sole proprietorship*).

You may operate the business in your own name, or alternatively you may use a business name, such as "Joanne's Consulting Services." (In formal terms this would be called a *fictitious* or *assumed name*.) From an estate-planning standpoint, sole ownership businesses have the advantage of being relatively simple. Your business is closely interwoven (some even substitute the term *intertangled*) with your personal financial and legal picture. As you inventory your estate, you need to remember a major chunk of your estate is your business.

However, sole ownership businesses have significant downsides that are downsides for your estate, specifically:

- ✔ **Responsibility for debts and liabilities.** If your business starts losing money and never recovers, you're responsible for all the business loans and other liabilities, such as leases on retail or office space. Consequently, if you have to cover those debts and liabilities, you can seriously damage your overall estate. You may even find yourself having to sell other non-business property — your stocks, or maybe even your home — to cover your business obligations. In the worst case, you don't have enough nonbusiness property to cover your debts and liabilities, and you may need to consider desperate measures up to and including bankruptcy.

- ✔ **Legal exposure.** Someone who sues your business is actually suing you, and even the nonbusiness side of your estate (that is, your personal investments and your home) can be severely damaged by having to pay for a judgment or a legal settlement.

  As we discuss in Chapter 17, several types of insurance provide protection against the financial loss and harm that can come from lawsuits. If you're in business, make sure that your current insurance coverage protects your estate from legal liability incurred by something that happens in your business. You can also broaden your current coverage for business-related exposure, or purchase liability insurance that specifically covers your business operations.

- ✔ **Succession planning.** We talk later in this chapter about the challenges of succession planning in family businesses (deciding who will take your place and under what circumstances). If you're the only owner, then you must look elsewhere to find someone to succeed you.

- ✔ **Business interruption.** If your sole ownership business is a small, one-person operation, and you become ill for an extended period of time or even permanently disabled, your business operations may not survive. Aside from the lost income, you may erode or even wipe out your estate by having to sell property to cover regular living expenses — even if you have adequate health insurance. As we discuss in Chapter 17, look into long-term disability and long-term care insurance, even if you're a business owner rather than an employee of another company to protect yourself.

Partnership — we're in the business together

Many family businesses begin as partnerships. You may go into business with your brother and sister, for example. Or perhaps your father has operated a family business as a sole ownership for more than a decade, but now that you've graduated from college, you decide to join the business as a partner.

All the estate-related downsides listed for sole ownership are usually downsides for partnerships, though sometimes with a twist. For example, the financial and legal exposure also spills over into the personal estates of the partners, but indeed can actually be even more of a problem. Why? Because any partner can create a financial or legal obligation on behalf of the partnership that, if things turn sour, obligate all the partners. For example, if you're partners with your two brothers and your youngest brother causes the business to be sued, you and your other brother are just as responsible as your youngest brother to pay any settlement or judgment.

Therefore, partnership forms of family business ownership can cause significant (and sudden) problems to the estates of all the owners, regardless of which partner caused the problem.

On the positive side, though, if your youngest brother turns out to be a business and financial genius and his ideas are the chief reason the business is wildly successful, your estate and your other brother's estate actually benefit from your youngest brother's ingenuity. Profits of the business flow through to each of the partners according to their ownership shares. Therefore, you sometimes find one or more partners going along for the ride on another partner's coattails — the one who turns out to be the driving force behind the business's success.

But back to the negative side: If you and your other brother are riding your younger brother's coattails, he may resent being the brains behind the business. He may decide that he really doesn't need to be in business with his two brothers. Leaving aside the family discord and estrangement (remember *Dallas* and all those Ewing family fights, one of which drove youngest brother Gary Ewing not only out of the family business, but also out of the show altogether to his own *Knot's Landing* spin-off!), if the owners begin fighting among themselves and decide to dissolve the partnership, they can damage the business. And, depending on the business's current status (how much debt is outstanding, what lease obligations exist, and so on), the dissolution may erode or wipe out all the partners' estates to cover the partnership's obligations.

I know my rights!

If your family business is a partnership, you and your partners must follow a couple of very simple rules to make sure you avoid confusion at estate-planning time.

First, make sure that you don't commingle your personal funds and property with the partnership.

Second, make sure that you and your partners decide and very clearly state in writing who owns what in the partnership. If, for example, you and your three sisters equally co-own a partnership business, then you need to create agreements and file all the applicable financial and tax paperwork that indicates that each of you owns 25 percent of the business. When it comes to your estate planning (as well as the estate planning of your sister-partners), that clearly stated 25 percent is important when determining the value of partnership property that needs to be included in your estate, any shares of partnership income that are due to your estate, and related estate-planning factors.

Even with multiple partners, business interruption can be a problem. If three brothers operate a music and video store, two brothers may cover management responsibilities if one brother becomes disabled or ill for an extended period. However, suppose those same three brothers operate a small consulting company, and each spends the majority of his time on billable work. If one of those brothers is absent from the business for an extended period of time, the other two won't be able to pick up the slack because each one is already spending most of his time working for and billing his own clients. The result may be that business revenues and profits drop significantly, possibly to the point where debt and lease obligations can't be fully covered. As a result, the partners have to dip into their own estates to make up for the revenue and earnings shortfall from the business interruption.

Corporation — limiting my liability

Corporations are an attractive form of business ownership for one primary reason: the corporation's owners generally have limited liability to the amount each owner has invested in the business. Unlike sole ownership and partnerships, where personal estates can be devastated if business turns bad or the business is successfully sued, in a corporation, most of an owner's estate may be protected against such an unfortunate turn of events.

We say "may" be protected because quite possibly, as an owner of a family business corporation, you may have almost all your property tied up in the business, with very little personal property outside your share of the corporation. So depending on your particular circumstances, if your family business corporation goes down the tubes, your estate can still be severely diminished as a result.

Don't automatically assume that a corporation has thousands or millions of owners (shareholders) and must be a multibillion-dollar global behemoth, like Microsoft or General Electric. Small or moderately sized family businesses are often structured as corporations primarily to receive the limited-liability benefit. However, a downside to corporate forms of ownership is *double taxation.* With double taxation, the IRS taxes business profits through corporate taxes, and the IRS again taxes the money that owners receive as dividends, salaries, and bonuses through personal income taxes.

A way around this double taxation is to structure your business as an "S corporation," which allows more money to be sheltered from various forms of taxes — and therefore increases the business owners' estates. But note that the rules for S corporations can be complicated, so consult with your tax adviser and attorney before electing S corporation status for your family business.

Family businesses structured as corporations are at least slightly less susceptible to estate-related problems, such as financial and legal obligations, business interruption, and succession planning, than sole ownership and partnership businesses. Depending on the breadth and size of the family corporation, you often find more official succession plans and strategies for business interruption than you do in relatively small family partnerships. As a result, the corporation and the owners' estates may not be affected as significantly if the business goes sour.

Limited partnership — a mix of corporation and partnership

Many family businesses that are heavily oriented toward investment activity, such as in real estate or thoroughbred racing horses, are structured as *limited partnerships.* A limited partnership possesses some of the characteristics of both a partnership and a corporation.

A limited partnership has two types of partners: general and limited. To qualify as a limited partnership, your business must have at least one of each type. Think of the general partner as the person in charge of the partnership. General partners are personally liable if the limited partnership can't pay its liabilities and debts.

A limited partner, however, is more like a shareholder of a corporation (including a family business corporation) with liability limited to the amount invested in the limited partnership. But a limited partner in a family enterprise (or any limited partnership) must take care not to get involved in daily operations of the business. The law says you can lose the protection of limited liability if you mess around in management.

Limited partnerships are taxed like regular partnerships. General and limited partners report all income and losses directly on their own tax returns.

If you're a limited partner in a family business, ask your accountant and attorney to double-check all paperwork to make sure that your estate isn't exposed to any unexpected liability because documents were filled out or filed incorrectly.

If you're a general partner in a family business, then you not only have the same estate-planning considerations we discuss for regular partnerships, such as debt and liability exposure for your estate, but you also have the responsibility of protecting the limited partners' investments. Irate limited partners can be nasty if your actions cause the investments to go sour — especially when those limited partners are your own relatives in a family limited partnership. Thanksgiving get-togethers may be a bit strained for a while if the estates of the limited partners take a big-time hit because investments go bad!

Limited liability company — the new kid on the block

A relatively newer form in which a family business can be organized is called a *limited liability company (LLC)*.

An LLC is a separate legal entity like a corporation. However, an LLC differs because its members report the LLC's financial results directly on their own tax forms without dealing with the double taxation issue. Furthermore, the LLC doesn't pay any taxes.

No member of an LLC is personally liable for the business's debts or liabilities. Furthermore, LLCs pass profits or losses directly to its members.

From an estate-planning perspective, the characteristics we mention for an LLC (limited personal liability, avoiding double taxation of profits, and so on) can benefit your estate's value by protecting the nonbusiness side of your estate if business goes bad, as well as helping to increase your estate's value by sending money that would otherwise get hit by double-taxation into your estate.

Many state laws restrict the life of an LLC to a maximum of 30 years.

Calculating the Value of Your Family Business

Before you begin to develop an estate plan for your business, you need to determine the value of the business just like any other property in your estate.

You most likely have some subjective feelings about your business, somewhere between "my business is my entire life" and "yeah, it's a nice investment, but that's about it." However, for valuation purposes, you need to go beyond your subjective feelings and arrive at a precise value.

We discuss the concept of valuing your property according to *fair market value* in Chapter 2. But to have a fair market value for any property, you need both a willing seller and a willing buyer. In the case of a family business, regardless of the form of ownership, you very often don't have a willing buyer because, quite simply, the business isn't for sale!

So where do you begin as you try to figure out your business's value? Start by looking at the business's financial performance. Financial analysis can include some of the following benchmarks:

- ✔ Book value
- ✔ Discounted cash flow
- ✔ Sales multiple
- ✔ Liquidation value

The following sections briefly examine these various benchmarks that you and your estate-planning team can use to figure out your business's value. You need this figure:

- ✔ When you plan to sell some or all your ownership portion of the business, perhaps as part of your estate-planning strategy
- ✔ Upon your death when one or more of your beneficiaries inherits your ownership share, and estate taxes need to be calculated

Book value

You use a simple formula to come up with your business's *book value:* assets minus liabilities equals net worth. Your business's assets include all money, property, and *receivables* (amounts owed to the business). The assets can further be classified as *capital or fixed assets* — those items that can't easily be turned into cash (like a building) — or as *current or liquid assets* that can be easily turned into cash (like whatever your business sells).

Business liabilities are all your business's legal obligations, debts (money owed), or responsibilities. Finally, the net worth is simply the difference between your business's assets and liabilities (and hopefully you have more assets than liabilities!).

Discounted cash flow

Discounted cash flow can be confusing, so talk to your attorney or accountant. To oversimplify a bit, the faster your business grows, the higher the value that you will arrive at using discounted cash flow calculations. Did you follow that? Take our advice and seek counsel.

Sales multiple

You get a *sales multiple* by multiplying your business's sales numbers by an industry-specific standard to obtain a valuation. Most types of businesses, whether retailers, manufacturers, or restaurants, have some type of industry-wide valuator (or *multiplier*). Take any business that falls within the industry and multiply a financial benchmark to obtain a valuation.

For example, you calculate the value of a family restaurant business by multiplying the restaurant's sales by the industry-wide restaurant multiplier.

Liquidation value

Your business's *liquidation value* is based on the amount of money your business would receive if all its assets were sold. Think of liquidation as it sounds — turning something into liquid (or cash), which is easier used than something in a solid state. (Isn't good old cherry gelatin easier to slurp when you're in a sickbed when the gelatin is liquefied and runny? Or, isn't cash easier to spend than a building or piece of equipment?)

Take your business's liquidated assets minus the debts and liabilities and you have the liquidation value.

Don't confuse liquidation value with book value, even though the equations are nearly identical! Often times, liquidation values are associated with a quick sale of a business's assets, such as a going-out of business sale, which means that many of the fixed assets (equipment and inventory, for example) are sold at less than book value to quickly raise cash. Therefore, a family business's liquidation value is typically lower than that same business's book value, the latter of which usually applies to a healthy, ongoing business operation.

Getting to the bottom line — with expert help

So how do you put all these calculations together and come up with the value of your family business? We advise that you obtain an independent third-party opinion.

You can get an independent valuation opinion in a few different ways. You can find software that is specifically designed to provide a valuation for your business. By using your business's various financial benchmarks we discuss earlier in this chapter, the software produces its opinion (actually, the opinion of the company who produces the software) of your business's valuation. Often times, however, you may prefer to actually hire someone who specializes in valuing businesses — specifically, a *business valuator*.

A business valuator determines your business's worth. (Think of the great business card tagline for a business valuator: "The business of valuing business!") The business valuator processes the relevant financial information to obtain a value.

If you determine that you need an independent person to value your family business, where do you find one? You may use your accountant — especially a Certified Public Accountant (CPA) — because your accountant already knows how your business operates. However, you may want to find someone who has a highly specialized background in business valuation.

Don't forget goodwill

A business valuator may give some value for your business's reputation and its built-up perception in your industry. This so-called *goodwill* is subjective and is additional value beyond your business's other assets. If, for example, you, your sister, and your brother are co-owners of a moderately sized chain of music and video stores that has been a landmark in your city for more than 30 years, and if business is still going strong, your business value may be pumped up by an additional amount for goodwill.

You can find CPAs who have received specific training through intense study, including a five-day training program and comprehensive exam, for the valuation of closely held businesses. These *Certified Valuation Analysts (CVAs)* are trained to apply a consistent standard of valuation for a closely held business. To find a CVA in your area, you can go to the National Association of Certified Valuation Analysts Web site at www.nacva.com.

Alternatively, you can engage a CPA who also has a designation as Accredited in Business Valuation (ABV). Though not as touted as a CVA, a CPA with an ABV (talk about acronym overload!) has also received specialized training in business valuation.

Your search for a business valuator may require you to look outside your geographical area. For example, if your family business specializes in manufacturing widgets (whatever widgets really are!), but the local business valuators you contact focus primarily in retail family businesses, you may want to search for a business valuator with manufacturing business valuation experience.

After you've done all your legwork — getting all your business's financial details together, informing your business valuator of the details of ownership structure (partnership, corporation, and so on) and percentage (how much of the overall business do you own?), your business valuator can tell you how much your business is worth. You can then factor this result into how your overall estate plans relate to your business plans.

Dealing with Business Evolution — Stuff Darwin Never Imagined

Another important challenge you must undertake is deciding how your business will evolve, when your business will evolve, and how that evolution will affect your estate's value and the estates of any other co-owners.

But you may have even more challenges. Scan the following list of possible business evolutionary twists. If any of them resonate with you (like setting off alarm bells), make a note to raise these topics with your co-owners and your professional advisers. Specifically:

✔ What happens if you own and operate a one-person sole ownership company, and you want your oldest son to take over the business from you — but he doesn't want to? Do you instead turn to another child, or maybe a nephew or niece? If so, do you adjust your estate plan to make up for your oldest son not having the business?

✔ What if your oldest son does want to take over your business from you, but you feel that he's not qualified? The good news (at least from a business continuity standpoint) is that your only daughter is a business whiz and you're confident that she'll grow the business far beyond what you ever could achieve. Whether you give or sell the business to your daughter, what (if anything) do you do about your oldest son in terms of your estate plan to make up for him not getting the business? Do you retain a small ownership of the business after your daughter takes over because you think that will turn into a great investment? If you do retain a small ownership, should you change the sole ownership structure to a partnership or a limited partnership with you as a limited partner, or perhaps a corporation? Do you expose your estate by retaining an ownership stake after your daughter takes over, just in case your opinion of her business skills is (to put it delicately) overrated? And will your oldest son and daughter ever speak to each other again?

✔ What happens if you and your brother are in business together in a partnership, and for whatever reason, the two of you become estranged? Does one of you buy the other out, or do you both sell the business and get out before you run the business — and your respective estates — into the ground?

✔ What if you and three of your siblings are actually getting along fairly well in your family business partnership, but suddenly one of your brothers needs to raise a large amount of cash for some personal matters in his family? He really doesn't want to sell out, and nobody else wants him to sell out, either. Do you adjust the ownership structure of the business, either temporarily or permanently? How is everyone else's estate affected by any temporary or permanent changes?

✔ What happens if one partner in a family business has financial or legal problems? As we discuss earlier in this chapter, one of the chief risks to many family businesses is exposure to liability. But suppose you have adequate insurance, or that your family business is structured as a corporation so you and the other owners have limited liability. Your business and your respective estates may still be at risk if, for example, the family member with the problems is really the brains of the operation and is now either distracted or totally absent from running the business.

Estate taxes may be a significant challenge to keeping a business viable, as we discuss in the next chapter, depending on how much of the business is in cash or is liquid enough to pay any taxes.

Make sure that you examine and understand the impact of your decisions on everyone involved in the family business.

In Chapter 16, we discuss some specific strategies and tactics you can use to mitigate many of these family business challenges and help protect your estate.

Chapter 16

Transferring Ownership and Paying Estate Taxes in a Family Business

*I*f you own 500 shares of stock in Home Depot and decide to sell part or all your stock, doing so is a breeze. You call your broker or go online and — presto, you no longer own those shares! At tax time, you figure your gain or loss and settle up with Uncle Sam.

But when you sell or give away your ownership in a family business, the process is much more complicated than buying and selling publicly traded stock. Yes, we agree with you that a family enterprise should be easier to navigate than a deal on the Big Board, but that's what makes family-business life "interesting." To complicate matters even more, the transfer of ownership in your family business can take place after you die, meaning that estate tax considerations come into play.

In this chapter, we present you with a concise overview of the family business equivalent to selling your 500 shares of Home Depot stock. We explain how to get out of the business whether you're alive or dead, as well as the estate tax consequences — and a few tax breaks to help save your estate some money.

Exploring the Ins and Outs of Buy-Sell Agreements

The name says it all. A *buy-sell agreement* is (get ready for a big bold statement of the obvious) an agreement in which you decide how you'll sell your ownership in a family business and who the buyer will be. A buy-sell agreement not only helps to protect your business by keeping it intact and operating, but it also helps protect your estate — and the estates of family members with whom you're in business — because your estates are likely to be so closely intertwined with, and dependent on the success of, your business.

Take note of this very important point about a buy-sell agreement: Create the agreement long before you actually plan to sell your family business ownership. Think of a buy-sell agreement as "an agreement on standby" that suddenly comes to life when some type of *triggering event* occurs.

A triggering event is (and here's one more statement of the obvious) some event that sets off the need for the buy-sell agreement to wake up from standby and guide you in the sale of your family business ownership. The buy-sell agreement may be triggered:

- ✔ If you become disabled
- ✔ When you die
- ✔ If you decide to retire
- ✔ If you divorce
- ✔ If you file for bankruptcy
- ✔ If you lose a professional license that is required to operate the business
- ✔ If you receive an offer by a third party to buy the business from you

Notice how the various triggering events include a mixture of items that relate to you personally (such as becoming disabled or when you die), while others relate primarily to the business (losing your professional license or receiving an offer to buy you out). Because your personal and professional lives and fortunes are usually so intertwined with a family business, consider triggering events from both your personal and business perspectives when planning a buy-sell agreement.

In the preceding list, you may only be able to predict and plan one of the triggering events years in advance — retirement. A few other triggering events, such as divorce or bankruptcy, may be anticipated (that is, you realize that you have marital problems or that your personal finances are on a downward spiral), but very often your warning period is so short that you won't be able to seek out favorable terms to sell your business ownership, resulting in your family business either collapsing, being sold for far less than it's worth, or (at best) being seriously disrupted. Finally, other triggering events can happen with no warning at all, such as your death or disability.

Therefore, even if you're immersed in running and growing your family business — and, consequently, your estate's value — look ahead to when you'll no longer want to or be able to be involved in your family business and plan now for what will happen then. Trust us, that day will come, sooner or later, and you may as well be prepared.

Looking at a typical buy-sell agreement

Buy-sell agreements are particularly appropriate when you're involved in a business with other family members. The typical buy-sell agreement may specify something like:

- ✔ If you die while you're still actively involved in the business, your estate must sell your share of the business to the other family members in the business that survive you, according to some predetermined "sales rules." For example, your ownership share may be split equally among all the surviving family business owners, or perhaps only one of your relative-partners may purchase your shares.

- ✔ If you retire from the business, you must first offer to sell your ownership stake to the other family members in the business, again in some way that you all see fit (equal split versus only one person buying you out versus some other type of arrangement). If, however, your relative-partners elect not to buy you out, you're then free to sell your ownership to some other third party, who may or may not be a relative.

In both of the sample triggering events and terms we describe, the buy-sell agreement clearly specifies what the purchase price of your ownership stake is.

In Chapter 15, we discuss various methods used to calculate the value of your ownership portion of a family business, and recommend that you seek professional assistance from a business valuator to help establish an accurate valuation.

Because a buy-sell agreement may not be triggered for many years after it's created, the agreement should specify a *method* for determining the sale price rather than an actual sale price. For example, the buy-sell agreement may specify that a particular industry-specific *sales multiple* (see Chapter 15) be used, or the agreement may simply state that the business will hire a business valuator who will value the business at the time of sale and, based on the results of the valuation, establish an appropriate sale price.

You may, however, include a specific purchase price in the buy-sell agreement, or perhaps a table of purchase prices for each of the next 50 years. Basically, you and the family members with whom you're in business can put whatever you all agree to in a buy-sell agreement, including some fixed sale price.

If your business and family relationships are fairly strained, a predetermined fixed price that one or more parties now feels is unfair could be the cause for a protracted (and expensive) legal battle as everyone wrangles over trying to break the agreement and reset the sales price.

Funding the buy-sell agreement

Suppose that you're in business with you brother as equal partners, and you've grown your small manufacturing company to be very successful — worth $4 million based on a recent independent business valuation. You have no intention of retiring, and want to keep working as long as you're healthy or until you die.

You and your brother put a simple buy-sell agreement in place, agreeing that when the first of you dies, the survivor will have the right to buy out the other's (technically, the decedent's) ownership, based on a revised business valuation that the survivor will obtain within 30 days after the first of you dies.

If you and your brother have been stashing cash away for years, then quite possibly you have $2 million handy that you can use to buy out the other if the triggering event occurs. But suppose that you don't quite have $2 million available in your bank accounts? If your brother dies first, how would you come up with the money to buy out his share from his estate?

You could, of course, try to take out a loan using your business assets as collateral. But suppose that for business or personal circumstances, taking on additional debt makes you queasy. After all, if you borrow a large amount of money, you're adding a significant loan to your financial picture and affecting your estate. What if the business suddenly starts doing poorly? You may still be on the hook for the loans (depending on the legal structure of your business, as we discuss in Chapter 15), which could dramatically reduce or even wipe out your estate.

A better strategy that is commonly used is to use life insurance to provide the cash to buy each other out. In Chapter 17, we discuss how you can use certain types of life insurance as part of business-related estate planning. One type is a *first-to-die* life insurance policy, in which (in this example, and to over-simplify a bit) your brother's estate receives a $2 million death benefit upon his death, and in turn, you take over his ownership of your business. Alternatively, if you were to die before your brother does, your estate receives the $2 million death benefit and your brother takes over sole ownership of the business.

Life insurance can allow you and family members with whom you're in business to actually fund a buy-sell agreement and to execute that agreement in one of several forms, including those we describe in the next section. So beyond any personal insurance that you have, such as life, disability, health, and so on (see Chapter 17), make sure that you look into business-oriented life insurance if you're involved in any kind of business, particularly a family business.

Selecting the right form of buy-sell agreement

Buy-sell agreements come in various flavors, and one may be more tempting than another. This section presents a brief overview of:

- ✔ Cross-purchase agreements
- ✔ Entity-purchase agreements
- ✔ No-sell buy-sell agreements

Cross-purchase agreements

If a buy-sell agreement is a *cross-purchase agreement,* each owner purchases an insurance policy on the other owner or owners so that a "cross over" in policies exists for each owner. Each owner owns and is a beneficiary of an insurance policy on the life of the other owner(s). Upon the death of any owner, the remaining owner or owners buy the now-deceased owner's interest in the business with the benefits paid by the insurance policy.

The advantages of a cross-purchase agreement include:

- ✔ Insurance policy death benefit amounts are usually free of income tax.
- ✔ Business creditors can't touch insurance policy proceeds because the business doesn't own the policy.

✔ In some instances, overall taxation may be more favorable than with an entity purchase. (See "Entity-purchase agreements," later in this chapter.)

But of course, with advantages also come some disadvantages:

✔ Administrative expenses increase and are more complex when more than a few family members are involved in the business, because each has to have an insurance policy on all other owners. (We cover how to get around this disadvantage later in this chapter.)

✔ The costs to policy owners vary because premiums are higher or lower based on the insured's age. For example, a younger owner pays higher premiums for a life insurance policy on an older owner due to insurance premiums based on age, while the older owner pays less for the younger owner's insurance policy. Therefore, you often have unequal (and inequitable) costs to each owner.

You can use a type of cross-purchase agreement that eliminates the inherent disadvantage if the business has more than two owners. For example, if the business is a corporation with six stockholders, 30 individual life insurance policies are required to fund a cross-purchase agreement! (Here's the math: Each stockholder has five individual life insurance policies on the other five stockholders, so six stockholders multiplied by five policies each is 30.) All these policies result in a higher cost than one larger policy, not to mention potential confusion. And you may have potential problems if one of the owners forgets to pay the premiums on one or more of the policies and the policy lapses.

To get around this problem, a *trusteed cross-purchase agreement* enables the corporation to set up a trust that owns one insurance policy on each stockholder. The corporation pays the insurance premium and then charges each shareholder's salary or dividend account his or her percentage share of ownership for the paid premium. When a stockholder dies, the insurance proceeds go to the trustee in exchange for the sale of the deceased's stock to the other stockholders.

Entity-purchase agreements

With an *entity-purchase agreement,* the company, rather than the owners individually, purchase disability and/or life insurance on each partner. The business has an agreement with each owner that in the event of death or disability, the company purchases the owner's interest, and each remaining owner's interest in the business increases because now the company has one less owner. The insurance policy's proceeds purchase the owner's interest.

Advantages of the entity-purchase form of a buy-sell agreement include:

✔ The company avoids several extra steps because it's buying the policies rather than all the individual owners doing so.

✔ The company pays the premium costs so owners themselves aren't subject to different premium costs based on age. Still, the company premium payments on the various owners may still be unequal based on each owner's age — but at least the company is absorbing those costs.

The disadvantages of entity purchase agreements include:

✔ Creditors may make claims against the proceeds of the insurance policies because the policies are owned by the business, not by the owners. So if your business owes any creditors and they try to go after the money from those insurance proceeds, your entire buyout plan can go down the drain.

✔ Insurance policy proceeds may amplify estate taxes by increasing the value of the business if the death benefits are added back into the business. (See our discussion in Chapters 14 and 17 about the life insurance estate tax trap and ways you can get around that problem.)

No-sell buy-sell agreements (yes, you read it right)

A *no-sell buy-sell agreement* (or is that the "she sells sea shells" agreement?) keeps the remaining business owner(s) in control of the business but provides the deceased owner's family with an interest in the business — meaning a stream of income, they hope.

Other advantages of the no-sell agreement include:

✔ The business can, on its tax return, deduct the insurance premiums paid as compensation to the owners.

✔ The deceased owner's family is still part of the business and can be part of its success (and their estates can correspondingly grow as the business continues to grow).

The chief disadvantage with a no-sell buy-sell agreement is that while the surviving owner or owners control and manage the business, a portion of the business's ownership is in other peoples' hands. In a close family, this nonmanagement ownership may not be a problem. For example, if you're in business with your three sisters and one dies, you and your other surviving sisters may have no problems with your now-deceased sister's surviving spouse and children having an ownership stake in the business. However, families with (how shall we put it) somewhat more adversarial and less congenial relationships may prefer (in psychological terms) closure to the ownership process if one of the owners dies, and no-sell buy-sell agreements may not be the best course.

If a no-sell buy-sell sounds like something you want to explore, talk with your attorney. The deal involves technical stuff like voting and nonvoting shares that only a legal eagle should explain.

Thinking through your buy-sell choices

With so many options available for buy-sell agreements, we run through a list of what-if scenarios to make sure that your specific buy-sell agreement achieves what you intend, not only for business purposes but also for your estate plan (as well as the estate plans of other family members involved in your business).

The following isn't an all-inclusive checklist, but is intended to provide you with some items to think about when contemplating entering into a buy-sell agreement:

 ✔ Decide if the buy-sell agreement applies just to current owners and shareholders, or to future ones as well — for example, if your oldest son and your brother's oldest daughter plan to join the business in a couple of years after they graduate from college.

 ✔ Decide if, upon the death of an owner, the company automatically buys out his or her interest or if the deceased owner's family (spouse and children, typically) has an opportunity to do so; making this decision helps determine what type of buy-sell agreement you want to have.

 ✔ Determine the time period in which to pay a shareholder or that person's estate in the event of a triggering event — within 90 days of someone dying? Within six months of becoming disabled? Over the next five years?

 ✔ When you're looking at the final agreement, clearly state that your buy-sell agreement is the most current and supersedes all other existing agreements regarding stock purchases among owners and shareholders. (If this scenario sounds familiar, you're right. You take the same step in your will to clearly state that your particular will is the most current one and supersedes all others — see Chapter 3.)

Transferring Ownership to a Family Member

You may want to transfer ownership of a family business to your children while you're still alive and maybe even still actively involved in the business, or as part of your estate. If you don't have any family members with whom you're currently in business, you don't have to worry about buy-sell agreements with your brother-partner, for example. Your business is your own, and you're free to do with its ownership what you want.

Sometimes, transferring ownership of your family business is cause for you to change the form of ownership. If your business is a sole ownership, for example, transferring ownership to your three children requires the business to be a partnership, corporation, or one of the other multiple-owner forms of business we discuss in Chapter 15.

And sometimes, transferring ownership and changing the ownership form can play into your estate plan. For example, if you convert your business to a corporation, you can do what is known as a *preferred stock recapitalization*. Think of recapitalization as beginning your business over again by changing how the business is set up. You can set up different ownership classes within the corporation.

When your business is recapitalized, you have created different classes of stock. Initially, you still own 100 percent of all the stock. But you can now begin to sell or gift the different classes of stock to family members, which enables you to begin the transfer of your business as you want while still achieving your goals.

If you gift your ownership interest over a period of years, you can take advantage of the gift tax annual exclusion we discuss in Chapter 11. As you gift, your estate's value decreases and the gifts you give are tax-free to the extent that they stay under the annual exclusion.

Suppose that to protect your estate, you still want to retain control of your business, even as you begin to give away portions of ownership as gifts. Your corporation can have *voting stock:* stock in a corporation that enables you to make the important decisions regarding how the business is managed and operated. Your family members, however, receive no-voting stock. You can still make the important strategic decisions for the business while you slowly bring other family members into the business operations.

You may also want to receive income from the business, even after you transfer much or all the ownership to other family members and perhaps head off into retirement. You can set up your preferred stock to receive dividends, so you (and your estate) can still benefit financially from the business that you built. Talk to your attorney about how to do this.

Identifying Estate Tax Considerations for Family Businesses

Estate taxes can cause the death (pun intended) of a family business if an owner dies, even if other family members who are also owners keep the business going and if everyone had put solid buy-sell agreements or family ownership transfer plans in place.

What's the problem? Sometimes a wealthy person may actually have access to very little cash because most of his or her property (and therefore his or her estate) is in *illiquid* assets, such as real estate and other property that can't easily be turned into cash. Or, even if you or your estate can turn some of that property into cash, you have to sell some property to make the cash available. In short, no matter how wealthy a person — or business — looks on paper, that person or business may actually be cash poor.

Assume that, for example, you're in business with your brother and two sisters and assume that your business is worth $20 million. Also suppose that outside of the portion of the business you own (25 percent because all four are equal co-owners), the rest of your estate consists of your house and some stock investments that haven't been doing very well lately. You do have several bank accounts and certificates with about $50,000 in total, so for most routine expenses you can get your hands on a decent amount of cash if you need it.

But now you die unexpectedly, and your estate needs to be settled. Suppose your estate's value totals just around $6 million — your $5 million that represents your portion of the family business, plus another $1 million in your house, bank accounts, collectibles, and other property. Assume also that you die in 2008, when the federal estate tax exemption amount is $2 million (see Chapter 13).

Finally, assume that you aren't currently married and therefore have no spouse to whom you can leave your estate and take advantage of the marital deduction.

Uh-oh! Your estate has to come up with a significant amount of cash to pay the federal estate taxes that it owes! Furthermore, if you live in a state with an estate or inheritance tax, your estate has to pay even more money.

But what's the problem? After all, if you have an estate valued at $6 million, why can't the appropriate amount of money be "subtracted" from the property in the estate to pay the taxes, and then whatever is left over, goes to your children or whomever you want to leave property in your estate?

Because your estate doesn't have enough cash! For argument sake, we assume that the total bill for federal and state estate taxes comes to $2.5 million. You don't have that amount of cash right now, and unless you sell your share of the business before you die (which, for purposes of this example, you haven't, which is why your estate has a problem), the money just isn't there to pay the taxes.

By now, you hopefully see the problem: The bill for estate-related taxes (federal and, if applicable, state) is based on the tax tables and rates, exemption amounts, and other factors that are in effect the year you die. But if you're still actively involved in a family business and if most of your estate's wealth is tied up in that business, then you and your family members with whom you're in business have a big problem on your hands. Where will the money come from to pay those taxes?

You can fund a buy-sell agreement with life insurance to help with a smooth transition of your business ownership. (Take a look at the beginning of this chapter, "Exploring the Ins and Outs of Buy-Sell Agreements.")

But even with a well-thought-out buy-sell agreement to smooth the transition and make the necessary cash available for the actual buyout, you still have estate tax issues to deal with if your estate is valuable enough to be in the tax zone.

We have some good news for you, though! You have some tax breaks and special tax treatment options available to you if you're an owner of a family business. We describe these breaks and special treatments in the following section.

As we discuss in Chapter 15, the IRS has some very specific rules and laws that determine whether or not your business is really a family business and can qualify for the breaks. Make sure that you receive a clear and precise ruling from your estate-planning team — particularly your accountant and attorney — that lets you know whether or not you and your business can take advantage of this special treatment when your estate is settled.

The most significant tax breaks for family businesses are:

- ✔ The qualified family-owned business (QFOB) exemption
- ✔ Spreading out estate-tax payments over several years
- ✔ Tax breaks on the value of business real estate
- ✔ Giving away minority interests in your business as gifts and using a *valuation discount* to reduce the value of your business for estate purposes

Watching as the family-owned business exemption sunsets

In Chapter 13, we discuss the federal estate tax exemption magic number that represents the amount of your estate that is free of estate taxes. Under the 2001 tax law, the exemption amount is $1 million for anybody's estate in 2003.

However, if you have a family-owned business (or, more formally, a qualified family-owned business, or QFOB), you actually have a slightly higher magic number — $1.3 million to be precise. Basically, you get up to an extra $300,000 of estate tax-free transfers above what someone who doesn't have a QFOB would have.

But just like that good old Broadway show *Bye-Bye Birdie,* come 2004 it's Bye-Bye QFOB! As we discuss in Chapter 13 (see Table 13-1), the exemption amount for federal estate taxes increases to $1.5 million for 2004 and 2005. Guess what? The extra $300,000 for QFOBs doesn't get added on to the $1.5 million. The writers of the 2001 tax law basically said, "You know what? Because $1.5 million is more than $1.3 million, we'll get rid of the QFOB extra exemption and put everyone — family business owner or not — at the same level."

So if the additional QFOB exemption is going away, why are we even discussing it? Two reasons:

- ✔ First, you quite possibly could be dealing with settling an estate for someone who died in 2002 or 2003 when the additional QFOB exemption amount is still in effect. Thus, you do need to know about its advantages.

- ✔ Second, recall that in 2011 the federal estate tax exemption amount may go back to $1 million if no further tax laws change it (see Chapter 13). Quite possibly, this once-again-lower exemption amount could bring additional tax relief in the form of a revived-QFOB deduction.

Doing it Moe's way: Spread out!

If you're a Three Stooges fan, the command "Spread out!" may bring a smile to your face, because Moe Howard frequently used that phrase. And if you're not a Stooges fan, well, all we have to say is "Ohhhh, wise guy!"

Slapstick aside, current tax law allows your estate to "spread out" — or delay having to start paying federal estate taxes for five years after your death and then to pay off any estate taxes over ten years, in equal installment payments. With that kind of time, hopefully your estate can raise enough cash through business operations or other means to prevent having to sell off crucial business assets to pay estate taxes — paying the taxman but possibly killing the business in the process.

To take advantage of delayed and spread out payments, your family business must be at least a certain portion of your estate — under current tax law, at least 50 percent of your taxable estate or 35 percent of your total estate. (See our discussion in Chapter 13 about the difference between taxable estate and total estate numbers.)

Valuing real estate for estate tax purposes

If you're a farmer or have a small factory or industrial plant, you may have special below-market valuations on your land and real estate for property taxes. These valuations are based on how you're using your property versus other ways the land could be used, such as a residential subdivision. For example, if your family business is a 250-acre farm, your land, barns, and other buildings are probably zoned and valued at some sort of agricultural rates that (depending on where you live) are significantly less valuable for tax purposes than 250 acres of farmland that is just waiting for a real estate developer to show up with the bulldozers.

But aside from property tax breaks, you may also have estate tax breaks on your real property. Current tax law allows you to value land you use for your farm or business according to how you currently use it rather than how it may be used — again, for example, developed and turned into a residential subdivision.

As with other tax laws and rules that apply to family-owned businesses, you find several restrictions that determine whether or not you can take advantage of this tax break. If you can, limitations also restrict how much you can reduce your estate taxes by including: a minimum percentage of the value of the real estate to your estate's total value, another minimum percentage of the value of the business to your overall estate, how many years you have used the real estate in business, and so on.

Rather than list all the rules, we suggest you check with your accountant. He or she can tell you exactly how much of a tax break — if any — you can plan on receiving. With this knowledge, you can do your estate planning and your business planning as accurately as possible.

Shopping for more discounts at the family-business store

Earlier in this chapter we discuss how you can transfer ownership in part or in full to other family members, a piece at a time by giving away minority ownership interest. Quite often, you can keep these individual gifts below the annual exclusion radar for gift taxes. Even if you don't, your gifts may be tax-free if the combined amount of gifts and what's left in your estate when you die doesn't exceed the exemption amount in the year you die.

But beyond the gift-based strategy of reducing your estate gradually, you may also take advantage of some additional discounts that further reduce your family business's value, at least for estate tax purposes.

When several family members own a minority interest in a family business and have restrictions on how they may sell their ownership (only to other members who already have stock in the family business, for example), then a *valuation discount* is applied to the family business's overall value. Basically, you can declare that the business's overall value is less than it would be because of the fragmented ownership picture (lots of people, restrictions onselling, and so on). If you tried to sell the business for what it may otherwise be worth according to the valuation methods we discuss in Chapter 15 (book value, sales multiple, and so forth), you won't be able to get what the business is worth.

As a result, some discount percentage is applied to the overall business value to "mark down" the value of everyone's shares, at least on paper. So not only is your share of the business suddenly worth less than it otherwise may be — and for estate tax purposes, "less" is good! — then as you make any future gifts to other family members, the valuation of those gifts is also deemed to be lower (for gift tax purposes) than if the valuation discount weren't in effect.

Essentially, you use the valuation discount to reduce your business's value on paper. Therefore, you can reduce applicable estate-related gift taxes —

federal estate taxes, gift taxes, and any state taxes — while you're in the process of transferring ownership of part or all your family business to other family members.

The IRS allows valuation discounts, but it isn't happy about them! If you need to file a gift tax return (Form 709, as we discuss in Chapter 11), you find a question (currently at the beginning of Schedule A of Form 709) asking you if any gifts you're declaring reflect a valuation discount. If so, you need to provide more information and answer several questions.

Make sure that whomever you may use for this purpose — your accountant, an outside business valuator, or perhaps both of them working together — advises you on the percentage number to use for any valuation discount you claim. Make sure you also receive a clearly written explanation of the rationale and justification for the percentage you're using. Trust us: The IRS wants to know why you used the percentage. If the IRS isn't satisfied with your explanation, it'll likely challenge the valuation discount and the value and tax liability of your gifts!

Part VI

Crafting a Comprehensive Estate Plan

In this part . . .

You almost certainly have various types of insurance policies, and are also looking forward to and planning for your retirement days. In this part, we discuss both of these fundamental personal finance subjects from an estate-planning basis — the specific "touch points" where you need to look at how these disciplines all relate to one another so you can plan ahead and prevent extremely unpleasant down-the-road surprises.

And speaking of surprises, Chapter 19 covers some of life's unexpected twists and turns that can complicate estate planning — divorce, for example. The chapter also contains estate-planning advice for unmarried couples, guardianship issues, and even estate-planning considerations for your pets!

Chapter 17

Factoring Insurance into Your Estate Plan

*I*n this book, we introduce the four members of your estate-planning team — financial planning adviser, accountant, insurance agent, and attorney — and we discuss how important each professional is to your estate planning.

In this chapter, we focus on insurance. We look at how various types of insurance factor into your estate plan and how your insurance agent fits into the planning process. And here's a heads-up: We take a broader perspective on insurance than many other estate-planning books do, going beyond simply basic life insurance. We think that health, disability, and auto insurance, for example, all are part of the picture, and we explain why.

For many people, an insurance agent provides this holistic view and can put together a comprehensive package of insurance plans to meet your specific needs. But many other people today bypass the agent and go directly to insurance companies by telephone and the Internet. This chapter also prepares you to deal effectively with customer service representatives who may not be familiar with all the important estate-planning details you need to know, such as ways to craft a life insurance policy to reduce or eliminate federal estate taxes. Our advice: If you do business with your insurance company without dealing with an agent, make sure you bounce your ideas off your financial planning adviser. (Please see our discussion in Chapter 1 about selecting that key adviser.)

Using Insurance to Protect Your Assets

Protection!

We say it again: Protection!

After all, as we mention at the very beginning of Chapter 1, estate planning is all about protection and control. When it comes to protection, make sure you have a comprehensive insurance strategy.

Insurance provides you with protection against various situations that can dramatically impact your estate, such as:

- Unexpected — and unexpectedly high — expenses, such as medical bills or long-term nursing home care that can cost you a lot of money and even force you to sell some of your assets — such as your home — to pay those expenses

- Dying before your time and leaving behind family (such as your spouse and children) or even a charity that has depended on your gifts and has anticipated future continuance of those gifts

- Becoming seriously disabled and unable to earn an income

- Lawsuits over an automobile accident, an injury that occurred on your property, or just about anything else where, if you lose, you may lose a lot

You may have heard the saying "only insure what you can't afford to lose," which is certainly sound advice when you decide on coverage for your automobile insurance and health insurance. Don't allow anyone — even your insurance agent — to talk you into buying more coverage than you need.

But with estate planning, modify the statement to "make sure you insure what you can't afford to lose!" Look at the four items listed earlier in this section. Do you want to see most or all your lifetime savings go to pay for medical coverage or nursing home care? Do you want an automobile accident to turn into a situation where you get sued and have to give up a significant portion of those same lifetime savings?

Insurance relates to your estate plan in three possible ways:

- Protecting assets that are currently part of your estate from being unexpectedly taken away for one of several reasons, such as a lawsuit against you or unexpected costs due to disability or nursing home care

✔ Protecting assets that aren't currently part of your estate but will almost certainly be part of your estate in the future

✔ Supplementing the assets that are currently part of your estate by providing additional cash for one or more beneficiaries as part of your estate plan

We discuss each of the preceding three strategies for linking insurance to your estate plan in this chapter. ***Note:*** However, for your particular circumstances, not all three may apply. For example, you may only be concerned about the first item — basic protection for assets you have. Alternatively (and very likely), all three can be of equal interest and concern to you.

Protecting what you've already got

As we discuss earlier in this chapter, people buy insurance for protection. In Chapter 2, we discuss how you need to conduct a thorough inventory to figure out your estate's value. Suppose, for example, you conduct just such an inventory and find out that your estate is worth $950,000 after any remaining debts and liabilities. You then decide how much to leave behind to take care of your spouse if you die first, as well as what you want to leave to your children and your grandchildren — and you decide that $950,000 is more than enough. So: (as Crocodile Dundee may have said) "No worries then, mate?"

Not quite! Suppose that you're involved in an automobile collision that is your fault, and you seriously injure one or more people in the other vehicle. You know that you'll be sued (all you have to do is watch enough television and see enough commercials for litigation attorneys that begin with "Have you been injured in an automobile accident?").

Without adequate liability coverage in your automobile insurance policy or other liability-related insurance (like umbrella insurance, which we discuss later), you may find your $950,000 estate worth far less after a legal judgment against you or an out-of-court settlement. Indeed, your entire estate can even be wiped out!

Now you may be thinking, "I'm a safe driver" or "I don't even own a car!" Are you safe from your estate being drastically diminished or wiped out? Sorry, the answer is "no!" Without sufficient insurance, a serious illness or automobile accident can cause you to lose some or all your estate.

Insurance and estate planning go hand-in-hand. Insurance covers you against various forms of liability and unexpectedly high expenses. Later in this chapter, we discuss different types of insurance that you need to check into to protect your estate.

Even if you declare bankruptcy and walk away from crushing debts and liabilities, you most likely have to give up almost all your assets as part of the bankruptcy proceedings. The rules vary — you may be able to keep your home, for example — but essentially, bankruptcy allows you to start over with many of your debts and liabilities behind you. *Note:* You also have to start over with your estate plan because you probably lost most, if not all, of your estate during the bankruptcy proceedings. If you file for bankruptcy, you need to revisit any estate-planning strategies.

Therefore, even though bankruptcy may help you get back on your feet again after a severe financial setback, for estate planning purposes, you're basically back at square one. The moral of the story: Make sure you have adequate protection-oriented insurance so you don't find yourself in such a predicament!

Insuring the future: Protecting what you hope to acquire

You need to include insurance in your estate planning to protect what you don't have right now, but expect to have in the future. No, we're not engaging in a bit of double-talk. Think about the basics of life insurance (which we discuss in more detail shortly). You pay a little money now so just in case you die before your time, your spouse, children, or other beneficiaries receive a larger amount of money.

Your life insurance agent can help you fill out worksheets to figure out how much "future-income insurance" you need, but here are a couple of general guidelines to help you begin working with your insurance agent:

- Have enough life insurance to cover a mortgage balance on your house. If you were to die tomorrow, you want your family to have the money to pay off the mortgage balance and stay in the house, right?

- Have enough life insurance to cover anywhere between five and nine years of lost income (that is, the salary, bonus, and so on, that you would have received if you were still alive). Factors to discuss with your insurance agent include whether or not your spouse also works (and if your spouse continues to work if you die, versus having to stay home to care for young children), and upcoming costs and expenses, such as college for your children, that aren't part of your budget right now, but will be soon, and so on.

You can reduce or even eliminate your future-income insurance needs if you have lots of assets (cash, money in treasury bills or bank certificates of deposit, and so on) that your family can use to pay the mortgage and live off for several years.

However, if most of your valuable estate is in stocks and mutual funds, watch out! You still need adequate insurance to cover the loss of future income if some — or maybe even most! — of those investments suddenly turn sour (think Enron, Worldcom, dot-com stocks, and so on). Similarly, if most of your high-value estate is tied up in real property (your primary home, your vacation home, real estate partnerships, and so forth), you also need adequate insurance against loss of your future income, particularly if most or all the real property value is in your primary residence that still has a sizable mortgage, or if selling your real estate suddenly isn't quite so easy.

Again, work with your insurance agent to figure out if you need to worry about including life insurance against lost income.

You may need more than life insurance for this particular strategy. As we discuss later, long-term disability insurance protects you against lost income if you're still alive but can't work because you're disabled, and long-term care insurance helps prevent your assets from having to go entirely towards nursing home fees or other very expensive alternatives, possibly for the rest of your life. So don't forget to work with your insurance agent on long-term disability needs, also!

Shielding the gifts you hope to leave behind

The first two insurance strategies we describe deal with protecting your assets and property: what you have right now, as well as what you reasonably expect to have as a result of your income. However, you may find that insurance (life insurance, in particular) can play a third, important role in your estate plan — essentially creating cash that goes to one or more of your beneficiaries after you die (and we're not talking about counterfeiting money and breaking the law).

Suppose that your estate is valued at $1.75 million, but it's comprised of two main pieces: your paid-off home worth $250,000, and your successful business that you began 25 years ago now worth $1.5 million. You have two children, a son and daughter. Your daughter has worked with you in the business since she was in high school and now runs the business's day-to-day operations, while your son decided to pursue a career in the military and now lives across the country from you.

Your big problem: How can you adequately and fairly divide up your estate between your two children?

Some options that you consider — and reject — include:

- ✔ Leaving the business and the house to both children. Not a good idea, you decide, because your son has no interest in the business and because of his military career, he isn't in a position to contribute to the business' success, even if he were made a silent co-owner with his sister. Essentially, your daughter would be doing all the work and your son would be sharing in the profits. Furthermore, your son may have little or no interest in the house, and not want to be burdened with real estate taxes, maintenance, and so on.

- ✔ Leaving the business and the house to your daughter with the provision that she pays your son to compensate for the ownership you don't leave to him. If you were to require that your daughter come up with $750,000 in cash to give to her brother for his "interest" in the business and another $125,000 for the house, she may very well have to either sell the business or take out large loans she doesn't want to assume; also not a good idea, you figure.

- ✔ Leaving the business to your daughter, and the house to your son. Sure, the business is far more valuable than the house, and maybe your son will be satisfied with his second-place status in your estate. However, if your son is still in the military and doesn't live anywhere near you, he may want nothing to do with the house, either as a potential home for his family in the future or as rental property.

Perplexed? Here's a simple solution for you: Leave the business and the house to your daughter, and purchase a life insurance policy for yourself with a death benefit of $1.75 million that has your son — and only your son — as the beneficiary. This way, each of your two children receives the same amount (more or less, depending on the current value of the business and your home) when you die, even though you don't have $3.5 million in your estate!

This third strategy allows you to use life insurance as a way to create cash when you die to balance the amounts your beneficiaries receive that you specify in your will or with other forms of ownership, such as joint tenancy with right of survivorship (see Chapter 6 on will substitutes).

One potential downside to this strategy is that the life insurance premiums (monthly, quarterly, annually, or so forth) become much more expensive the older you get. So although you're relatively young — in your 40s, for example — that $1.75 million policy payable to your son may cost you $2,000 to $3,000 per year (for a term life policy, which we briefly discuss later in this chapter), depending on factors, such as whether or not you smoke, other aspects of your health, and so on. But by the time you reach your 60s, you pay significantly more each year to maintain that same level of coverage.

Therefore, you need to work with your insurance agent to look at various scenarios, such as using the preceding strategy to create cash for some period of time (for example, 15 to 20 years) and then perhaps switching to some alternative way to divide up your estate when life insurance becomes prohibitively expensive. Perhaps when life insurance is unaffordable (or maybe even unattainable, if you can no longer find coverage) your son will have retired from the military and now be looking at a second career, perhaps even working with his sister in the family business after all this time.

You need to be flexible and adjust your plans to the situation. Life insurance may work for ten or twenty years, but afterwards, some other technique or strategy may be better for you and your beneficiaries. Make sure to adjust as necessary!

Additionally, as we discuss later in this chapter, your life insurance proceeds may be subject to federal estate taxes, depending on how you structure the policy's ownership. So if you're using life insurance to equalize what your beneficiaries receive, make sure that you set up the policy correctly (as we discuss) to prevent a significant amount of money going to pay federal estate taxes and resulting in the same imbalance among your beneficiaries that you were trying to avoid in the first place!

Sorting Out the Kinds of Coverage You Need

For your estate planning, as well as your day-to-day needs, consider the following types of insurance, each of which is discussed in one of the following sections:

- ✔ Life insurance
- ✔ Health insurance
- ✔ Disability income insurance
- ✔ Long-term care insurance
- ✔ Automobile insurance
- ✔ Homeowner's (or renter's) insurance
- ✔ Umbrella liability insurance

Yes, we know that you probably already have at least a couple types of these insurances — automobile and health, in particular — but we give you an estate-planning perspective on insurance that you may not have thought about before.

Make a consolidated list of all insurance coverage you have from all the listed types, including the name(s) of insurance companies, contact information at the insurance company, policy numbers, and the location of the actual policy documents that are probably jumbled amidst all kinds of other important papers somewhere in your house!

For a far more comprehensive discussion about various types of insurance than we can provide in the limited space we have, check out *Insurance For Dummies* by Jack Hungelmann (Wiley Publishing, Inc.).

Life insurance

Life insurance works on a very simple premise. If you die while you have a life insurance policy in effect, the insurance company pays money to your beneficiaries. Of course, the details are a bit more complicated, particularly who receives the money and how much.

Because life insurance is such an integral part of your estate planning, we have an entirely separate section later in this chapter that takes you inside various types of life insurance. For now, we focus on why you need life insurance, such as the following reasons:

- **Replacing your income if you die.** You may plan on living until your retirement years, earning income from your job or business along the way and not only paying your family's regular bills but also socking away a tidy sum to cover expenses during your retirement. But suppose you die at a rather young age? Can your family get by on what you've saved so far plus your spouse's income? Or will your family be forced to sell the house and scale back dramatically to try and make ends meet because you're no longer around to provide for your family? Of course, you need to match your particular situation with your insurance needs. If you're unmarried and have no dependents, and haven't planned on leaving your life savings to another family member or to your favorite charity, your untimely death may not have quite the financially devastating impact as if you had a spouse and several young children. Still, the main point to remember is that one of the primary purposes of life insurance is to replace income that you would have otherwise earned if you were still alive.

✔ **Improving your estate's liquidity.** *Liquidity* is a financial term that basically means readily available cash or an asset that can be quickly turned into cash. Suppose that when you die you have a substantial estate worth $5 million, but almost all your estate is in your primary residence, your two vacation homes, and your investment in your business. You may have heard the old saying, "Rich people don't have any money," or the one that goes, "All his money is tied up in wealth." The point is, even if you're well off financially your personal representative may not be able to distribute large sums of cash very easily, depending on the particular investment portfolio. So if your family needs money for living expenses or for some other substantial cash needs after you die, life insurance can be an important tool to provide cash without your family or other beneficiaries having to sell property that they otherwise wouldn't.

✔ **Paying off your debts.** Life insurance can provide money to pay off your estate's debts — mortgages on real property, business loans, and even sizable personal loans.

✔ **Providing money for estate taxes.** Rather than your family having to sell property to come up with money for estate taxes, life insurance proceeds can do the trick.

See the section, "Looking Closer at Life Insurance" later in this chapter for more about life insurance.

What if you don't have a spouse and children?

The common conventional wisdom about life insurance is that you need to provide money for your spouse and dependent children in the event of your death. But if you don't have to worry about paying for your children's college education after you're gone, or to provide money for your spouse to keep paying the mortgage on your house, then you probably don't need insurance. Therefore, the equation may be stated as "no spouse and kids = no life insurance needed."

Not so fast! Suppose that you are an avid supporter of a charitable cause, such as a small local animal shelter, and you regularly give hundreds of dollars each month to the charity, and

plan to do so for years to come. Perhaps, you're one of the shelter's primary benefactors. So what happens if you die suddenly, especially if you have a fairly modest estate without a lot of assets? Even if you leave your entire estate to the charity, you're only talking about a fraction of the total amount of money that would otherwise be available if you remain alive for many years and keep making your regular monthly contributions.

In this case, you may want a life insurance policy to make sure that even if you were to suddenly die, money is available for the charity as if you were still alive and donating a portion of your salary every month.

Health insurance

We hope you have some form of health insurance, either through your job or business or through some other source (such as an association to which you belong). Because if you don't have health insurance, you run a very high risk of watching much of your estate suddenly get whisked away to pay for medical bills.

Many people are accustomed to health insurance in the form of Health Maintenance Organization (HMO) or Preferred Provider Organization (PPO) coverage, where your primary interaction (and concern) is how much your deductible is for office visits and prescriptions. But at the most basic level, you must view health insurance as a means to help you pay for very high (and usually unexpected) health-related costs, such as extended treatment for cancer, care and rehabilitation after a heart attack or stroke, or any one of numerous other medical catastrophes that could befall you.

So from an estate-planning perspective, make sure that you clearly understand the details of your health insurance policy beyond the deductible amounts printed on your insurance card. Pay particular attention to any maximum amounts associated with your policy, such as the maximum payment for a particular incident or any maximum lifetime benefits. Also understand deductible amounts (if any) for hospitalization. If your insurance policy covers 80 percent of hospitalization costs (versus 100 percent) and you find yourself paying 20 percent of a very expensive prolonged stay for a serious accident or illness, your estate could get hit with a fairly heavy bill.

For example, take a look at Jack Sprat. Jack is 55 years old and works for a company that another company bought out last year. Thankful that he survived the mass layoff frenzy, Jack doesn't give a second thought to the new list of health insurance options during the company's most recent open enrollment period. He simply signs up for the plan with the lowest premium payment each paycheck as he always did.

Stressed out from the pressure at the new company (profits are down, the stock price is down, rumors of new layoffs are circulating), Jack — who isn't in the greatest physical shape anyway — suffers a heart attack that puts him in the hospital for several weeks. After several more weeks at home recuperating, Jack goes back to work, only to suffer another heart attack, this one putting him in the hospital for a month.

Because Jack didn't really pay much attention to what his health insurance policy did and didn't cover, he is shocked (and almost suffers yet another heart attack!) when he starts receiving bill after bill for various doctors and hospital stays, all adding up to a total of $45,000 that Jack has to pay.

(Remember, his policy only covered 80 percent of hospitalization and related doctor charges.) And in Jack's particular circumstances, having to come up with $45,000 isn't quite that easy. He has to cash in stock investments, sell collectibles, empty his bank accounts, and so on.

Now most of Jack's estate planning is in ruins. Various giving clauses in his will (see Chapter 3) are no longer valid because they reference certain tangible personal property (specifically, certain collectibles) that Jack had planned to leave to his oldest son, but now no longer owns. He also had to sell his small share of a real estate investment partnership in which he had a joint tenancy with right of survivorship form of ownership.

The moral of the story: If Jack had adequate health insurance coverage for his particular situation, his estate plan may not have been turned topsy-turvy because of the unfortunate sequence of heart attacks and the resulting medical expenses.

"No big deal," you may be thinking. "For my situation, I have plenty of cash and I can come up with $45,000 without any problem." Perhaps, but suppose that you suffered some type of illness or injury that resulted not in hundreds of thousands of dollars in medical bills, but instead several million dollars in hospitalization, doctors, prescription drugs, and other costs.

Suddenly, the out-of-pocket equivalent is a lot of money to anyone, and consequently can dramatically disrupt anyone's estate plan!

Selecting the most appropriate health insurance coverage isn't simply a matter of looking for a plan with the lowest possible premium payments or "first dollar coverage" (that is, all medical expenses are covered by the insurance, but you pay a much higher premium). You need to look at what's covered and what isn't — and how much the "what isn't" may cost you — and consider the impact on your estate plan if any worst-case scenarios come to pass and you need to lay out a lot of money.

Disability income insurance

Disability income insurance (often referred to as simply disability insurance) provides you with protection against a serious illness or injury that affects your ability to earn a living. Basically, if you get hurt or sick and can't work — but unlike with life insurance, you're still alive — disability insurance provides payments to cover living expenses and replace income.

You typically come across two different types of disability insurance, usually provided by or made available through your employer (though if you're self-employed, you can buy disability policies, just like you can buy health insurance or other forms of insurance). The two types are:

- Short-term disability, which usually covers a period of three months (sometimes longer) and is often provided by using your current and sometimes future vacation balance

- Long-term disability, which as you may guess from the name covers long periods of time — up to many years — by replacing a sizable portion of your income

You find all kinds of variations with long-term disability insurance, so make sure you fully understand what your benefits are if you need to use the insurance. For example, some policies cover a fixed percentage of your salary — often around 60 to 67 percent — while other policies give you a choice as to how much of your salary is provided, ranging from 50 to 75 percent (with correspondingly higher or lower premium payments).

Other policies only come into effect if you're totally disabled, while still other more expensive policies may come into effect if you can't work in your chosen profession but still can perform some other type of paid work.

Some policies have a cost-of-living adjustment feature (that is, the payments go up each year according to increases in inflation rates or some other cost-of-living measure) — something to pay attention to if you're dealing with several decades of coverage because of disability.

Finally, most long-term disability policies provide coverage until the age of 65 (at which time government-provided health benefits can kick in), unless you want to buy coverage for a shorter period of time (for lower costs, of course).

In Chapter 18, we discuss Social Security disability benefits that you may receive in addition to long-term disability insurance that you purchase. When you're figuring out how much disability insurance you need, check to see what your expected Social Security disability benefit will be if you become disabled and factor that amount into the equation. You can probably purchase a smaller amount of long-term disability insurance and pay lower premiums while still providing the coverage you want and need because of what you receive from Social Security.

From an estate-planning perspective, the relationship between long-term disability insurance and protecting your estate is fairly straightforward. Earlier in this chapter, we discuss how part of your insurance-to-estate planning relationship likely is to protect against the loss of future income, in addition to protecting property that is currently part of your estate. Long-term disability, along with life insurance, is a very important part of this strategy.

If you can't work due to an illness or injury and you don't have long-term disability insurance, you can lose nearly everything. You may have to cash in your accounts and sell all your personal and real property to make up for the lost income. From a medical perspective, you can at least receive rudimentary care through government-provided programs for those who can't pay, but at quite a price. Essentially, if you fail to protect against the loss of future income, you may lose everything you already have.

Long-term care insurance

Long-term care insurance is somewhat similar to long-term disability insurance. Whereas long-term disability insurance provides you a salary when you're unable to work, long-term care insurance covers the costs of long-term health care, such as nursing home coverage.

You need to look at both long-term disability insurance and long-term care insurance in concert with one another, evaluating income replacement needs, what amount of health care costs you need to cover, and other financial and personal factors.

Keep in mind that long-term care insurance is an important part of your estate plan, not only for your elderly years but also in the event of a debilitating injury.

Think of long-term care insurance as a cross between health insurance and long-term disability insurance. Ask your insurance agent to help you figure out how much coverage you need to cover medical expenses, and how this coverage can be tied into your long-term disability insurance. Also ask if the insurance policies have any gaps in how they relate to one another. For example, you max out your health insurance, but a particular long-term care policy doesn't kick in for one reason or another, essentially leaving you without coverage (and subjecting your estate to the lack of protection that you're trying to avoid in the first place through insurance).

Automobile insurance

For estate-planning purposes, you really only need to focus on the liability coverage provided by your automobile insurance policy.

Many people gloss over the confusing language in automobile policies about liability limits, wondering what's the big deal about "per person" and "per accident" amounts. Work with your insurance agent — or if you don't have an insurance agent, an insurance company representative with whom you speak over the phone when you set up or modify your policy — to thoroughly understand what the language in your policy (or the policy you're considering) means.

When working with your insurance agent, go through several accident scenarios involving one or more vehicles, one or more other people, and other factors to understand what your policy covers, and — even more important — what your policy doesn't cover. Then take a look at the impact on your estate plan, particularly how the policy can help protect what you have (in this case, from the result of a lawsuit or out-of-court settlement).

Homeowner's or renter's insurance

As with automobile insurance, you must consider the liability protection component with your homeowner's or renter's insurance policy if an accident happens on your property and someone sues you. Make sure that you clearly understand what's covered and what isn't.

As with most types of insurance, you're trying to prevent assets you currently have from being taken away. Ask your insurance agent to clearly explain any worst-case scenarios that may be expensive and may adversely impact your estate plan.

Umbrella liability insurance

Even though you probably have some degree of liability coverage through your automobile and homeowner's or renter's insurance policy, you may need additional liability insurance. Basically, the more your estate is worth, the more likely it is that someone will sue you in the event of an automobile accident or an injury on your property.

An umbrella policy provides — as the name implies — additional coverage above and beyond your other liability coverage. Furthermore, the policy helps protect you against a financially devastating judgment in a lawsuit (or even a settlement to which you agree). As with the other types of insurance coverage we discuss in this chapter, stress to your insurance agent that you want to protect the property in your estate.

Remember the question that we use several times in this chapter — "What is the worst-case scenario, and how will my estate plan be affected?" You must always ask your insurance agent this question about any type of insurance and the various policy options you consider. Make sure that you clearly understand the answer and that you balance all the insurance costs with what you have at stake. Again, a good insurance agent can help you protect what you can't afford to lose without trying to gouge you with very expensive coverage that essentially over-insures you.

Looking Closer at Life Insurance

In the following sections, we provide you with a concise overview of life insurance that may be pertinent to your particular estate plan. You can find additional, much more detailed information in many Internet sources, as well as (as we mention earlier) *Life Insurance For Dummies* by Jack Hungelmann (Wiley Publishing, Inc.)

Many people need to first decide if they need life insurance or not and if the insurance policy is permanent — that is, the policy builds up a *cash value* (sort of like a savings account in addition to providing insurance coverage). Another option is a *term insurance* policy, in which no cash value is built up (but is typically less expensive in your younger years).

Rather than go into all the details of this decision, check with your agent to discuss all the factors. In this chapter, we provide a brief explanation of various types of policies you may encounter.

Whole life insurance

A *whole life* policy is sort of the "granddaddy" (or grandma) of life insurance, and for many years was the staple of many Americans' life insurance needs. You pay a premium (typically every quarter or every year) and receive insurance coverage, and along the way a portion of your payment is set aside and earns interest, sort of like a bank savings account. The cash value is yours, and you can take loans against the value while the policy is still in effect or, if you cancel the policy, you get the cash value as the proceeds.

A variation of whole life insurance is *universal life,* which became popular in the high-inflation, high-interest rate early 1980s. Universal life can get complicated but basically, you can get a guaranteed minimum return just like with a whole life policy, but you also have the opportunity to earn more based on factors spelled out in your policy. If your return is high enough, you may not even have to make premium payments for some period of time because the premium is taken out of your gains. But as with whole life, the important point to note is that universal life policies build up a cash value.

With a *variable life* insurance policy, you have a say in how some of your premiums are invested by the insurance company, such as in bonds or even in the stock market. However, your principal is at risk and you can actually lose some or all your principal, as in the case of poor stock market performance. Be careful about going the variable life route, and know what you're getting into if you go down that path.

Term insurance — no cash value while you're alive

Many people choose to stick with *term insurance* for their life insurance needs. You can think of term insurance as pure insurance. If you die and the policy is in effect, the insurance company pays your death benefit. If, however, you no longer have the policy in effect for any reason when you die, then the insurance company doesn't pay anything.

As with the various types of permanent, cash-value insurance policies, you find all kinds of variations offered to you by insurance companies. Some policies are called *annual renewal term* policies, and your death benefit stays the same as your premium payments go up periodically (for example, every three years while you're very young, and then annually once you reach a certain age). Other term policies allow you to lock in a fixed premium price for some period of time — typically from 10 to 20 years — rather than have those premiums increase over time. Still other *decreasing-term* policies leave the premium payments the same but over time decrease the death benefit of the policy.

From an estate-planning perspective, various forms of life insurance play different roles as part of the three-pronged strategy we discuss earlier in this chapter. Specifically

- ✔ Life insurance primarily protects against the loss of future income, as well as protects your assets from being sold to cover your future income that is now lost because you've died.

- ✔ Life insurance creates cash if a significant portion of your estate is concentrated in an asset that can't be easily divided, such as your business.

- ✔ You can leave various life insurance policies that build up a cash value to one or more beneficiaries along with other property in your estate, such as stocks and bonds.

Variations on the life insurance theme

Most insurance policies feature periodic premium payments as long as the policy is in effect, regardless of whether those payments stay the same for the policy's duration. Additionally, life insurance typically covers only one person: you. However, you may find variations along the way that you may want to consider. For example:

✔ A *single-premium policy* is one in which you pay a rather sizable amount of money up front when the policy goes into effect.

✔ A *first-to-die* policy covers you and another person on a single policy (as contrasted with each of you having your own life insurance policies), and the insurance company issues payment whenever the first of you dies.

✔ A *second-to-die* policy also covers you and another person, but the insurance company issues payment when the second person dies.

You need to review with your insurance agent and financial planner any of these variations you may be interested in — as well as new policies that insurance companies develop — to make sure that they make sense for you and your estate.

Business-provided life insurance

You can receive other life insurance courtesy of your employer or the business you own or co-own. *Key-person insurance* is life insurance on (as you can guess from the term) a key person in a company, such as the chief executive or one of three partners of a small closely held family business. (You most likely see the term *key-man* insurance but we prefer the gender-neutral terminology.)

Split-dollar insurance is a rather complicated insurance mechanism that is often used by companies to insure the lives of executives at or above a certain level (for example, all assistant vice presidents, vice presidents, senior vice presidents, and up) and to provide those executives with a company-paid benefit in the form of a cash value insurance policy. If you have a split-dollar policy through your employer, ask someone knowledgeable in your human resources organization to walk you through the details.

In Chapters 15 and 16, we discuss estate-planning needs for family businesses. You definitely need to look at business-oriented life insurance — particularly key-person insurance — as part of your strategy to keep your business viable if something happens to you or someone with whom you're in business.

Other company-provided life insurance

Even if you're not a senior company executive, you may have company-provided life insurance, and not even know it! Beyond basic life insurance coverage available to every employee as well as optional coverage employees can buy, many companies provide their employees with additional life insurance in the case of accidental death while on company business or travel. Check with your human resources department or on your company's internal Web site for details, and factor any additional contingency life insurance into your estate plan. Make sure your family and personal representative are also aware of the coverage you have!

Understanding Life Insurance Tax Implications

Even if you've taken great care to protect your estate with adequate amounts of life insurance, you may unwittingly create a federal estate tax trap that can cost your estate lots of money!

If you "have control" over your life insurance policy (more on what "have control" means in a moment), the death benefit of the life insurance is added into your estate's value, just as if that money were in a savings account.

For example, suppose that you die in 2007 when the exemption amount for federal estate taxes is $2 million and the total value of all the savings accounts, stocks, bonds, real estate, and collectibles in your estate is $1.5 million. So you won't owe any federal estate taxes at all because you're $500,000 under the exemption amount that federal estate taxes kick in, right?

Not so fast! Suppose that you have a term life insurance policy that pays $750,000 to your oldest daughter upon your death, but that you "have control" over that policy. According to the rules of the federal estate tax game, $750,000 is added to the total value of your stocks, bonds, savings, and property, so now your taxable estate is valued at $2.25 million (the $1.5 million plus the $750,000 death benefit of the life insurance policy). So now estate taxes kick in because your taxable estate, including your life insurance, is above the exemption amount in the year you die.

So you're pretty much out of luck when it comes to federal estate taxes on your life insurance, right? Not quite. First, realize that even with the death benefit amount of your life insurance added in, you may still not have to worry about federal estate taxes at all. Assuming the same details as the above example, if you were to die in 2009 — when the federal estate tax exemption amount is $3.5 million (again, see Table 13-1) — then your taxable estate of $2.25 million including your life insurance is still under the exemption amount — so no estate taxes for you!

Even with the lower exemption amounts in the early and mid-2000s, and possibly in 2011 if the federal estate tax comes back after being gone for a year, you still may not have to worry about estate taxes if the value of your estate is fairly modest. For example, an estate of $250,000 augmented by an additional $250,000 in life insurance is free of federal estate taxes in all cases. (See Chapter 13 for more on the death tax.)

But what if you're above the exemption amount with your estate and your life insurance? Good news! You have a couple tricks up your sleeve. Basically, you can "give up control" over your life insurance policy to have the value of the death benefit excluded from your estate for federal estate tax purposes. You can give up control in several ways, the most popular being:

✔ You can simply transfer the ownership of the policy to someone else, such as a family member or friend. By doing so, you give up the right to change beneficiaries and make other changes to your policy, but the policy is no longer considered to be within your control. Transferring a life insurance policy could result in gift taxes or federal estate taxes, though; check with your estate planning team for the details on your particular situation. You also need to be aware of the three-year "tax timer" on life insurance policy transfers (see "The pesky little details" sidebar).

✔ You can use an *irrevocable life insurance trust,* as discussed in Chapter 8, as an ownership vehicle for the policy. Again, you give up control but now no longer have to worry about the death benefit being included in your estate. But again, gift or federal estate tax issues may apply.

WARNING! You need to work with both your insurance agent (who may focus primarily on selling you an appropriate amount of coverage rather than worrying about estate tax implications) and also your attorney (who is knowledgeable about the rules that determine whether or not you have adequately given up control).

The pesky little details

Uncle Sam doesn't make it easy for you if you're trying to give up control of an insurance policy. You need to be concerned with some of the small details. Of particular concern is the *three-year rule* that states if you transfer ownership of a life insurance policy within three years of your death, then the death benefit of that policy is added into your estate, even if another person owns the policy or if you've created an irrevocable life insurance trust. Check with your attorney to make sure these details don't burn you.

Particularly, if you want to set up an irrevocable life insurance trust, you definitely need to work with your attorney.

You also need to get up-to-date advice on the relationships involved for the beneficiary or beneficiaries of your policy, who owns the policy, and who pays for the policy. Make sure that when all the pieces of the puzzle are put together the end result is life insurance that is estate-tax free. Also, state tax laws vary, so check with your attorney about any state-level considerations that affect your life insurance.

Asking the Right Estate-Related Questions About Insurance

You already know some of the critical questions to ask your insurance agent, company HR department, or whoever is responsible for signing you up for any type of insurance. You need to find out what the policy covers, when it kicks in (for example, when the life insurance is paid after you die, when health insurance is paid after you go to a doctor or get taken to the hospital), how much the policy costs, and so forth.

Other specific questions you need to ask about all types of insurance include:

- ✔ **What is my worst-case scenario?** We already mention this question several times, but we can't emphasize it enough. You find all kinds of limitations and exclusions buried in the fine print of any insurance policy, from your basic automobile policy to life insurance. You want to find out, and you may want to phrase the question this way: "If I buy this policy and pay all my premiums, what can happen to me that *won't* be covered by this policy and will cost me lots and lots of money?" The answer to this question can help you decide if an insurance policy provides what you are looking for — protection against the worst case scenarios — and if that particular policy is worth the cost or not.

- ✔ **What assets of mine are at risk?** Your state may have laws that put everything you have at risk if your insurance coverage isn't sufficient to cover a lawsuit, medical expenses, or whatever — or perhaps certain assets are exempt, such as your primary residence. Make sure you clearly understand what you can keep if you don't have adequate insurance and you (or your family) must start selling off assets to raise enough cash to cover the insurance shortfall.

- ✔ **When does this insurance coverage end?** Estate planning is a long-term proposition, stretching from now until after you die. Sometimes you can keep insurance coverage for the rest of your life if you want. In other situations, your coverage may only last until you reach a certain age, if your employer is acquired by another company, if you're successfully sued (because your insurance company can then drop you), or something else occurs. Part of your estate-planning responsibility is to make sure that you have adequate control and protection and that as you get close to death, your estate isn't unreasonably exposed to losing everything.

✔ **What safety nets exist beyond this insurance, and what are the catches?** If you need long-term medical or nursing home care and simply don't have the money or adequate long-term care coverage, the state provides the care you need, with a catch. As we discuss in Chapter 10, the *Estate Recovery Act* requires your state to go after your estate to recover the costs they put out. So the good news is that you do have a safety net, but the bad news is that much, or perhaps most, of whatever is left in your estate may go to pay for that safety net after you die. Make sure that you clearly understand the relationship between insurance and any down-the-road impacts on your estate, such as the state coming after your property because you were forced to use that safety net.

Chapter 18

Connecting Your Retirement Funds to Your Estate Plans

*Y*our retirement accounts, such as pension plans, Individual Retirement Accounts (IRAs), and 401(k) plans, are like any other asset you own when it comes to estate planning. First, you decide how to use them — more or less — to fund your retirement. After you die, the amount left is part of your total estate's value when somebody (like your attorney or personal representative) figures your final tax bill, if any.

You also need to cover these retirement-related assets in your will, and decide how you want to divide up these accounts like the other assets in your estate. (You know, your spouse gets the proceeds from your 401(k), while Junior receives the proceeds from one of your IRA accounts.)

This chapter helps you make some decisions concerning your retirement-related assets — and understand how to best use expert advice.

Deciding What Your Nest Eggs Are Really For

You can take one of two approaches to linking your retirement plan with your estate plan:

- ✔ Using most or all your property to fund your retirement, and only leaving behind a few leftovers in your estate when you die

- ✔ Using part of your property to fund your retirement and then having specific and significant estate-related goals for what's left in your estate after you die

We discuss each of these two approaches in the following sections. Essentially the question you need to ask yourself is this: "Are my retirement funds really for my retirement?"

No matter which of the two following strategies you follow, discussing what you plan to do with your nest eggs is a key topic when you talk with your financial adviser.

Uh, I thought my retirement accounts were for retirement

Use your retirement accounts for things other than retirement? That idea may sound silly, but keep in mind that you may never need to tap into your IRA, 401(k), or other special retirement accounts during your retirement years. After all, you can defer income taxes on gains (interest, capital gains on stock price appreciation, dividends, and so on) on these special retirement accounts, even though the proceeds from those gains are still left in the retirement account. And in many cases, you can leave money in these accounts for years, essentially giving you a tremendous advantage when it comes to income keeping taxes at bay.

Suppose that you have plenty of money in your nonretirement CDs, stocks, mutual funds, and other accounts — not to mention a pension plan from your employer that pays you enough to cover your living expenses for the rest of your life. All together, these accounts provide more than enough money to fund your golden years of retirement.

If you're fortunate to have so much nonretirement money that you never have to touch your retirement accounts until you absolutely must, you may view your retirement assets as something you pass on to your children, a charity, or some other beneficiary after you die.

On the other, more unfortunate side, if you don't adequately plan for your retirement, you may run out of money and have to tap into assets you had earmarked for estate-related purposes, such as money for your grandchildren, property you had wanted to leave to your favorite charity, and so on.

Strategy No. 1: Satisfy your needs and plop the leftovers away

With this approach, essentially you're stating, "Leaving money behind isn't important to me. I've worked hard all my life and I want to use my money to enjoy my retirement years!"

You may still have specific plans about who gets what in terms of property in your estate, but in your case, you're thinking more of the antique dining room furniture and your antique collectibles and not your bank accounts, CDs, stocks, and bonds — the accounts that you'll use to fund your retirement years. When you die, whatever is left — whether your estate's value is a teensy little bit or a lot — goes to one or more beneficiaries.

To accomplish this, you'll work with a financial adviser on retirement planning and fill out some moderately complex worksheets that detail what assets you currently have and any debts you have (such as a mortgage, credit card balances, and so forth). Your adviser plugs these numbers into various formulas that make assumptions about factors, such as:

- Your accounts' annual earnings (for example, interest on your bank accounts, gains on your stocks, and so on)

- Your current age, your target retirement age, and life expectancy

- The type of retirement lifestyle you plan (Stay mostly at home? Travel the world?)

Your financial adviser tries to figure out as closely as possible how much money you need to have, how much more you need to save and invest, and how much your current and post-retirement spending is. Your adviser wants to make sure you have enough money to fund your retirement and not run out. You don't have to worry about specific amounts to leave behind as part of your estate (more on this topic in a moment).

Strategy No. 2: Walk the balance beam between retirement needs and estate plans

The second — and probably more common — approach to linking your retirement planning and estate planning is trying to balance the two disciplines. You want to not only fund a comfortable retirement, but you also want to have a specific plan for your estate, as we stress throughout this book.

This second approach makes sense when you know the amounts of money you plan to leave your children, grandchildren, or charities.

We say it again and again: Make sure you make plans with your financial adviser.

When we say *money* in the preceding paragraphs, we're referring to your estate's property value. As we note in Chapter 1, property can be both real (real estate) and personal (either tangible or intangible) such as your collectibles and your mutual funds, respectively.

Linking Retirement and Estate Planning: A Tough Job, But You Can Do It

In this chapter, we assume that you don't want to focus on your retirement plan with the intention of leaving behind only what you didn't use up. Chances are that you're equally concerned about making sure you also have enough money to meet specific estate-planning goals.

As you may guess, you have several factors to work out with your financial adviser to achieve this balancing act: your pension plan (if you have one), your retirement accounts, and Social Security. The following sections discuss how various retirement-oriented assets and investments apply to your estate plan.

Tapping into a traditional pension plan

Pension plan.

Those two words together conjure up some interesting impressions, depending largely on your particular background:

✔ Many people, particularly those who came into the workforce during or after the mid- to late 1970s, have little or no familiarity with pension plans and think that pension plans are a relic from a bygone era when people worked at the same company for most or all their careers before retiring.

✔ Other people, who have worked for a company that still maintained an old-style pension plan (one that pays you a predetermined amount of money, typically every month, during your retirement years), can't even utter those two words together without bitterly thinking about the years they put into a now-bankrupt, now-scandal-ridden company that essentially has robbed them of promised retirement benefits because the pension plan is also now bankrupt.

✔ Yet other people — particularly government workers, including those in the military — see a pension plan that starts paying retirement benefits while people are in their 30s or 40s (still young enough to start on an entirely new career) as a just reward for spending a first career with salaries lower than they could have earned elsewhere in the private sector.

Pension plan basics

Surprise! Pension plans do still exist today. If your company offers them, pension plans can very well make up an important part of your estate, which means two important things for you: contingency planning and death tax implications of down-the-road lump sum payments.

Contingency plans

First, you need to have some type of contingency, or backup, plan, particularly if you don't work for a government organization (federal, state, county, or local). If you work for a private company that has a traditional pension plan and the company sinks into the morass of a financial scandal (as we've seen in the early 2000s time and time again), your pension benefits may be at risk!

You need to know two things: Is your pension insured and, if it is insured, does the insurance cover all or only part of its value.

The good news is that the Pension Benefit Guarantee Corporation (PBGC), a federal agency, may protect some or all your pension benefits, even if your company fails. As noted on the PBGC Web site at www.pbgc.gov, PBGC protects approximately 44 million American workers' retirement incomes in more than 35,000 defined benefit pension plans.

Keep in mind, though, that PBGC insures some, but not all pension plans. The PBGC usually doesn't insure pension plans offered by professional service firms, such as a doctor's office or a law firm that employs fewer than 26 employees. Similarly, church pension plans and government worker pension plans aren't typically insured. Check with your employer's pension plan administrator and ask if your company's plan is PBGC-insured.

Another item of concern — or maybe not — for you is whether all or part of your pension benefit is insured. Maximum amounts change each year, but for 2002 up to $3,579.55 per month, or $42,954.60 annually, is insured. Additionally, the guaranteed amount is adjusted lower if you begin receiving payments before age 65, or if your pension plan includes benefits for a survivor or some other beneficiary.

As companies usually say on TV and radio commercials for various products and special offers, "other restrictions and limitations may apply," so if you have a pension plan, carefully read through the material on PBGC's Web site. Some specific topics and Web pages you may want to check out include:

- ✔ Retirement planning and estate planning — www.pbgc.gov/retire/default.htm

- ✔ Applying for PBGC benefits if you need them — www.pbgc.gov/forms/view700.htm

- ✔ Frequently asked questions — www.pbgc.gov/faqs.htm

If one of the preceding Web pages has changed, go to the site's home page at www.pbgc.gov. Continually check the home page to see what is new since the last time you checked out the site.

Even with possible PBGC insurance on your pension plan, double-check from a retirement-planning perspective as well as an estate-planning perspective that you have backup plans (money in your IRA account and your other non-retirement savings, for example), in case your pension benefits either evaporate suddenly or never materialize as promised.

Lump-sum payments

In addition to any regular monthly payments you receive from your pension plan, stay aware of any down-the-road lump-sum payments that may be coming in, particularly any lump-sum amounts that may be paid upon your death to your spouse or some other beneficiary in lieu of future monthly payments. Make sure that you discuss these payments with your financial planner and attorney to understand any estate tax implications.

Key items for your estate plan and your pension

A pension plan can affect your estate plan — for better of for worse — in three ways. Those three considerations are:

- ✔ Covering expenses during your retirement years
- ✔ Having a backup plan if your pension income is disrupted
- ✔ Planning for inflation

Covering expenses during your retirement years

From a retirement-planning perspective, your monthly pension-plan payments must match your regular expenses, such as housing, food, planned travel, medical and health care, and so on. So far, we're not talking about rocket science, or even anything out of the ordinary! But now you need to go back to what you determined to be your philosophy about how your retirement planning and estate planning are linked (the spend-it-all versus balanced approaches that we discuss earlier in the chapter). Specifically:

✔ If your strategy is to balance your retirement and estate plans, and your anticipated pension plan income is roughly equivalent to your anticipated retirement expenses, then you have all the rest of your assets — CDs, IRAs (which we discuss later in this chapter), stocks, and so on — available to include in your estate plan. That is, if you don't intend to spend it all, then you can start giving away property as gifts (see Chapter 11). In your will, you can make provisions to leave other property to your children, grandchildren, or any other beneficiaries.

✔ If your strategy is to spend all your retirement money (and your anticipated pension plan income and retirement expenses are about the same), then you actually have additional money available for your retirement years (in addition to your pension income). You can move into a nicer apartment or house, travel extensively, or otherwise spend as much of your money as you can while you're still alive. Gifts of property to your children? Significant bequests in your will? Nope, not for you. You can start whittling away at your savings, spending additional money to improve the quality of your retirement years. (Don't forget to set aside at least some of that extra money just in case you find yourself facing significant unanticipated expenses.)

✔ If your pension plan income is less than your expected expenses and cost of living, then you need to plan to "draw down" (that is, slowly tap into) your assets to cover the shortfall. Again, your retirement-versus-estate planning philosophy comes into play here. If you don't really plan to set any of your property aside to be left to beneficiaries after your death, then you have a bit more money to work with than if you leave behind specific amounts of money as part of your estate. Make sure that your financial adviser knows what approach you want to take as you put together a retirement "draw down" plan so your plan can reflect your desires.

✔ If you're one of the lucky pensioners whose pension income exceeds your anticipated retirement expenses, then you have a pleasant problem on your hands. Specifically, you need to account for money being added to your estate during your retirement years! (Unless of course, you want to spend the extra money by taking elaborate trips to India and Tahiti and dine at five-star restaurants weekly.) And no, you don't need to be the retired CEO of a major corporation, drawing a pension of more than a million dollars each year (not to mention access to the company jet), to have this problem on your hands. If you paid off the mortgage on your home years ago and plan to live there during your retirement years, and if you don't eat out much or don't like to travel, then even a modest pension can put you into the income-greater-than-expenses category. So even if your philosophy is to take care of your retirement and not worry about your estate plan, you still need to worry about your estate plan! If you don't have any family to whom you want to leave your property (or if you do have family, but don't want to leave them any property), you can always give some of your extra pension income to your favorite charity or to some other cause, such as your local symphony. Remember that you want to have control of where that extra pension income goes, rather than accumulating it in your bank accounts and then having your state's intestate laws make that determination for you after you die.

Having a backup plan if your pension income is disrupted

As we discuss in the previous section, you always run the risk of your pension income being reduced or even being totally lost. Or, on a positive note, one day your pension income may exceed your expenses. Plan accordingly by leaving behind significant bequests to your children and your favorite charities. However, a short time later (and on a negative note), you find your pension income significantly reduced because only part of the payments are covered by pension insurance. Consequently, you may need to shift your retirement plans to begin to draw down some of your savings to cover living expenses. Furthermore, you also may find yourself in a situation where you simply don't have enough money to take care of your retirement years' expenses and also to fulfill the estate-planning goals you once had. Therefore, you probably need to go back to the drawing board and adjust your will and make other changes to your estate plans as necessary.

Planning for inflation

Inflation hasn't been much of a problem in recent years, but if you're getting close to your retirement years (or are already there), you most likely remember the late 1970s and early 1980s with double-digit inflation. Even the years immediately before and after that period (early 1970s and mid- to late 1980s) were hallmarked by modest inflation that often was around 5 to 6 percent, and sometimes even higher. Many pension plans have payments that adjust for inflation, but suppose that yours doesn't? If high inflation comes roaring back, you may find yourself in a situation where you need to adjust your retirement plans to use more of your savings to supplement your pension than you had originally anticipated. You need to make sure that none of the giving clauses in your will are suddenly invalid because you've had to sell an asset or use more money than you had anticipated, and money or property that you had planned to leave to a beneficiary is no longer available.

Managing your IRA accounts

Very few investment vehicles have undergone as many changes over the years as Individual Retirement Accounts (IRAs). IRAs became very popular in the early 1980s as a tax shelter for taxpayers to deduct up to $2,000 of earned income from an individual tax return (more for joint married tax returns). Taxpayers put the money into a special account where it could grow through interest, dividends, and capital gains tax-free until withdrawn.

But soon, the tax laws changed so only people not covered by traditional pension plans where they worked could put "pre-tax" money into an IRA. Soon, the rules for deductibility of contributions started changing every couple of years, plus variations of IRAs such as the Roth IRA (for after-tax contributions rather than pre-tax contributions) were introduced. Self-employed individuals also had still other variations, such as the SEP-IRA ("SEP" standing for self-employed).

Under the latest tax law, tax-deductible contributions are back, but only if your income is under a certain amount; otherwise you can still put money into an IRA, but you can't take a tax deduction.

Additionally, Congress reset the amount you can put into an IRA at $3,000 for 2002 to 2004, $4,000 for 2005 to 2007, and then $5,000 in 2008 with inflation-indexed increases afterwards.

If you're 50 years old or older, you can also make catch-up contributions — make sure you work with your financial planner to figure out the details.

So far, IRAs sound just like any other savings account or CD (for IRAs invested in fixed income assets, such as interest-bearing accounts), or for riskier stock-based IRAs, like any mutual fund or other stock investment. So what's the big deal for estate planning? The answer: three key points that we discuss in the following sections, including:

✔ Naming a beneficiary

✔ Decoding tax implications for your beneficiary

✔ Adapting your retirement-versus-estate philosophy to your IRAs

Even beyond tax and estate-planning implications, you need to get up-to-date information about various IRAs and how they can affect your retirement. Basically, the world of IRAs can be very confusing, so ask your financial adviser.

Naming your IRA beneficiary

When you create an IRA account, you can name a beneficiary for that account, just like a life insurance policy (see Chapter 17). Upon your death, IRA proceeds go to your beneficiary and don't go through probate.

As we discuss in Chapters 5 and 6, your estate is technically comprised of two parts: your probate estate — your property that is transferred to others through your will or your state's intestate laws if you don't have a will — and your nonprobate estate, or assets transferred outside of probate, such as through a will substitute like joint tenancy with the right of survivorship.

Again, IRA assets that go to a named beneficiary don't go through probate, meaning that all the advantages of avoiding probate that we discuss in Chapter 5 (speed, privacy, and so forth) come into play. You should also consider naming a contingent beneficiary for your IRA.

Decoding your beneficiary's tax implications

Certain IRA assets can increase your beneficiary's income taxes! For example, say you live long enough to totally withdraw all your IRA contributions that you made over the years that were tax-deductible. Because you were fortunate enough to avoid taxes on that money on the way into your IRA, guess what: the IRS wants its cut of the money on the way out!

If you die before you withdraw all (or any) your money, the IRS still wants a cut as if you were still alive. As a result, your traditional IRA's beneficiary has to pay income taxes on the amount received just as if you had received the money.

Adapting your retirement-versus-estate philosophy to your IRA's value

If you intend to spend as much of your money as possible during your retirement years and not worry about leaving behind specific amounts as part of your estate plan, then you and your financial planner can plan for you to draw down your IRA balance during your expected lifespan.

If, however, you want to fund specific goals as part of your estate plan, then you need to set aside a certain portion of your IRA balance for estate-planning purposes. (For example, you set aside money for your grandchildren and great-grandchildren's education, even after you've died, [see the sidebar, "Setting aside college money"].)

If you want to leave behind specific amounts and not put those amounts at risk, you need to make sure that a significant portion of your IRA is in safe investments, such as CDs, rather than in riskier investments, such as stocks.

Estate planning for 401(k) and similar plans

401(k) plans are, in many ways, a cross between IRAs and traditional pension plans. Specifically

- ✔ 401(k) plans are structured very similarly to IRAs, though with different limits (and a few restrictions) on contribution amounts.
- ✔ Many companies that no longer have (or that have never had) traditional company-funded pension plans instead offer 401(k) plans as the primary retirement vehicle for their employees.

401(k) plans cover employees of privately held or publicly traded companies, while the very similar 403(b) and 457 plans cover government workers and those who work at tax-exempt organizations. Check with your employer's human resources department to see what plan your company offers and what the rules are.

Your company may offer some amount of matching contribution in addition to your own contributions to your 401(k)-like accounts. Very often, companies offer some type of *matching program* — typically an additional 10-20 percent of your contribution that they add into your account for you, sometimes much more depending on your employer. Also, your 401(k) is a portable retirement vehicle. If you leave your employer, you have a certain period of time to move that money into another tax-advantaged account (such as doing an *IRA rollover,* or transferring your money into an IRA account) to avoid penalties.

From an estate-planning perspective, if you're married, you must name your spouse as your 401(k) account's beneficiary (unlike an IRA), unless your spouse signs a waiver. And if you die, your spouse can elect to get your 401(k) account's proceeds paid out over time rather than in a lump sum. You and your spouse definitely need to work with your financial planner to understand payment plan possibilities, advantages, and limitations.

As with IRAs, your 401(k) beneficiary or beneficiaries may owe income tax on distributions they receive because of the tax-deductible contributions you made along the way. And also as with IRAs, proceeds left to a named beneficiary — your spouse or, if your spouse signs a waiver, someone else — don't pass through probate.

Social Security and your estate planning

Social Security bashing has almost become an American sport. From complaining about how much Social Security tax is withheld from our paychecks each year, to fearing that when we retire, the system may have little or nothing left despite how much tax we've paid over the years, Social Security gets as much respect as . . . well, as Rodney Dangerfield!

Not so fast, though. With estate planning (not to mention your retirement planning), don't overlook the benefits that Social Security can provide you. Specifically, your estate planning can benefit from:

- ✔ Social Security retirement payments — the pension portion of Social Security

- ✔ Disability benefits — payments you can receive if you become disabled that help to protect part or all your estate

- ✔ Survivors' benefits — like life insurance payments from Social Security that may go to your family members after you die

✔ Supplemental security income — additional money available from Social Security for the truly needy

We discuss each of the preceding items in the following section.

Social Security retirement payments

Perhaps you're getting close to your retirement years and as you take stock of everything that your estate comprises — your bank accounts, stocks and bonds, retirement funds, home and other real estate, collectibles, and so on — you're starting to worry. You don't have a pension plan where you work, and your IRAs and 401(k) plans haven't been doing so great lately because of stock market losses.

You sit down with your financial adviser to talk about your retirement plan and estate plan. You tell your adviser that you have specific estate-planning goals with regards to leaving certain property behind for your children and your favorite charity. You really don't want to have to sell your collectibles, sell your house, or take out a second mortgage. However, you're not sure if you have enough money available for your retirement years without having to make tough decisions that may cause you to fall short of your estate planning goals.

Depending on factors, such as how many years you've been working and your income, plus the age at which you expect to retire, you can probably expect to receive anywhere between $1,000 and $2,500 per month.

From a retirement-planning perspective, you certainly want to factor this income into other retirement income and thus balance that total against anticipated regular expenses, travel, and so on. More important, though (for purposes of this book, anyway), your Social Security retirement payments operate similar to a company-provided pension plan — money for your retirement years that supplements other income you have or amounts that you draw from your savings. Depending on your retirement-versus-estate philosophy, you can either:

✔ Have more money available to use up during your retirement years

✔ Draw less from your savings and assets to fund your retirement, thus leaving more available for your beneficiaries after you die

For many people, Social Security retirement payments augment pension plan income or withdrawals from savings and IRAs and often are enough to cover routine and even some unanticipated expenses. For you, these payments may mean that you don't have to sell collectibles and antiques that you want to leave to your children, or sell the family home that you want to keep until you die and then leave behind for your spouse or perhaps one of your children.

So even though you may think of Social Security retirement payments only in the context of retirement planning, remember that Social Security also affects your estate planning because you use less of your savings and investments to cover expenses during your retirement years.

Disability benefits

In Chapter 17, we discuss how long-term disability insurance can be an important part of your estate planning. Long-term disability protects property in your estate by providing income if you become disabled (therefore preventing you or your family from having to sell much or all your estate to make up for lost income).

In addition to long-term disability insurance that you purchase from an insurance company, you may also be eligible to receive Social Security disability payments (depending on how many *credits* you build up during your working years — consult the Social Security Administration for more information) that provide a modest amount of money to help pay for expenses. As a result, Social Security can help protect your estate by allowing you to avoid selling off property that you'd like to keep — at least for a while, assuming you have enough money coming in from Social Security disability benefits and any long-term disability insurance that you purchase.

If you become disabled and begin receiving Social Security disability payments, you do so until you reach the age of 65, at which time those benefits automatically convert to Social Security retirement benefits — but you still receive the same amount of money.

From an estate-planning perspective, Social Security disability benefits help protect your estate, but they most likely don't come close to covering your living expenses (and, if applicable, your family's living expenses). Therefore, to help protect your estate, don't forget about long-term disability insurance before you need it. (See Chapter 17 for details.)

Survivors' benefits

A significant portion of your estate plan is figuring out who gets what. You want to designate who gets property that you currently have. And as we discuss in Chapter 17, you can use life insurance to create money to go to one or more beneficiaries after you die.

Another piece of the who-gets-what picture also comes from the Social Security corner: survivors' benefits. Survivors' benefits provide payments to certain family members, such as spouses (widows or widowers), children, and dependent parents.

Even certain divorced spouses may qualify for survivors' benefits. For example, if you were married for at least ten years, your former spouse may be eligible for the same benefits as if you were still married when you die. Even if you were married for a shorter time, your former spouse may be eligible to receive survivors' benefits if he or she is caring for your child who is under the age of 16.

Essentially, survivors' benefits act in much the same way as life insurance (see Chapter 17). However the amount of money that Social Security provides probably won't be enough to maintain your family's quality of life without causing a serious impact on your estate — specifically, forcing your family to sell property that you left them that they had planned on keeping.

Make sure you include your Social Security benefits with your private insurance benefits when you're looking to taking care of your family and protecting your property when you die.

Keeping track of your Social Security benefits

The Social Security Administration sends you a statement every few years that tells you:

✔ Your adjusted gross income each year you've been working

✔ The amount of your adjusted gross income subject to Social Security taxes (if you've earned more than the maximum taxable amount, only some of your adjusted gross income is subject to Social Security taxes)

✔ The amount of Social Security taxes withheld each year from all your paychecks that, essentially, comprises your personal Social Security account

On this form you also receive a projection from the Social Security Administration of the amount of money you can expect to receive each month, with various scenarios depending on the year in which you elect to begin receiving Social Security payments. Basically, the earlier you start receiving payments, the less you get each month, and conversely the longer you wait to start receiving payments the more you receive each month. (The projections are based on assumptions of your annual earnings between now — the date of the statement — and when you retire, and are only estimates!)

Be aware of all kinds of rules that not only govern how much you receive, but also rules that affect additional Social Security benefits (such as for disability), what happens if you or your spouse dies, what happens to your benefits if you get divorced, and whether or not your Social Security payments are taxed (depending largely on your additional earnings). You can get details of these and other aspects of Social Security from various publications that describe your benefits in detail, as well as from the Social Security Administration's Web site at www.ssa.gov. Some specific Web page addresses include:

✔ Disability — www.ssa.gov/disability/

✔ Death benefits — www.ssa.gov/pubs/deathbenefits.htm

✔ Supplemental security income — www.ssa.gov/notices/supplemental-security-income/

Supplemental security income

Supplemental security income (SSI) is a Social Security program that provides benefits to the *truly needy* — people who have very little property, who are blind, or who have other disabilities.

From an estate-planning perspective, SSI comes into play as sort of a last resort if the most unfortunate, tragic circumstances come to bear in your life and all your estate planning has gone down the drain. If you've had to sell all the property in your estate because of some unfortunate turn of events, you can at least turn to SSI for some amount of subsistence.

Nobody really plans for such a turn of events in life, and certainly if your circumstances are such that you need to apply for SSI, almost everything else that we discuss in this book is irrelevant. However, in the interest of completeness with regards to our Social Security discussion, we at least want to mention SSI so you know the program is available if the worst comes to pass.

Chapter 19

Estate Planning in Exceptional Situations

*E*ven the most orderly estate plans can be cast to the winds by some unforeseen event. Don't despair! Not only is estate planning about putting together an orderly, comprehensive strategy to address your will, estate taxes, insurance, and all the rest, but also it's about planning for the unplannable.

Take divorce, for example. Most of estate planning is built around and based on traditional family structures: a never-before-married couple that stays married for their entire lives and has 2.64 natural-born children (or whatever the statistical average number of children is these days). Just thumb through the pages of this book and notice how often we refer to "your spouse" or "your children." We're simply reflecting the fact that laws governing estate-related matters, such as those for wills and taxes, focus primarily on the traditional family structures most common when those laws were first written.

But if your family or personal situation doesn't look like The Cleavers from *Leave it to Beaver,* you've come to the right place. In this chapter, we discuss how divorce, unmarried couples (either same-sex or opposite-sex), and incompetence (in a legal sense, not "being unable to get the hang of something") can affect your estate planning.

You have two main choices: you can do nothing or you can do something else. We explain what happens if you choose to do nothing — leave your estate's fate in the hands of relevant laws — as well as ways in which you can do something else to better match your estate-planning goals.

Working a Divorce into the Plan

When divorce happens to anyone who is key to your estate planning — you (and, by extension, your spouse), your former spouse, your children, your parents, your brothers or sisters — everything becomes unsettled as the divorcing couple divides up their property. Unfortunately, most people in the middle of a divorce focus on the present instead of the future — how marital property is divided, for example, or (in less congenial divorces) how much of the other person's property they can grab as part of the divorce settlement.

In the following sections, we discuss your choices for two important parts of your estate — and your life — that divorce affects: property and children. We describe:

- ✔ What's likely to happen if you don't do anything
- ✔ What your options are if you decide to do something

You may want to work with an attorney who specializes in divorce in addition to your estate-planning attorney, who may not do much divorce work. Make sure that these two attorneys coordinate their activities and that you clearly understand what each is doing (or trying to do) and how particular tactics affect your estate planning.

Divvying up the stuff — and ignoring the estate plan?

When people divorce, they divide up their property.

"No kidding," you're probably thinking. Even if you've never gone through a divorce yourself or know someone who has, you've probably seen hundreds of TV shows and movies in which two people getting divorced go through the he-gets-this, she-gets-that exercise.

Very often, though, people going through divorce focus primarily on the here and now of dividing up property and don't really consider the impact on each person's estate planning.

Look at it this way: Before you divorce, you have an estate plan that thoroughly covers property you jointly own with your spouse, as well as your own individual property. Your spouse has a similar estate plan. Most likely, you and your spouse plan to leave most, maybe even all, of your respective estates to each other. You also have plans for your children, plus maybe each person's siblings, parents, nieces and nephews, and so on.

But after you divorce, both you and your spouse are back to square one. One way or another, your property has been divided — perhaps 50 percent to each of you, or maybe 95 percent to one spouse and only 5 percent to the other — meaning that the total value of each person's estate has now changed. Individual items (for example, tangible personal property, such as an antique grandfather clock) that you may have included in your will now belong exclusively to your ex-spouse.

In this section, we discuss how divorce affects your estate planning if you do nothing and let state law run its course, or if you take a more active role.

Figuring out what happens to your property if you do nothing

Married people usually think in terms of "our property" rather than "my property and his (or her) property." They fill out applications for car loans and mortgages and include all family assets and debts regardless of whose name a brokerage account is in or who really owns that coin collection tucked away in the safe. In fact, estate planning is often the first time married couples take a hard look at how much of "our property" is really "our property" (that is, jointly owned marital property) and how much actually belongs solely to one spouse or another.

But if divorce happens, then suddenly the long-standing view of "our property" goes out the window. Claims and accusations of "You never liked that Tiffany lamp anyway!" and "I used my money to buy the vacation home!" often start to fly and the more adversarial a divorce becomes, the more contentious the process of dividing up the property.

Depending on various state laws, divorce can cause ownership rules to change, which not only complicates the divorce process but also later affects the estates of each person.

For example, suppose that the husband purchases a cabin at a lakefront lot as a getaway for him and his poker buddies, and keeps the property titled in his name only. He is free (in most states) to later sell the property without having to include his wife in the transaction. Similarly, if the wife purchases a condo in Vail where she goes to have some quiet time to write books and articles, and if the condo is titled only in her name, in most states she can later sell that property without her husband getting involved in the sale.

However, if the couple goes through a divorce, the rules change. Specifically, the concept of *marital property* comes into play, meaning that property acquired during marriage is considered to belong to both parties to one degree or another. In *community property* states (see Chapter 4), the law applies a fixed ownership percentage to property acquired during marriage (typically 50 percent for each), regardless of whose money is used or other factors. In other noncommunity property states, the courts determine the ownership ratio of each spouse in an attempt to create a fair and equitable distribution of marital property. The bottom line: Property that a couple acquires during their marriage probably is split up in some way if they divorce, with the courts and state law making the divisions.

After the divorce is settled, the estates of both former spouses have been "shuffled" and the "who owns what" picture for what was once marital property is changed.

In most states (including community property states), property that each spouse owned before getting married doesn't become marital property at the time of divorce. That means if the couple divorces, each person keeps what he or she originally had (before the marriage) within their respective estates after the divorce is finalized.

However, you need to be aware of a potential complication. If the property that each spouse owned before the marriage has appreciated in value during the marriage, the appreciated value usually will be considered to be "marital property" subject to court division. If the marital property cannot be divided in kind along with available liquid assets (cash, bank accounts, and so on) to achieve the required equitable split, the court may be required to sell assets (including appreciated assets acquired before marriage) in order to achieve the necessary division.

Ownership of property often changes automatically when two people divorce. In states where a married couple can own assets as joint tenants with the right of survivorship or as tenants by the entirety (see Chapter 6), the ownership usually changes to a common ownership after a divorce. So whereas before the divorce when either the husband or wife would automatically acquire the full ownership after the other died, the rules have now changed. Now, because the ex-spouses own a common and equal interest with the other but without the right of survivorship, each person's ownership percentage of the property becomes part of their respective estates. Furthermore, those assets, like any other probate assets (see Chapter 5), will be subject to each person's will (or if none, the intestate laws of the state).

After a divorce, you must at least take the following steps concerning the estate plan:

✔ Revise or overhaul any estate and gift tax marital deductions.

✔ Prepare a new will to reflect your new marital status and remove any property you no longer own as a result of the divorce settlement from your will's giving clauses (see Chapter 3).

✔ Make new arrangements for the transfers of your property after your death. (You need to revise your beneficiaries so that your ex-spouse doesn't receive any of your property unless you still want your ex-spouse to receive some of your property.)

Getting more proactive: Additional options for your property

After your divorce is finalized, your ex-spouse is just like any other unrelated person in regards to your estate planning. Suppose, though, that your divorce was a particularly congenial one, and you and your spouse get along very well as you both continue to play important roles in your children's lives? Suppose that you two remain good friends and you want your former spouse to receive part of your estate after you die?

If that's what you want to do, then nothing is stopping you! You just need to explicitly mention your former spouse in your new will and the property that you want to leave him or her, just as you would your best friend from college, your next-door neighbor, or any other unrelated person.

Looking at marital agreements

You can also use a *marital agreement* to make legally binding arrangements for additional out-of-the-ordinary property transfers that affect your estate and that of your former spouse. (You can specify that certain assets will go to your former spouse.)

Couples also often use marital agreements to specify who won't get what if a divorce occurs.

Marital agreements and your estate

You probably recognize a marital agreement by the more common nickname of prenuptial agreement, or "pre-nup" for short — a marital agreement that is signed before you marry. However, nothing prevents you and your spouse from entering into a marital agreement after you marry, thus creating a "postnuptial agreement."

You may also come across the term "ante-nuptial agreement," which is another way of referring to a prenuptial agreement that is created before you marry.

Whether the marital agreement is a "pre-nup" or a "post-nup," its terms and provisions represent the wishes of both parties and are governed by state law. The primary purpose is to establish property rights of each spouse, now and in the future. The marital agreement customarily establishes who owns what assets. If any assets are considered to be marital assets, the marital agreement will specify how those assets are to be divided between the parties at death or upon the termination of the marriage.

An important part of many marital agreements is the *waiver* of the right of the parties to share in or claim a right in the estate of the other, now, upon divorce, and at death. Each person usually expressly gives up the right to participate in the other's estate or to claim any property rights in the other's estate. The parties to a marital agreement also are free to create nonprobate assets, such as joint tenancy with right of survivorship (see Chapter 6) that are held jointly or by only one of the spouses along with one or more other people, or to make outright transfers to each other, to children, or to other third parties.

State inheritance taxes can become an issue if you leave property to your former spouse. You need to know if your state has an inheritance tax with different rates depending on the relationship of the beneficiary to you. If you're still married, your state may have no inheritance tax or only a small inheritance tax percentage, but if you're divorced, a much larger percentage for someone who isn't related to you, such as your ex-spouse.

A common concern to divorced people is deciding how to honor moral agreements and obligations from their married days. Very often, these moral issues can conflict with the expectations and the legal rights of your current spouse and family (if you remarry). And even if your current spouse decides to go along with your previously made plans, the law in your state may dictate otherwise.

Suppose, for example, that you and your former spouse had an understanding while both of you were alive that whoever died last would leave a specific (and large) amount of money — let's say $750,000 — to a certain charity. Suppose also that your spouse died first, but you remarry. Finally, suppose that for whatever reason you don't have enough money when you die to make that $750,000 gift without adversely affecting the welfare of your new spouse and your children or stepchildren if you die before your new spouse does.

In Chapter 4, we discuss how noncommunity property states typically have will statutes that govern *spousal elective shares* (essentially, the right for your spouse to receive at least a minimum amount of your estate even if you have specified otherwise in your will). Most likely, your new spouse can exercise his or her right to receive that minimum amount, even if that means not enough money is left for your intended $750,000 charitable gift.

Your solution: If you want to honor some type of moral issue or obligation from a prior marriage, especially if that obligation involves property transfers after you die, work with your attorney to set up the appropriate type of trust (see Chapters 7, 8, and 9). You can create a trust that benefits both surviving family members and a charity (or charities) to one degree or another.

Considering children and divorce

One of the most tried and true recipes for bad TV movies (particularly back in the '70s and '80s) involved a second or third marriage, children from a previous marriage as well as a current marriage, and "broken promises" (or at least a change in plans) regarding who would inherit what property after someone died. The scheming and double-crossing, the yelling and screaming . . . yeah, those were the days!

In real life, unfortunately, the most contentious issues regarding estate planning and subsequent marriages often arise from that very same recipe. In order to prevent your life from turning into one of those TV movies, you need to take a particularly close look at how your remarriage affects any planned property transfers to your children from a previous marriage. Many families today have mix-and-match situations: natural-born children (that is, the family's husband and wife are the children's biological parents), stepchildren, and adopted children from either spouse's prior marriage(s).

Just because you have a household that contains, say, eight children, all children may not be treated equally or fairly in inheritance and other estate-planning matters, because of those children's respective relationships with you and your spouse.

Therefore, you need to be aware of two considerations:

- ✔ How applicable property transfers normally occur as governed by law, and how some children may find themselves cut out of inheriting property
- ✔ What ways you can change the normal order of property transfer to better meet your needs and desires and treat children from various marital combinations more equitably

Discovering what happens with your children if you don't adjust the estate plan

In first families (that is, neither spouse has ever been married before), wills tend to be relatively straightforward. (Intestate laws are also straightforward in regards to who is involved — spouses get something, children typically get something, and so on.) However, if a spouse in a subsequent marriage (second, third, and so forth) dies intestate — without a will — the state's intestate laws get a bit more complicated. Complications typically include:

- ✔ Stepchildren — the stepchildren of the spouse who dies (that is, the non-blood-related children who aren't adopted by the person who just died) likely won't receive anything under intestate laws

> ✔ If most or all the just-deceased person's assets are held jointly with his or her spouse in this subsequent marriage, then little or nothing is available to go to that deceased person's children from a prior marriage, even if that had been the plan all along after getting remarried

Continuing with the example, if the surviving spouse later dies without a will, intestate laws likely transfer that person's property to his or her children — including property that was once owned by that person's deceased spouse — meaning that the prior deceased spouse's children probably get nothing!

Even with valid wills that keep intestate laws at bay, children from multiple families complicate matters. Suppose that each spouse has a will, and both wills provide for some mutually agreed equitable distribution among all the children from all family combinations: his children from a prior marriage, her children from a prior marriage, and their children from their current marriage. But suppose the wife dies first. What prevents the husband from changing his will afterwards to cut out her children? Nothing!

Adoption also changes the complexion of your family, forcing changes in your estate planning. Basically, when you adopt someone, that person (*adoptee* in legalese) is considered to be in the same position within your family as any of your biological children.

So if you adopt a child — it doesn't matter whether that child comes from an orphanage across town, from another country, or is the biological child of your new spouse in a subsequent marriage — the law treats the child the same as if he or she were born to you. Furthermore, the court no longer considers the child to be a member of his or her former family.

For example, suppose that you and your spouse are each in your first marriages, and the two of you have three biological children. Then you both adopt a child. If your will specifies that you are leaving $400,000 to be divided equally among all your children, then each child — your three biological children and your adopted child — each receive $100,000 ($400,000 divided by 4).

In contrast, your adopted child has no claim on his or her biological parents' estates.

Making different choices for children and your estate

You can override inheritance laws for various parent-child relationships (natural children, stepchildren, and so on) if you want. In order to do so fairly easily in your will, you can use estate-planning mechanisms, such as trusts and life insurance death benefit proceeds (see Chapter 7 on trusts and

Chapter 17 on life insurance). However, as we point out earlier in this chapter, you need to think ahead — particularly for stepchildren and adopted children — and consider how to counter any possible complications, such as your surviving spouse changing his or her will after you die to cut out your children from your first marriage. Some general approaches you can take include:

- ✔ **Use gifts.** If your estate-planning strategy includes giving gifts to your children (and possibly others), you can also give gifts to your stepchildren. As we discuss in Chapter 11, you can make tax-free gifts by keeping the amounts of those gifts below the gift tax radar (the annual exemption amount).

- ✔ **Be explicit in your will.** If you want to include stepchildren on an equal footing with natural and adopted children in your will, use specific provisions in your will (see Chapter 3) to explicitly specify what property you want each to have. If you want to be absolutely certain that property in your estate goes to your children — natural children, stepchildren, or adopted children — then you must leave that property directly to them rather than indirectly (for example, leaving the property to your current spouse who then is supposed to leave any remaining property as part of his or her will to the children).

- ✔ **Use trusts.** If appropriate, set up trusts with property earmarked specifically for one or more of your children, even including stepchildren.

- ✔ **Use marital agreements.** You can use prenuptial or any other type of marital agreement to obligate your spouse to honor agreements that the two of you make to take care of each other's children, even after one of you dies.

Estate-related taxes and stepchildren

As a general rule, estate-related tax issues are the same no matter if you're talking about a first or subsequent marriage, except for a few complications. One possible complication you may have is tax treatment on assets passing to stepchildren, as contrasted with your natural-born children or adopted children (including the children of your new spouse from his or her previous marriage or marriages). Make sure that you work with your attorney to understand laws and rules relating to transferring property to your stepchildren, particularly at the state level if your state's inheritance taxes apply where you live and particularly if different tax rates apply depending on the relationship between various recipients and you.

Planning for Unmarried Relationships

As we mention at the beginning of this chapter, much of estate planning — will statutes, tax law, and so on — is oriented toward traditional male-female, legally married relationships. If you're involved in an unmarried relationship, how is your estate planning affected?

Unless a valid common-law marriage can be proven (see "Common-law marriages: We don't advise 'em"), unmarried cohabitants — that is, people who live together — don't usually have the benefits or obligations of a conventional marital relationship. However, some exceptions do exist, such as:

✔ A few jurisdictions where same-sex marriages are recognized. If legally recognized, same-sex marriages are likely to create the same rights and obligations as are created by more conventional marital relationships.

✔ The concept of *palimony,* (basically, "alimony for unmarried couples") which is recognized in some states. Keep in mind, however, that any palimony rights are based more on the relationship itself rather than on any finding if a "marriage" exists between the parties. But because palimony rights do create and affect property rights, they must be recognized for the rights and obligations they create.

A valid common-law marriage involves a couple that considers themselves husband and wife with the intent to be married, even though they've never had a civil or religious ceremony. If a court recognizes their relationship as a common-law marriage, both people are entitled to the same rights and are subject to the same obligations as any married couple.

Note: Just because a couple lives together for a while doesn't mean they have a right to a common-law marriage. Generally a court finding determines that a common-law marriage does or did exist. In fact, the court normally becomes involved after a possible common-law marriage has dissolved, when one of the parties tries to establish property or some other rights relating to the relationship.

For the most part, we advise against common-law marriages. If you intend to get married, do so. Otherwise, even if you and someone else live together, don't try to treat an unmarried relationship as the same as if you were married. Otherwise, you may face a palimony situation. Or you may require a divorce to legally terminate a common-law marriage.

However, you may be involved in an unmarried, cohabitating relationship with someone — either same-sex or opposite-sex — in which you and the other person do want to provide for each other in some way as part of your respective estate planning. If so, you must work with your attorney (or attorneys, if you each have a different attorney) to properly and adequately establish your respective estate plans.

First and foremost, make sure that each of you has a will in which you very explicitly refer to the other person and you also very clearly specify what you want to leave to that person. Or perhaps you each want to leave your entire estate to the other. The choice is yours; just make sure you factor any such plans in with other beneficiaries.

If you want your partner to receive the house that you share, or any other particular property rather than any of your blood relatives (children, siblings, parents, and so on), you may use the joint tenancy with right of survivorship form of will substitute (see Chapter 6). Remember that property owned as joint tenants with right of survivorship passes outside of probate, so property — such as your house — is less likely to get tangled up in legal dealings or challenges from disgruntled relatives who may want to stake a claim to that property.

You can also use trusts and other estate-planning vehicles to establish plans for each other. For example, you may set up a trust that provides periodic payments to your partner for some period of time after you die. You also have life insurance proceeds (see Chapter 17) as another means to provide money to your partner.

If you don't have a will, and if you don't adequately use proper will substitutes or trusts, you run a very high risk of not being able to transfer property to a partner in a unmarried relationship! Remember that intestate laws govern property transfers for your probate estate that you haven't included in a valid will, meaning that the state decides what happens to your estate and to whom receives it. Trust us, your estate isn't likely to go to your unmarried partner, no matter what the two of you have agreed, no matter how committed your relationship was, or any other factors! So make sure that you work closely with your attorney to adequately and thoroughly set up your estate plans to accomplish your wishes.

Untangling the Complexities of Guardianship and Your Estate

Guardianship is an essential part of estate planning that people often overlook as they concentrate on more quantifiable aspects, such as the property in their estates or estate-related tax planning. But you do need to understand two different types of guardianship, as described in the sections below:

- ✔ For your children
- ✔ For yourself

Guardianship for your children

Most people recognize the terms *guardian* and *guardianship,* at least when it comes to deciding who will watch after their children if both parents die while the children are still young.

You need to give careful thought to issues of guardianship as part of your estate planning, too.

One of the most common guardianship-related decisions relates to your minor children. By federal law, the *age of majority* is considered to be 18, and until a person reaches that age, that person is a minor. Under normal circumstances, a minor's parents provide and make almost all the decisions. However, two main types of guardianship may come into play if normal circumstances cease to exist, such as if both parents die.

You actually need to consider two different types of guardianship: *Guardianship of the Person,* the care-and-decisions form of guardianship, and *Guardianship of the Estate* in which someone is appointed to specifically control the minor's property, but not necessarily provide care to and make decisions for a minor.

Guardianship of the Person is the aspect of guardianship that most people are at least somewhat familiar with. A minor becomes a *ward* of his or her guardian and typically goes to live with that person. However, the second, less familiar form — *Guardianship of the Estate* — exists when a person or some entity (such as a bank's trust department) has the responsibility to invest a minor's money, watch out for the minor's assets, and generally take care of that minor's property until some point in the future.

When a minor reaches the age of majority (again, 18), the need for guardianship ends, and the former minor can now legally make decisions, live where he or she wants, and generally live as any other adult would. The guardian then simply turns the assets over to the former minor unless court approval is required. In this case, the guardian files an accounting of his or her activity, and after receiving court approval, turns everything over to the minor.

If junior has a lot of wild oats left in his bag

If you're worried that one of your offspring may not be able to handle his inheritance until sometime after age 21, no problem. Other avenues are available to control and protect those assets. You can put the assets in trust, for example, and keep them there for as long or short a period as you think is necessary.

Until that point, however, you need to be sure that care will be provided for the minor. And if the minor in question is your child — which most likely means that you died while your child was still young — then you hopefully have made provisions in your estate plan for guardians for your child. If not, the courts appoint a guardian, which may not be the person or institution that you would choose. So why leave things up to chance? Make sure that you adequately take care of guardianship as part of your estate planning along with your property, insurance, taxes, and all the rest!

Guardianship for yourself

Suppose you aren't able to adequately take care of yourself or to make decisions, possibly as a result of advanced age or in the aftermath of a serious injury? What happens then?

As we discuss in the next section, you may have a guardian yourself: someone who the court appoints to look after your best interests, much as a guardian is designated or court-appointed to look after your child's interests.

However, as we discuss, guardianship is only one option you have when dealing with situations where you can't adequately care for yourself or aren't capable of making decisions. You can consider other mechanisms — a durable power of attorney and a living will, specifically — as part of your estate planning. (See the following section for more on power of attorney and living wills.)

Doomsday Stuff: Factoring Incompetence and Death into Your Plan

You need to plan for what will happen to your estate if you become *incapacitated,* or incompetent, and the choices you have for how your care will be provided. Furthermore, you need to think beyond incompetency and incapacity about what may happen if you are about to die. As described in this section, you need to be aware of adult guardianship issues, but you also need to complete a *durable power of attorney* and a *living will* as part of your estate planning.

The three basic documents that everyone needs to have as part of a thorough estate-planning effort are a will (see Chapter 3), a durable power of attorney, and a living will.

A durable power of attorney — your personal representative while you're alive

In general, a *power of attorney* is a document by which a person appoints someone else to act as his or her agent to do one or more acts. The powers granted can be limited or pervasive, can continue indefinitely or can terminate at a particular time, can be effective immediately or at some future time, or upon the happening of some event (such as incapacity), and generally authorize another to do all or only some of the things the person can do themselves.

A *durable power of attorney* is one that continues to be valid and enforceable even after the person making it becomes incompetent or incapacitated. The durability power is required in order to help avoid a guardianship proceeding in the case of incompetency, and allows the agent to continue to act for the incompetent person.

As compared with guardianship, a durable power of attorney has several advantages, such as:

- ✔ The agent (again, the person in control) can usually act on most matters on behalf of the incompetent person without court approval.
- ✔ No regular court filings are required.
- ✔ Matters are more private and less embarrassing.
- ✔ The agent is chosen by you and not the court.

If an agent is unable to continue to serve under a durable power of attorney, a family member or some other interested party can always request the court to appoint a guardian at a later time even if the incompetent person's care started out under a durable power of attorney.

A durable power of attorney usually is one of the following forms:

✔ A *general* or *business* power, which allows the agent to carry on the day-to-day affairs of the incompetent

✔ A *health-care* power, which allows the agent to make health-related decisions for the incompetent

(The two powers listed above can name the same or different agents.)

You need to have a durable power of attorney as part of your overall estate planning along with your will, trusts you set up, your tax planning, and all the rest. If you suddenly become incompetent and don't have a valid and proper durable power of attorney, the court may have no alternative but to appoint a guardian for you with all the associated cost, cumbersome processes, and lack of privacy.

Think of your durable power of attorney in the same context as your will, and court-appointed guardianship in the same context as your state's intestate laws. You absolutely want to create a durable power of attorney and a will so the court doesn't have to appoint a guardian or your state's intestate laws don't come into play.

Just like with your will and every other legal document, you can execute a power of attorney only if you're legally competent at the time. If you are, in fact, incompetent, a power of attorney you attempt to execute will likely be considered invalid even if you can physically sign your name.

Your competency and the validity of the documents you have signed may become an issue in a later guardianship proceeding or other legal action brought by a family member or some other interested party.

The living will — giving directions when you can't communicate

In a living will, you express your wishes that certain care be provided or not provided when you aren't able to make those decisions for yourself. Usually a living will directs doctors, hospital, and nursing home staff to stop life-sustaining treatment that simply serves to prolong the dying process when you're otherwise in a terminal condition or death is imminent. The living will allows your wishes to be carried out when you are incompetent, unconscious, or otherwise unable to communicate.

The living will is usually coupled with a durable power of attorney appointing someone to act as your agent. Essentially, you use the durable power of attorney to determine who acts on your behalf to execute the instructions contained in your living will.

Like all powers of attorney and other documents in which a person is appointed to act for you, take care of you, or take care of your property, you need to carefully choose someone trustworthy and reliable. You also need to appoint a *successor agent* so that if the primary agent whom you've designated dies (and you don't subsequently update your living will or, for that matter, your durable power of attorney) or is unable to perform the required duties, someone else can step in to make sure that your wishes are carried out. (Just like in your will, you designate a successor agent in case your first choice can't fulfill his or her duties.)

Many people tend to shy away from living wills even more than regular wills (see Chapter 3). Perhaps many people can't deal with the thought of the last days of a terminal illness or a catastrophic accident. Maybe, they view these thoughts as more troubling than death itself and the subsequent considerations, such as how property will be distributed. Regardless, don't ignore the importance of having a living will as a part of your estate planning.

Realizing why the court appoints a guardian when you're incompetent

What if you don't make a durable power of attorney? Who will take care of you and make decisions for you? If you do become incompetent or incapacitated, the court may appoint a guardian for you and your estate. The court wants to protect your estate from the chances of being squandered or robbed by those people with, shall we say, less than noble intentions. Additionally, the court also sees that you receive appropriate care, depending on the reason of incompetency or incapacity (for example, Alzheimer's Disease, hospitalization because of an automobile accident-induced coma, and so on).

If you don't have a living will, any wish that you have not to be kept alive by artificial means is unlikely to be carried out, whether or not you have a guardian.

And — on the positive side — if your condition improves enough that you are no longer considered incompetent or incapacitated — the court will terminate the guardianship, essentially once again giving you control over your decisions and property.

Legalese alert!

Incompetent and *incapacitated* (as with *incompetency* and *incapacity*) are often used interchangeably, but very subtle differences do exist that we want to point out. The difference relates to the kind of guardianship law that exists in a particular state. Under the older laws in some states, a person's competency was either so diminished as to require a guardian (in which case the person was incompetent), or if the requisite proof and extent of diminished capacity was not shown, the person was considered to be competent and the appointment of a guardian wasn't necessary.

Many states have now adopted the concept of *limited guardianships* and now use the term

incapacitated instead. In those states there can be a limited guardian or a plenary guardian, depending on the extent of incapacity. To complicate matters a tiny bit more, the term *conservator* sometimes is used to distinguish a Guardian of the Estate (that is, property) from a Guardian of the Person, who is simply referred to as the *guardian*. (We introduce these two types of guardians in the section, "Untangling the Complexities of Guardianship and Your Estate.") As in the case of a minor, the incompetent person is the *ward* of the guardian of the person, and the property of the incompetent is simply referred to as the estate.

In legalese, the word *incompetent* has nothing to do with how the word is typically used in general conversation, as a not-so-polite synonym for *unqualified*. An incompetent person is one who can't adequately care for himself or herself and needs help. Incompetency can result from mental or physical problems before or during birth, later-in-life medical causes (for example, a stroke or Alzheimer's Disease), an automobile accident that someone survives but is in a coma for the rest of his or her life, or some other cause. An incompetent person can't legally make decisions for himself or herself, and needs special protections

Even though guardianship acts like a sort of safety net for incompetent people, drawbacks do exist. A guardian is always answerable to the court, creating a somewhat cumbersome relationship in which the guardian must file regular reports, and the court always keeps an eye on the situation. The guardian must obtain court approval before taking anything other than rather minor action on behalf of the incompetent.

Also, the guardian may be required to post a bond or other security with the court and to keep the bond current.

Perhaps the primary disadvantage is that guardianship is a legal process that requires the filing of a petition or similar pleading, with notice to all parties in interest and proof of incompetency. Quite often, these proceedings are contested and result in extensive (and expensive) litigation. Even if the proceeding is more run-of-the-mill and uncontested, it's still fairly expensive. And, of course, having someone, such as family member or close friend subjected to a court proceeding to determine competency, can be unpleasant and embarrassing.

Taking Care of Fluffy, Spot, and Bootsie

If you have a pet — or, like many people, more than one pet — you need to consider your pets in your estate plan. Most likely you won't write your will to leave the majority of your property to your eight cats, although you've probably seen those occasional human-interest (or maybe animal-interest) stories in which an elderly man died and made provisions for his beloved cats and dogs to live in his house for the rest of their lives, with a trusted friend or relative taking care of those pets in addition for eventually taking ownership of the house.

You can do pretty much whatever you want in your estate plan when it comes to your pets, but just like with your spouse, your children, other relatives, and friends, you need to write everything down and make sure that your personal representative and the rest of your family clearly understands what you want to happen.

Some of what you need to specify is fairly obvious: how you want your pets cared for, by whom, and where. Do you want your oldest son to take the two dogs into his home, or maybe your long-time next-door neighbor is the person whom you want to care for the dogs after you die, rather than ship them across the country to where you son lives? You also need to calculate how much money will be needed to care for your pets, and make sure that you leave that money to the caregiver. You may simply leave the required money as part or your will (though you need to be aware of any delays caused by a prolonged probate process, as we discuss in Chapter 5), or set up a trust from which the money can be withdrawn as needed.

But beyond the basic care instructions and the financial provisions, you also need to write down any additional requirements or restrictions, some of which may seem silly to your relatives and friends who don't have any pets or perhaps only have a single dog or cat. For example:

✔ You may want "special friends" to stay together rather than be split up. If you have several dogs or cats or horses or other animals, you likely have noticed how often two (or sometimes three or more) pets form special bonds with each other (two cats who always nap together and walk side by side everywhere they go, or two dogs who play together constantly). Too often, people make somewhat haphazard provisions for their animals' care after they die, resulting in two animals who spend all their time with each other being split up — one cat or dog to one home, and his or her best friend to another place. Sadly, the result is that one or both often become very depressed, now having lost their owner and their best animal friend. And — seriously — depressed animals often suffer the same effects as depressed people, such as being more susceptible to physical ailments.

✔ Specify what should happen to your pets when they die. You may want them to be buried in your backyard (subject to local ordinances), in a pet cemetery, or on your farm or ranch. Or you may want them to be cremated and their ashes dispersed in some particular location, such as where they spent the last years of their lives or on a nearby mountaintop. Whatever your intentions, make sure that the person or people who assume responsibility for your special friends are aware of what you want for your pets' final resting place.

✔ Don't forget to plan for estate-related taxes on any pets that, from an estate-planning perspective, can be like investment property . . . a valuable racing or event horse, for example.

Part VII
The Part of Tens

The 5th Wave   By Rich Tennant

"Living trust? Avoid probate? I say we stick the money in the ground like always, and then feed this peddler to the sharks."

In this part . . .

This part contains several concise, easy-to-remember lists to help you begin making decisions about estate planning. If you want to feel like you're taking charge, take a look!

Chapter 20

Ten Questions to Get You Rolling on Your Estate Plan

*Y*our estate-planning efforts can be relatively easy or very complex (rather inexpensive or quite costly). No matter the cost or difficulty, your estate plan must reflect your situation. And who knows more about your situation than you do?

So don't worry! Talking to yourself isn't a worrisome sign when it comes to estate planning. Ask yourself the questions in this chapter, and then answer them to help you discover how to get started on your estate plan!

Why Do I Even Need an Estate Plan?

"What the heck, I don't want to take any responsibility for what happens to all my property. I'll just let someone else decide. And I think I'll turn over as much of my property as possible to the government while I'm at it."

Can you see yourself uttering the preceding sentences? Of course not! But if you don't actively plan for what may happen to your estate — not only after you die, but also when you're alive, as well — then you're essentially giving up any hope for control over what happens to your property. Furthermore, your estate will likely suffer a larger tax bite than otherwise necessary.

So if you need to psyche yourself up for what lies ahead in your estate-planning efforts, ask yourself this seemingly rhetorical question and think about how you respond. As we emphasize throughout this book, your two main estate-planning objectives are protection and control, and you need to answer your own question in that context!

If I Need an Estate Plan, Why Doesn't Everyone Have One?

Remember the standard childhood admonition from a parent to a child: "Well, if Johnny jumped off a bridge, would you do the same thing?"

Just because others haven't done their estate planning doesn't mean their shortcomings have to be your downfall! After all, we're talking about your hard-earned estate, not theirs!

And if your close family members or friends have been negligent with their estate planning, let them learn from your example after you get your own estate plan in order!

What Are My Top Three Estate-Planning Goals?

Estate planning is very much a matter of give and take, checks and balances, yin and yang — you get the idea. You need to look at all sides and come up with the optimal solution.

So because of the give and take that occurs in your estate planning — particularly if your estate situation is rather complex — you need to identify your top three goals for you and your estate-planning team's consideration. Are you trying to assure that all your children receive roughly the same amount of your property after you die? Are you trying to minimize the overall tax bite on your sizable estate? Are you trying to protect as much of your estate if you need to tap into government-funded health care or if you need to move to an expensive nursing home? Do you want to leave a lasting legacy that benefits one or more charities? Are you trying to make sure that someone in your family doesn't get anything from your estate?

Make a list of ten estate-planning objectives and then check off the ones that you see as your top three, and concentrate your efforts on them.

Whom Do I Want to Take Care Of?

In the broadest sense, you can use your will, trusts, will substitutes, and other estate planning tools to take care of everyone you are even remotely related to, including your 19th cousin, twice-removed who lives in Latvia (and whom you have never met in person). As a practical matter, however, you probably want to concentrate your efforts on your closest relatives: your children, grandchildren, siblings, and (if they're still alive) parents and grandparents.

However, you still need to make some key decisions about your closest relatives regarding your estate plan. For example, you may want to simply leave all your estate to your children, who in turn will someday leave that property (or, more accurately, whatever is left) to their own children. Conversely, if your children are particularly well off, you may want to leave the majority of your estate directly to your grandchildren (perhaps in trust). Or you may have a favorite cousin who has always been like a sister to you, and you want to help her out, perhaps even ahead of your own children and grandchildren.

Hey, it's your estate and your family, so you make the decisions! But before you start worrying about what to put in your will and what trusts to set up, make sure you identify who in your family is at the top of the line.

What's the Best Way to Protect My Children?

You have many considerations for your children regarding your estate plan. What happens when you die? Is your spouse still alive? Are you still married to your children's other parent, or are you divorced? Are your own parents still alive and well enough to raise grandchildren, if the need arises? And how much money does your children's guardian need to raise your children if you aren't around?

The answers to these questions help guide what you do in your estate plan for insurance, guardianship, trusts, and other important considerations. So make sure you think about the big picture when it comes to protecting your children — not just financially, but overall.

How Much Help Do 1 Need?

In Chapter 1, we introduce your estate-planning team members and note that depending on your particular needs, you may rely on some (for example, your accountant and attorney) more than others (such as your financial planner and insurance agent). Someone else — your brother, for example — may require a different "weighting" of assistance because of his own professional background or different personal and family circumstances.

Make sure you ask yourself how comfortable you are with estate planning and what you feel comfortable doing yourself. Be wary of do-it-yourself kits, such as for wills and certain simplistic trusts, because mistakes and omissions can be very costly!

What's My Budget for Estate Planning?

To put it bluntly, you can spend lots of money on estate-planning help, even if your estate-planning needs are rather modest. You can meet with your attorney two or three times a year to review your will, for example, or sit down with your accountant every time your portfolio undergoes some minor changes, but why?

Make no mistake about it, you have to spend some money for estate-planning assistance, but before you spend a single penny, you need to have a general idea of what those costs are for at least the foreseeable future. This way, you can maintain better control over the fees and charges you have to pay and resist some of the more shady estate planning "deals" out there, such as questionable investments.

Does My Attorney Have the Right Experience?

Is your attorney estate savvy? The law is a broad field with many specialty areas — criminal, civil, real estate, and so on. You may have an existing relationship with an attorney, but you definitely need to assess that person's capabilities with respect to estate-planning knowledge.

Ask your attorney questions such as:

✔ Have you worked on estate-planning–related documents like wills and trusts for other clients?

✔ How many clients have you previously worked with or currently work with on estate planning?

✔ What percentage of your business involves estate planning?

✔ What are the trickiest estate-planning problems you've seen for someone with basically the same situation as me?

Based on your attorney's answers, determine if you feel comfortable with your attorney handling the delicate matters of your estate plan.

Who Are My Confidants about These Plans?

Your estate planning involves an element of soul searching because it forces you to think beyond the present and into the future — a future where you are deceased. So you may want to think about which family members are going to be a part of your estate-planning process.

Perhaps you feel comfortable talking about your estate plan with your siblings, children, parents, and other family members. Or maybe you see your estate plan as a relatively private matter, for you and your spouse only.

Or perhaps you don't want your spouse to know anything about your estate plan because of some rather serious lack-of-trust issues. (We certainly don't mean to be flippant, but these situations happen!)

Whatever your situation, decide how much various people should know, and make sure that you keep everyone up-to-date with your estate-planning strategy.

How Do I Know I Can Do My Estate Plan?

Quite possibly you're a bit overwhelmed by the topics we cover in this book, and are leaning toward saying: "What the heck, I don't want to worry about estate planning."

Trust us: Anyone can do a reasonably good job at basic estate planning, especially with a little help from some trusted and experienced professionals. So ask yourself what your confidence level is about estate planning. If you're still on the skeptical side, sit down with your accountant or attorney and pick one or two simple areas — such as your will, if you don't have one or haven't updated yours in a while — as a starting point. Before you know it, you'll be reciting Latin estate-planning phrases with the best of them!

Chapter 21

Avoiding Ten Common Mistakes and Problems in Your Will

In This Chapter
▶ Sidestepping the booby traps
▶ Taking enough time to get your will right

Making sure that you prepare a valid will is a key part of your estate plan. Your will can be very simple or very complicated, depending on factors such as your personal and family situation and your estate's value. But whether simple or complicated, you can still make several mistakes in your will.

Use this chapter as a checklist of what not to do when you prepare your will.

Forgetting to Review Your Will Annually

In the business world, the term *living document* is used to describe a document that changes over time to reflect new or changed circumstances. Although calling your will — a document in which you discuss what happens after you die — a living document may seem like a contradiction, the term actually fits perfectly!

In Chapter 3, we discuss many different reasons that can cause you to update your will, such as getting married, getting divorced, or having a major change in your financial fortunes.

Unless you review your will at least once a year, you run a very serious risk of having an out-of-date will — possibly a very out-of-date will — when you die.

So pick a date, any date, that you set aside each year to review your will to see if you need to make any updates to the document.

(You can always make a game out of your annual review, pretending that you are in a movie reading your will out loud in front of your family and then imagining each person's reaction.)

Conduct your annual will review and if you have any questions or doubts about whether or not you need to do any updates, get in touch with your attorney.

Forgetting to Include a Residuary ("Leftovers") Clause

Your will's residuary clause (see Chapter 3) can either cover the "leftovers" of your estate (if you want to be very explicit in your will about who will get what property), or it can actually be the main clause you use if you just want to treat most or all of your estate as one big pool to be divided up among your main beneficiaries.

But regardless of your strategy, if you forget to include a *residuary clause* to cover property that you don't specifically mention elsewhere in your will, the law — not you — will dictate how any property that you have not otherwise mentioned will be distributed, and to whom. You will now have died *partially intestate,* meaning that only some of your property is covered by your valid will.

This point is a no-brainer: Make sure that whoever prepares your will includes a residuary clause to take care of those leftovers.

Forgetting the "Just in Case" Contingencies

In sports, every baseball, football, hockey, or basketball player has a backup — someone to fill in if something happens, such as the player being injured. In the theater, an actor usually has an understudy — someone who can step in if laryngitis sets in one night, or if the actor just needs time to take a break.

In your will, you need to make sure you include those backups and understudies, or *contingencies.* Specifically, include *contingent beneficiaries* who will "fill in" if your main beneficiary dies before you do. Additionally, you must also name a contingent personal representative who can serve in that all-important role if the person whom you've designated for some reason can't do the job.

If you forget to include contingencies, all sorts of complications can set in. Because one of the main goals of spending time on your will is to avoid complications, you are better off focusing a bit more effort on those just-in-case contingencies and making sure they are included in your will.

Sticking With Your Personal Representative When You Really Need a Substitute

After you die, your personal representative needs to make sure that your wishes and instructions are carried out for all aspects of your estate.

But just as you need to review your will annually, you must also periodically ask yourself if the person or institution you selected as your personal representative is still the best choice. You may be having second thoughts for several reasons. For example, you may have selected your sister as your personal representative five years ago, but now she is estranged from the family, or perhaps severely disabled from an automobile accident.

Or you may have selected a small-town bank as your personal representative because you've done business with them for more than 30 years. However, last year a behemoth, out-of-state financial institution purchased the bank and the people at the branch have all been laid off.

Even though your instincts may be to avoid making any changes in your estate plan after you have your will and other aspects in place, you need to strongly consider designating a new personal representative if you're now concerned for any reason about your original choice.

Forgetting About All Those Pesky Statutes that Affect Wills

Remember that the laws of the state in which you live play an important role in what happens to your estate. As we discuss in Chapter 4, you can "override" some of those *statutes* in your will, while other statutes are "carved in stone." (So that would make them sort of "statue statutes," right?)

Anyway, as you're deciding what you want to write in your will, keep in mind the statutes that you need to deal with. For example, remember that *abatement statutes* come into play when your estate is not valuable enough to meet all of your obligations (such as money you still owe) plus what you've specified in your will about what your beneficiaries are supposed to get.

Work with your attorney on a number of "what if" scenarios. (For example, what if the value of your stock portfolio falls dramatically, how does that affect what you want to do in your will?) When you do your annual will review, be sure to make any necessary changes to keep unfavorable statutes from coming into play.

Getting Too Precise in Your Will

If you state specific dollar amounts in your will, you risk having your estate being distributed in a way that you really didn't intend. Instead, use percentages wherever possible, particularly for the larger shares of your estate among your beneficiaries.

For example, suppose that your estate is valued at $500,000 when you create your will, and you decide to leave most of it to your only daughter, except for $50,000 that you want to go to your only brother. Your intention is that your daughter will get 90 percent of your estate. But when you draft your will, you don't state the particular percentage in your will; but instead, you state that $50,000 will go to your brother. (You figure that if the value of your estate rises your daughter will get even more, but you want to keep your brother's amount fixed at $50,000).

But suppose that before you die the value of your estate decreases dramatically for some reason, such as a costly medical expense that uses up most of your estate. When you die, your estate is now worth $75,000. By preparing your will as described above, your brother will still get $50,000, but now your daughter will only get $25,000!

If, however, you had specified in your will that your daughter receive 90 percent and your brother 10 percent, then even though both will receive far less than they would have if your estate were still worth $500,000, at least your intentions of leaving most of your estate to your daughter will still be in effect.

Using Your Beneficiaries as Will Witnesses

Never use a beneficiary as a witness to your will. Doing so is a legal conflict of interest and could result in your beneficiary not receiving what you have stated in your will.

The same person as both a beneficiary and a will witness casts a shadow of doubt about what influence that person may have had on you, and could open the door for other beneficiaries to claim that you were influenced by that "unscrupulous" person.

If you use an attorney, have his or her office staff members serve as witnesses. If you don't use an attorney, make sure that your witnesses are not named as beneficiaries in your will.

Failing to Factor in the Personal Side

The decisions you make about your estate that are specified in your will should include your "non-monetary," or personal, objectives in addition to your monetary (financial) goals. Don't just go "by the numbers;" instead, really think through the choices you make and consider family, emotional, and other considerations.

For example, suppose you have three children. Two of them are very well off financially and the third is a struggling would-be social worker. Family tradition may dictate that you split your estate equally among your three children, but you may wish to reconsider this tradition and leave more to your not-so-well-off child and less to the others. The choice is yours.

Keeping Important Information From Your Attorney

Make sure you tell your attorney everything that you can think of — even personal, sometimes painful, or embarrassing items — when you are deciding what to put in your will. Even if you don't think some long-ago item is relevant, err on the side of too much information.

For example, if long ago as a teenager you were an unmarried parent, make sure that your attorney is aware of this fact as well as what happened to the child. Are you legally the child's parent? Did you place the child up for adoption? Answers to similar questions will help your attorney put the correct legal language in your will to reflect what you want — or don't want — to happen with your estate with regards to that child.

Tell your attorney if your business is having difficulties, or if you and your spouse are having marital problems and divorce looks like a possibility. Your will must be one step ahead of life changes that you may be able to anticipate.

Rushing Through Your Will

Take your time!

Even if you think you have a relatively uncomplicated family and financial situation and preparing your will can be a snap, you must still go through a number of what-if scenarios to make sure that you have thought of every-thing. Even when working with your attorney, prompt him or her with the same what-if questions to see if the questions spark any thoughts about potential problems that you need to address.

The last thing you want to happen is that you think you have a valid will that accurately reflects what you want to happen with your estate, and then after you die, all kinds of problems surface because you failed to address what you thought were nitpicky details that turned out to be very important.

Chapter 22

Ten Estate-Planning Resources on the Internet

In This Chapter

▶ Flying solo in cyberspace

▶ Zeroing in on numerous resources

*O*kay, an entire "new economy" made up exclusively of dot.com and other Internet-related companies isn't a possibility. But you still can't beat the Internet for at-your-fingertips access to a wide range of help for pretty much anything you're interested in, including estate planning.

The ten Web sites listed in this chapter contain lots of information about one or more of the estate-planning topics covered in this book, and of course, the Internet has hundreds of other resources available for even more information.

Because the Internet is such a dynamic, ever-changing organism, make sure that you get an up-to-date list of Web sites whenever you need to check out something about estate planning, particularly if you're trying to stay abreast of late-breaking news (such as Congress's latest work with the federal estate tax). Use your favorite search engine, such as Google (www.google.com) or Yahoo! (www.yahoo.com), to find late-breaking news as well as lists of new estate-planning Web sites that may not have existed last time you checked.

If you aren't very familiar with the Internet and related terminology, such as *home page* or *search engine,* then you can check out *The Internet For Dummies,* 8th edition, (published by John Wiley Publishing, Inc.) to get up to speed with the technology and the lingo. Don't worry — using the Internet is easy!

Smartmoney.com

Smartmoney.com (`www.smartmoney.com`) bills itself as an Internet site for information about investing, saving, and personal finance. One topic that certainly fits into that category is estate planning, and if you go to `www.smartmoney.com/estate`, you can find articles about estate planning and worksheets, such as the Net Worth Calculator, to help you figure out your estate's value.

You can also access Smartmoney.com's estate-planning pages by following links from the site's home page, currently accessible from the Personal Finance link.

Sometimes magazine-oriented Web sites change how their pages are linked together, so you can also use the site's search capability to get to the estate-planning information.

Estateretirementplanning.com

Estateretirementplanning.com (`www.estateretirementplanning.com`) focuses on the related topics of estate planning and retirement planning. A number of links are included to assist you with information about trusts, wills, financial advisers, plus retirement savings plans, such as your 401(k) and annuities. If you're interested in doing additional early research into wills before speaking with your attorney, you can go to `www.estateretirementplanning.com/makewill.html` (also available from the site's Wills link) for up-to-date information about topics you need to consider.

Estateplanning.com

Estateplanning.com (`www.estateplanning.com`) is a site that serves both the general public and estate-planning professionals, such as Certified Financial Planners (CFPs) and Certified Life Underwriters (CLUs). On the general public side of the site, you can locate estate-planning-related articles plus find out about seminars near you.

Savewealth.com

Savewealth.com (`www.savewealth.com`) gives you current news about estate planning, taxes, and retirement, along with interesting and thought-provoking articles. For example, "Bluesman's Estate Finally Settles 62 Years After Death" discusses a 1930s-era blues musician named Robert L. Johnson who died in 1938 without a will and with no children. Similar to many entertainers and artists, Johnson's music continued to earn royalties, and his estate wound up in turmoil for years. The estate was further complicated when an album of his recordings was released in 1990, generating a whole new flow of income. By reading about Johnson's difficulties (or, more accurately, his estate's difficulties), you may be further inspired to get your own estate in order!

Moneycentral.msn.com

The Microsoft Network (MSN) and the CNBC financial network jointly operate a Money Central site, (moneycentral.msn.com). On the site's Planning link that is accessible from the home page, you can go to information about retirement and estate planning.

The direct address to get to that information at the time of writing is moneycentral.msn.com/retire/home.asp. If the site operators reorganize their site and that address doesn't work, you can also use the site's search capability and enter "estate planning" or a particular subject, such as "wills," that you want to find.

Estateplanforyou.com

The site at www.estateplanforyou.com is operated by the American Academy of Estate Planning Attorneys (AAEPA) and provides the general public access to free information: news and articles, special reports about subjects such as wills, and checklists of topics such as estate-planning techniques. You can also use the site to find an estate-planning attorney near you, and if you happen to be an attorney, then you can find out how to join the AAEPA.

Law.freeadvice.com

Law.freeadvice.com provides exactly what the Web site's name says: free, basic legal advice about many different legal topics, including estate planning. Estate-planning topics include asset protection, elder law, probate, trusts, and wills. You can get to these topics by either following the Web site's links or, if you know the address of the particular subject you want, by entering that directly into your Web browser.

Actec.org

The American College of Trust and Estate Counsel (ACTEC) Web site at www. actec.org (note that the site uses *org* and not *com*) includes an area for the general public. The public area gives you access to free articles and materials that you can purchase, such as a video called *Death & Taxes* and the *ACTEC Trust and Estate Accounting Package for Quicken.*

You can also locate an ACTEC Fellow to assist you with your estate planning. The site states "(ACTEC) Fellows are selected on the basis of professional reputation and ability in the fields of trusts and estates and on the basis of having made substantial contributions to these fields through lecturing, writing, teaching and bar activities."

Nolo.com

Nolo.com (www.nolo.com) is a Web site billed as "Law for all" and "Putting the law into plain English." You can purchase legal forms, books, and software for a variety of law-related matters, including estate planning. The site operates a number of law centers, including one for estate planning (accessible from the site's home page). If you're really into law, you can also conduct research into state and federal laws, Supreme Court cases, and various types of courts.

Nafep.com

The National Association of Financial and Estate Planning (NAFEP) site at www.nafep.com features a Web site that covers a broad range of estate planning topics, discusses problems and pitfalls, and provides tools to help you with your estate planning. (For example, follow the link from the home page to find information about charitable foundations and your estate planning.) Other information on the site will be of particular interest to you if you are an owner or co-owner of a family business (see Chapter 15). Follow the "Business Entities" link from the home page or go directly to www.nafep.com/business_entities/.

Index

• *M* •

• *Y* •

Notes

Notes

Notes

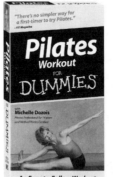

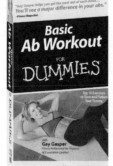

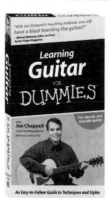

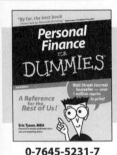

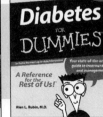
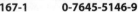

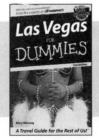

FOR DUMMIES®

Plain-English solutions for everyday challenges

FOR DUMMIES

The advice and explanations you need to succeed

FOR DUMMIES®

We take the mystery out of complicated subjects